KOOK

WHAT SURFING TAUGHT ME ABOUT LOVE, LIFE, AND CATCHING THE PERFECT WAVE

PETER HELLER

FREE PRESS

NEW YORK   LONDON   TORONTO   SYDNEY

Free Press
A Division of Simon & Schuster, Inc.
1230 Avenue of the Americas
New York, NY 10020

Copyright © 2010 by Peter Heller

First Free Press trade paperback edition July 2010

FREE PRESS and colophon are trademarks of Simon & Schuster, Inc.

For information about special discounts for bulk purchases,
please contact Simon & Schuster Special Sales at
1-866-506-1949 or business@simonandschuster.com

The Simon & Schuster Speakers Bureau can bring authors to your live event.
For more information or to book an event contact the Simon & Schuster Speakers
Bureau at 1-866-248-3049 or visit our website at simonspeakers.com.

Designed by Carla Jayne Jones

Manufactured in the United States of America

10   9   8   7

Library of Congress Cataloging-in-Publication Data
Heller, Peter
    Kook: what surfing taught me about love, life, and catching the perfect wave / Peter
Heller.
        p.   cm.
1. Surfing.   2. Heller, Peter   3. Surfers—Anecdotes.   I. Title.
GV840.S8H44   2010
797.3'2092—dc22
[B]   2009045508

ISBN 978-0-7432-9420-1
ISBN 978-1-4391-7181-3 (ebook)

TO KIM

For He hath founded it upon the seas, and established it upon the floods.

Genesis

"Somebody help the chicken!"

Surf's Up

The story in these pages actually happened. Some of the geography, however, you will never find on any map. I have changed the names of some people and places for everyone's protection, especially my own.

WITNESS

I had watched the seal catch two waves. Now his head popped up beside me where I sat on my board. I almost fell off in surprise. "Hi," I stammered. He blinked, unafraid and curious. *Oh, man*, I thought, *he wants to be my friend*. "Right?" I proffered. The seal didn't seem to be into conversation. He turned his head toward the open ocean, just like a surfer looking for a set. Wow. These are the kind of moments we dream about. He had position on me. I mean that, technically, he was closer to the peak where the waves broke and so the next wave belonged to him. But no rule of surf etiquette said I had to yield to a pinniped. *I'm going*, I thought. *Next good wave is mine. You can catch waves all day long.*

He turned his sleek head and looked at me with such frank and kindly condescension that I winced. *What on earth are you doing in my house?* he seemed to say. *You are such a kook.*

Kook means "beginner surfer." It is not a neutral term; it

carries a slug of derision, a brand for the clueless, for those without hope, without grace, without rhythm. To be a kook is to be consigned to a kind of beginner's hell. The seal disappeared in a swirl of green water. Good. I always messed up when someone was watching. I needed a little alone time.

I sat on the board and focused on the horizon. My ocean-sharpened eyes were hunting set waves—the distinctly bigger, more powerful swells that came like big fat birthday presents out of the Pacific. One was bound to have my name on it.

Was that one? Way, way out? Yes! I turned the board and lay down. Ready!

Surfers, people who actually knew how to surf, spun their boards just under the wave and took off. Not me. I needed a lot of lead time. I started paddling. My wave might not get here for a while, but I'd have some momentum.

The seal's head popped up, not ten feet away. Now he was about to burst with glee. Evidently he thought I was hilarious. He kept his head half turned, eyes unblinking and locked on mine as he effortlessly cruised beside me on my right. *Go ahead, laugh!* I thought. *You won't be the first, but I'm getting this wave.* I already suspected he could read my mind, so I added, *Big shot.*

I looked once over my shoulder. Oh, man, there it was, the building wall, barreling in just behind, steepening, lifting. This was it. The wave picked up my tail and shot me forward. Yes! Okay, okay, pop up!

In the split second it took to attempt the most crucial move in surfing—from passenger-prone to standing and in control—two thoughts flashed: *Anything is possible.* And: *What the hell am I doing here?*

THE CALL

I was in the middle of my life. I had just finished a book on a dangerous expedition through Tibet's deepest gorge, a chasm with tigers in the bottom and raging twenty-five-thousand-foot peaks on top. I had clung to the side of the canyon, struggled over high passes in the middle of the Himalayan winter. The two-month expedition was so strenuous that when I got home I slept for two weeks. Now, after completing a book about it, I was exhausted in a different way. I sat on my porch in Denver and watched spring snows sweep over the mountains to the west. I drank coffee and listened to the crows argue in the big maple across the street. Sometimes a solitary corvid would cry a single rising note that hung in the air, and it sounded to me like a question thrown against the sky.

How does one make a life?

I had done a Big Thing. Now what was I supposed to do?

Was I supposed to do another Big Thing? Or could I do some small things for a while? Was it enough to string together things of any size until I died? Did it matter, as long as I had friends, family, a community?

I had always sought solace and meaning in wild places. I loved exploring rivers in a kayak, which is a very versatile little craft, and I had found a way to write about these trips and make a living and keep going back. But more and more, wherever I traveled, I could see that we were degrading these places as fast as we could. It drove me crazy. Sometimes I imagined God blowing His whistle and saying to all of us, *Everybody out of the pool! I entrusted you with this paradise and look what you've done.*

And what about love? I mean romantic love. Wasn't that supposed to help define everything? I hadn't done so well in that category. I had loved several women deeply, but I was always traveling and when I came back I was on deadline and I never could fully commit. I was a moving target. I pushed the patience of my lovers to the breaking point and then I was heartbroken when they left. I was a fool. Now I was with a truly lovely woman named Kim, but the Tibet trip and my inability to promise anything had strained us, and everything seemed up in the air.

I had this idea that maybe my job here was just to pay attention. I liked that. Very simple. But then I wasn't sure what to pay attention to. Is it enough to listen to other people who are as lost as I am? Or to the wind, which pours through the trees in a language I cannot decipher? Or these crows, who seem talkative but restless?

At this point in his life, Dante met Virgil and went on a long vacation to hell. It was the mother of all midlife crises. I got a call from Huntington Beach, Surf City USA.

BOYS

The call came from a friend's wife. Andy had been one of my closest buddies since college. He had grown up on the wrong side of the tracks in Camden, South Carolina. His father died very young and his mother did all the mechanic work on their old station wagon. In college, he took law school entrance exams and scored so high that he ended up with a full scholarship to Columbia. He didn't really want to be a lawyer, but the offer was too good to refuse, so off he went. He aced school, despite not studying much, and went through a series of jobs at private law firms where he didn't fit in. Finally he landed at the legal department of a giant manufacturing company, where he began to thrive. He moved with his family into an old house on a tree-lined street in a midwestern city, got as comfortable as he'd ever been, and promptly got transferred to Orange County, California.

When his wife called me, she sounded desperate. She said that Andy was having a tough year. He'd been brought in to clean up the legal department of a subsidiary, and he was emphatically not a disciplinarian. When he had to call some cowboy lawyer on the carpet, his natural inclination was to tell him a long parable about bass fishing. He hated the constant conflict of the job and he wasn't sleeping. He had a vacation coming up, he had wanted to learn to surf, would I come out and learn with him?

Definitely, yes. I'd seen the Gidget movies and *The Endless Summer*. I booked a ticket and in early April I flew into John Wayne Airport, Orange County, California.

Andy picked me up wearing a Hawaiian shirt with surfboards all over it. We drove with the windows down. I was excited, he was excited. We were going to be boys, have an adventure. The first thing we needed to do was get me a board.

My first surfboard was an egg; that's the name of a classic design. They are ideal for beginners because they are usually forgiving. This one was not prepossessing. Neither longboard nor shortboard, it was eight feet long and as oval as a platter. It did not edge a straight line or turn particularly fast. It was not nimble and not stable. The shaper who made it must have been a genius, as it is almost impossible to make a surfboard that is *not* every desirable quality. It didn't do anything well, really, except hatch my career as a surfer.

It was an old board, pre-owned, covered in tiny vines—a hand-painted tangle of no plant that ever lived on earth. Most graphics on surfboards are laid down under the fiberglass so that the board is smooth to the touch: no matter how exuberant or violent the picture or color, close your eyes and your hand passes over the deck of the board like it was polished bone. Not the Egg. This was paint dabbed atop the gel coat—the first owner paying tribute to her most modest egg, or maybe an attempt to gussy it up after it surfed like a brick.

I guess Skip at Board 'n Bean would have felt bad charging me for a week with the board. He ran the last true surf shack in Huntington Beach, part board shop, part café, part betting parlor (I think), part other stuff. It sat on the Pacific Coast Highway beside a cluster of trashy palms, and it caught my eye as Andy and I drove past. There was a rack of brightly colored old boards out front with a sign that said BIG SALE.

"Nah, just take it," Skip said, handing me the egg. "Put me in an article. Hey, what size are you? You're gonna need this."

He threw me an orange full-length wetsuit. He was wearing a sleeveless T and his arms were like anvils.

"Got a leash?"

I shook my head. There was a muffled roar from the two TVs in the shop. Skip glanced up at the one mounted above the doorway to his new board room. "Fucking Dodgers. If I wanted to watch *The Simpsons*—know what I mean, Domino?"

Domino? No one had ever called me that. I liked it.

"Here." He unhooked a leash from a peg. I took it. Something in the way I looked at it as he handed it to me made him laugh and wince up his bloodshot blue eyes. He lifted his trucker's cap and his bleached blond hair spilled to his shoulders. The cap had a pair of the naked mud-flap girls on the brim.

"You don't know how to put it on, do you? Dude, you *are* a kook. Here."

He shook out the eight feet of plastic cable, ripped apart the Velcro tab, and attached it to the little loop of cord at the tail of the board.

"Hey, you need some wax. Got wax?" He tossed me two little bricks.

"Use the board for a week. When you decide you want to get your own, I've got one for you. No plastic, though, Domino, cash only. Cool?" He was hoping I would; there were some Lakers games later in the week he wanted to cover.

There's a feeling I will always remember: walking out of the shop with my first surfboard under my arm. This was cool. I bet the people in the cars passing on the Pacific Coast Highway thought I was a real surfer. I felt like a real surfer. I had a board, wax, a wetsuit. The whole Pacific Ocean in front of me.

A NOTE ON WAX

A standard modern surfboard is made of lightweight, rigid, porous foam shaped as need and art require, then skinned with layers of fiberglass. The result is a platform that's smooth as bone, slippery when wet. The early surfers in the U.S. and Australia dripped paraffin on their boards for traction. When push came to shove, the droplets of hardened wax didn't stay on very well. Various companies in both countries experimented with softening the wax and marketing it for surfers, but it was two outfits in 1972 that swept the surfing world: Mr. Zog's Sex Wax and Wax Research. Sex Wax came in round bricks a little bigger than a hockey puck. An old surfer told me that this was because the first production runs were poured into tuna tins—lucky they added perfume. Before a session a surfer rubbed the bar over the deck of his board, everywhere his feet might land. Sometimes he waxed the rails up front, a hand's-width patch where, when paddling out and confronted with a wave breaking in front of him, he would grab the board for a duck-dive.

Genius name, Sex Wax. Cool, edgy, adolescent, which strikes to the heart of surf culture. The ritual: squatting, shortboard over knee, waxing the tapered weapon. Or the pro pose, in transit to the water: little board cocked on hip, flexing the knee up for support, reaching across, and waxing quickly with the free hand. Leftover crumb of wax stuffed back in pocket. Or a longboard: laying it on the ground, moving along its length, addressing it with the wax, rubbing and rubbing, tip to tail. Is there anything more sexy except sex? It's preparing the rigid phallus for the act, or it *is* the act, I haven't decided.

In '92, Wax Research introduced Sticky Bumps, which sounds more like the yucky disease you might get if you didn't properly protect while using Sex Wax. But wildly popular to this day because it works. It comes in little square bricks with a deep groove down the middle so you can break it in two and shove one half in the pocket of your board shorts. Rub it on lightly and small deckles adhere; rub more, careful not to be too firm, and voilà!, little bumps. That are pretty sticky. You may pop up, miss your timing and get clobbered, driven to the rock reef, knocked in the teeth by your tumbling board, but it won't be because your feet slipped.

Wax sometimes, especially in the Third World, is hard to get. Or you left it back in the car, or the $1.25 a brick is more than you can afford because you have no job and you are crashing on your cousin's couch in Huntington and you'd rather spend that money on beer. Or the guy at Dukes on the Pier hasn't called you back about the busboy job, and you are living on peanut butter sandwiches and surfing your brains, what's left of them, out every morning north of the pier, and the guy in the parking lot cut you dead when you said, "Hey, bro, could I get a hit of wax?," just turned away, and you have, really, about a year's-worth of wax on your board already, but it gets flattened and smooth and greasy with time, then what do you do?

You use a wax comb.

My first pair of board shorts came with one looped into the pocket. Here's the funny thing about buying board shorts in Huntington Beach. You mostly can't wear them surfing. The water, for all but a couple of months of the year, is too cold to wear anything but a wetsuit. Thick, long-sleeve, and long-leg neoprene suits in the winter, short and light in the spring and summer. So unless you're one of the kids who take pride in trunking it, in being that tough, you're gonna be surfing in a wetsuit all year. So why buy board shorts? The shorts that tie at the waist and hang down past my knee and make me look like an elf?

Because they're cool. Period. What's wrong with you?

The wax comb is slick because it is another tool, multi-use, you can use to tune up your board. Just what it says: a two- or three-inch-wide plastic comb you rub hitch-hatch over the wax on your board to give it new grip. The back side of the comb is usually plastic-knife sharp, usually straight, for scraping off old wax. If it's really sophisticated, one side of the scraper is curved inward for running the wax off the rounded rails. My first pair of board shorts were tan and blue Quicksilver with the sturdiness of canvas, but a soft nap almost like suede. It had a surprise wax comb tied into the pocket on a loop of elastic cord, like a toy in a Cracker Jack box. Inspection revealed not only the translucent, heavy-duty comb, but also a fin key that slotted into it. A fin key is a very small Allen wrench that turns the screws that hold the removable fins in the tail of your board into their slots. How cool was this? Not only did you get hip shorts, you got a comb, a scraper, a fin key. With your board and a wave, you had all you needed.

First Blood

From Board 'n Bean, Andy and I drove south a few blocks to the parking lot of the Huntington Beach Pier. This pier, according to my contact Nathan Myers at *Surfing* magazine, had made and broken more surfing careers than anyplace on earth. It was tall; the heavy pilings lifted the deck some twenty feet off the water. The waves thundered white through the posts like an avalanche. Out over deep water beyond the break, a line of fishermen dropped their lines over the rails.

On the sand a few towels, a few sunbathers, not many. It was a Monday in April.

We teetered the boards off the rack of Andy's minivan. Stretched on our wetsuits, helped each other zip up the backs, lay our boards on the pavement of the parking lot, and waxed them, didn't know how, just rubbed hard and caked it on. This was already fun. Neither of us had ever used a surfboard before. The smart thing would have been to take a lesson, but we had both taught ourselves to kayak in college, picking up tips haphazardly from friends, and we figured surfing was a lot less complicated. I mean, there were no hydraulics, eddies, eddy lines, strainers, ledges, haystacks, horizon lines, or box canyons. There were just waves. We blinked at the bright water and surveyed them. They were about as tall as charging water buffalo. Over by the pilings was a bunch of surfers.

"Okay," Andy said. "Let's stay away from those dudes." To us, all surfers were dudes, which term we found out was about a decade out of date. He took a deep breath. "Try not to drown."

"Got it."

We jogged to the water on the south side of the pier. I was knee-deep in heavy wave wash before I had a plan; all I knew was that I was going surfing now. I had body-surfed all through my childhood. I understood that you positioned yourself, faced the beach, and when a wave came you paddled to get launched. Then I figured you stood up. Simple.

I waded until I was waist-deep, then pushed the board into the onrushing foam and bellied onto it. The foam spun me sideways and dumped me. Okay, no problem. I waded deeper, waited for the next surge to pass, then jumped on, spread my legs wide for stability, and paddled like a fool. Exactly like a fool. Windmilling arms, big splashes.

Phew. Somehow made it past the main break and into smooth water. Andy was already here. First triumph. I looked at the knot of younger shortboarders over near the pier and figured they must know something we didn't.

"C'mon, Andy, that's where the waves are!"

"Don't go over there."

"Why not? C'mon!"

I didn't want to get in their way, so I paddled over to them, but not too close. They sat on their tiny boards, which were so small they barely floated. I could do that, sit in the lineup like a pro.

I wriggled up on the egg and straddled it, wobbled, and capsized. Whoops, tippy damn thing.

I came up and blinked the water out of my eyes. Nobody had seen it. The surfer dudes weren't paying me any attention. They were looking seaward, quietly, or talking among themselves. Phew. I decided to just lie on the board and wait for a wave. It came, as waves do, in a few seconds. Humped up, rolled in.

Here was the wall. I paddled like a maniac, got picked up, bucked, yelled, stood up, sort of, a fraction of a second. Pitched forward, flew in air, then foam. The wave shoved me to the bottom. I flailed for sunlight and hit my head on the underside of the egg. When I finally cleared water and breathed, there was a long-haired kid five feet away yelling at me. Mid-twenties. He had a snake tattoo running down the side of his neck, and right then the snake was negotiating extruding corded tendons, throbbing arteries. His eyes were wild. *Jeez, dude, calm down.*

"You fucking Goddamn KOOK! Get the fuck out of the water!"

"*What?* I was way out of your way—"

"Fuck! Move the fuck down there!" He waved his arm. "Way the fuck down. See you here again I'll *fuck you up!*"

He shook his head, disgusted, and paddled off. As he went I noticed how fast his board moved, how he paddled way up on the front with his back arched, his chest way off the deck and his legs pinned together. He was an asshole, but he sure looked competent.

Smarting, I paddled over to Andy, who was already way south, sitting on his board, watching.

"You see that?"

"Yeah."

"What'd I do?"

"You cut him off. Cold, dude. Dropped in on him. I thought he was going to kill you."

"Me, too."

"You gotta watch. Thought that was the end of the line for my buddy." Andy pointed to the wave breaking just this side of the pier and explained to me how good waves don't just dump but begin breaking at a peak, and continue collapsing in a traveling line that moves sideways along the shore.

"See?" he said. "The peak, where it starts breaking, is over there by the pier. That's why those guys are there. They hop on it just as it begins to break and then they travel kind of sideways all the way down the face." He explained that that was why a surfer who jumped on near the pier and stayed just ahead of the white pocket could end up way down here in my lap.

I stared. "There's a whole bunch there. How do they know who gets the wave? Or do they just yell, *Get the hell out of my way?*"

"The surfer just closest to the peak where the wave starts breaking has priority. See?" Andy explained that everybody had to get out of his way as he zoomed and turned across the face. He said that a "left" means a wave that is moving left from the surfer's point of view as he's surfing it, a "right" means he's surfing along to his right.

"Oh," I said.

We wrestled with the foam for two hours. I felt less like a surfer than ammo in a human slingshot. I was so tired I couldn't lift my arms to paddle. We'd stood up for a combined cumulative time of four seconds. I thought I'd understood what Andy had said about the peak and the surfer with priority, but when I finally got out past the break I couldn't figure out where the peak was. I didn't know how far away from the other surfers was safe to sit, and I must have gotten it wrong, because another dude collided with me and asked me if I was born on Planet Kook. That really hurt my feelings. Andy and I crawled out onto the sand and went for a late breakfast at the Sugar Shack, a block and a half from the pier on Main. It was always packed. Working people, tourists, surfers. We squeezed into a table against the wall, an arm's-length from the backs of the guys at the counter, and I ordered eggs over easy with bacon and coffee. Andy asked for poached eggs on dry toast. The brisk young gal in a black Shack T-shirt snagged a pen from behind her ear, blew away a wisp of ponytail, and asked us how the waves were. How did she know? The tangled hair? My osprey eyes? I was thrilled. She had broad shoulders and strong forearms.

"Waist-high, kinda mushy," I said, repeating something I'd heard in the parking lot.

The walls were covered in surfing photos. We sat under a framed cover from *Surfer* magazine: a guy standing straight up and relaxed, like he was waiting for a bus, in the middle of a barrel about as big as the Holland Tunnel. Above that was a signed blowup photo of someone riding a giant, and next to it were two local Shack-sponsored kids' surf teams and a framed memorial to a young surfer who had died somehow. He must have been sixteen. Below his head shot, very blond and forthright, were the words:

> *Whenever you are riding,*
> *We hope the waves are forever*
> *glassy and hollow*

The guy in the tube was Timmy Turner. Timmy was behind the counter punching orders into the register. Timmy was twenty-six, and he'd been surfing for twenty years. He wore a black T, and it hung loosely on his wide shoulders and he seemed thin, almost slight, for being one of the most hard-core surfers around. His mom, Michelle, had bought the Shack twenty-five years before from her own parents and was known for feeding full meals to homeless people, and for sponsoring local school-age surfers. The kids got one free meal a week, salad through milkshake. I loved the place right away. The generosity of spirit, the rock-solid values of decency and civil duty, seemed to permeate the whole restaurant. It was there in the respectful way the young waitresses talked to the broken-down beachcomber at the end of the counter, the way everyone who passed asked if we needed more coffee.

Andy burst the yolk of his egg over his single piece of butterless bread.

"I love surfing," I confided.

Andy sipped his coffee and studied me over his cup, through his round gold wire-rims. "How do you know?" he said.

"Well . . ."

He smiled. "Maybe tomorrow we should try Bolsa Chica. It'll probably be closed out, but it won't matter. We need some time in the whitewater."

That sounded good. I didn't know what "closed out" meant, but I liked the idea of giving it all another go, maybe miles from any tatted-up dudes who kept saying fuck when talking to me.

Bolsa Chica State Park begins two and a half miles north of the Huntington Beach Pier. It is three miles of wide sand beach along a lightly curving southwest-facing coast. At the southern end, the Bolsa Chica estuary runs out through a cut in the beach. A rich tidal wetland, the estuary is one of the great American success stories of grassroots conservation and surfer activism. Once one of the largest oil-drilling fields in the world, the estuary and much of the beach were slated in the nineties for development as a mega-marina. The critical habitat would have gone the way of the rest of Southern California's 75 to 90 percent of coastal wetlands lost to development. This single lagoon was so important because the Pacific Flyway is one of the largest north-south bird migration routes on the planet, and many species are forced to skip much of Southern California because the tidal marshes where they used to stop over have been destroyed in order to build ports, marinas, and houses. The marina at Bolsa Chica would also have probably wrecked a favorite local surfing spot. A consortium of environmental groups led by the Surfrider Foundation stopped the project, and in 1997 got the state to put up $91 million to restore the marsh and to widen a cut through the beach to increase crucial tidal flow. At 880 acres, it has been one of the biggest and most successful coastal wetland restoration projects in the country, and has reestablished a stepping-stone in the flyway for migrating waterfowl. Now, every day, a few hundred yards from scores of surfers, bird-watchers can be seen walking the wood-plank trails in the marsh with their binoculars. Endangered birds such as the light-footed clapper rail are nesting there again. And outraged surfers led the charge. Go figure. The Surfrider Foundation is mostly made up of surfers, and today it has over fifty thousand members in the U.S. In '91 they won the second largest Clean Water Act lawsuit in American history, against two pulp mills in Humboldt County. More recently, they have worked with Laguna Beach to mitigate coastal water pollution from runoff, and they stopped Orange County from dumping 240 million gallons per day of partially treated sewage into the sea. Why should it surprise me? Surfers are an intense bunch and they love their coast the way they love their mothers.

We pulled up to the beach in a stiff offshore wind. Numbered lifeguard towers sat at two-hundred-yard intervals along the sand; the numbers went up as the towers marched northward. We would find out later that the towers served as landmarks for surfers—a few friends might decide to meet at Tower 21, or if it's too crowded or the waves are dumping, they'd go south to 18.

Bolsa Chica was pretty, but it was no picnic. We trotted out to an empty part of the beach and jogged into the surf. As soon as we stepped off the sand it was like walking into a swift river. We got swept south by the strong riptide. When I did manage to get through the surf to calm water, I was beat, but happy to be way past where any waves were breaking. I looked out to sea and blinked, transfixed like a highway deer. What the hell was *that*? *That* was a set wave. Bigger than anything yet and breaking much farther out. I got squashed.

Having learned my lesson, I paddled way, way out. No set wave would catch me inside again. Out here, it was pretty but it wasn't surfing. I clambered onto my board to sit—which in itself was a tenuous operation. I breathed, gut hollow with exhaustion, arms and back burning with lactic acid, and looked around. Relief to be out of the crashing mayhem. Just easy rolling swell. Phew. Three dolphins swam lazily by, heading north, their backs glossy and dark. Now, this was the life. But no waves broke so far out, so I edged back in. And then another wave, much larger than the others, walled up and broke on my head. It tumbled me back inshore, right into the impact zone, which is where the brunt of the waves collapse. It was also the worst part of the riptide, and I got trundled south, and the first wave's posse clobbered me one after another.

Was this fun? Two-foot waves were turning me into Play Doh. On the fifth wave, I managed to crawl up and stand and just as fast flew through the air like a catapulted cow. I know now that with the waves dumping the way they were, and the length of our boards and our skill level, we didn't stand a chance. Once, in sheer frustration, I rode the egg in on my belly, just to feel some speed. I got off it in ankle-deep water, and turned and lifted the heavy board. I carried it back into the white foam in front of me and across my body and got slammed by the next sweep of whitewater, and the egg leveled me like a snowplow. I unpeeled myself from the sand inch by inch the way Wile E. Coyote detaches himself from the pavement after Road Runner drives over him with a cement mixer.

I took a breather on the beach. Then, on the wet sand, carelessly attaching the Velcro of the leash to my ankle, I let the egg wallow in two inches of wash, and the next surge sent it sideways into me and nearly broke my legs. It could have snapped them like dry sticks had my feet been set.

If two inches of afterthought from a waist-high wave

could do that to me, what would a real wave do? The forces a surfer deals with are beyond reckoning.

That night, covered with bruises, aching everywhere, I lay on Andy's fold-out couch in the library. I revisited the last two days and winced. I was such a kook. In surf slang, kook doesn't just mean beginner; it means outrageous, awkward, clueless novice who cuts people off on waves, thrashes around speaking to other surfers like it's a cocktail party, hollers rebel yells when he does manage to stand up for a split second, has no tact, no respect for the finely tuned protocol of surf, and is dangerous to boot, because when he drops in on a wave without looking, boards and bodies collide. That was me. I had called my girlfriend Kim and she was sympathetic to a point. She was getting sick of me being away all the time. She did not demand that I change, but she pointed out that it was hard to stay close. Ouch. It dawned on me that kook also perfectly described my aptitude with women.

I was unwilling to turn out the light and let sleep claim me before I had salvaged something of the day. Andy's old shepherd Cody lay on my legs and watched me with a concerned expression. I had known him for years. Now he seemed to sense that I was wrestling with powerful forces: vanity, pride, surf.

I rubbed his forehead with my fist and slid a notebook off the side table. I glanced up at the bookcase that occupied the entire wall opposite. A thousand spines, a thousand reverberating names, the best efforts of the truest minds. I scanned across the modern canon and their antecedents. Eliot, Coleridge, Proust, Stein, Dickinson, Brecht, W. C. Williams, Plato, Faulkner, Homer, Rilke, Cervantes. Waves of their own, waves that broke over reefs of readers and worked their own geologic power. I felt small. What the hell was I doing here? I had hoped to write some fiction and I was setting that aside for the moment to take up a new sport that everybody said was consuming. Why do that to myself at forty-five? Why take the risk? If I was going to get any good writing done, I needed every minute I could get. I knew myself—the king of distraction.

The last title that popped out made me laugh. When I did, Cody lifted and cocked his head.

"It's nothing," I said. *"Don Quixote.* I'd read it to you, but it would drive a dog like you nuts."

I opened the notebook and wrote at the top of a page: *SURFING,* then *What I Learned Today.*

Set waves break farther out than you think and then you're screwed.

Do not get the surfboard between you and the wave. Keep it beside or down-wave from you.

Set waves are not alone. They come in . . . sets. D'oh!

Now we were getting somewhere. I closed the notebook and went to sleep.

We woke up just at first light on the third day. I eased my feet out from under the weight of Cody and found my shorts. The air coming through the open windows was brisk. I put on a thick sweatshirt. People think of Southern California as hot, but it's not, at least not by the water. Everything on my body hurt. My shins were bruised; my head was tender from the knock the first morning; my shoulders and back were stiff and sore. We made instant coffee in the kitchen while Andy's family slept. We each ate a bowl of cornflakes. We took the bottle of Advil out of the cabinet with the coffee mugs and each ate four. As the salty gray air lightened, we gathered our heavy wetsuits from their pegs without much enthusiasm.

We were sluggish, and I know my body was tired through and through. It's exhausting getting battered. Demoralizing getting yelled at. I think now that if we'd had another day of surfing like the first two, we might just have hung it up.

Then again, I doubt it. Most sports, at first entry, balance the initial strangeness and difficulty with some immediate rewards. In kayaking, you launch down your first riffling whitewater, take the first little waves over your bow, feel the speed like a revelation as the current tongues into a smooth V between rocks. You may dump and swim but you've had that rush. Skiing is the same; the bunny slope gives you that first alien and wonderful sense of slide and acceleration, though you may not know how to stop or turn.

Everything works this way except surfing.

Surfing is one of the only pursuits on earth that can drub you into numb exhaustion and blunt trauma time and again and give you nothing in return; nothing but sand in your crotch, salt-stung eyes, banged temple, chipped tooth, screaming back, and sunburned ears—gives you all of this and not a single stand-up ride. Time and again. Day after day. Gives you nothing back but tumbles, wipeouts, thumpings, scares. And you return. You are glad to do it. In fact, you can think of nothing you'd rather do.

WHAT WE THINK ABOUT WHEN WE THINK ABOUT SURF

Have you seen *Beach Blanket Bingo?*
   The Endless Summer? Step into Liquid? Riding Giants? Point Break? Baywatch?

When we imagine surfing we probably see images from these classics. Maybe in another dream there are old woody station wagons pulled up to the beach and some guys playing ukuleles. Maybe there's a leaned-over surf shack covered in bougainvillea and an empty curve of Mexican beach with perfect combers breaking white along the bay. A bucket of sweating Corona. Maybe there are three happy-go-lucky *Endless Summer* kids trading waves and you can hear their whoops on the wind. Maybe there are lifeguard towers every quarter mile and Pamela Anderson is driving a pickup, and maybe the beach is Malibu and there are five surfers hanging ten all together on one wave. Or maybe we are the rare dreamer and we see one giant mountain of water, some *Jaws* rogue wave, and there's a lone figure, small as a swallow, arcing down its face.

Either way, scientists and anthropologists agree that for 95 percent of us our fantasy will involve eight standard components:

1. A beautiful setting, invigorated by the wild nature of the sea.
2. Beautiful chicks, bikinis, the promise of sex in the air like the smell of hibiscus—hibiscuses—hibisci—
3. Aloha spirit—a generous, blissed-out bonhomie, on the waves and off.
4. Hair-raising prowess on the wave—muscled and graceful.
5. Machismo: the only possible result when combining numbers 2 and 4.
6. A party, lots of booze and pot.
7. Happy, danceable music in the background.
8. The wave itself. The lead character. However you conceive it. Like God.

What we have just concocted without realizing it is the Garden before the Fall. Maybe surfing was like this once. Maybe, after the red heifer and the Antichrist and a Great Fire, it will be so again.

But for now, let's review and correct.

1.   The raw power of the sea *is* beautiful. Even at Orange County river mouths where you are sitting on your board and look down and see what can only be strands of feces and undissolved toilet paper floating by your vulnerable toes. Even in Mexican bays where they have yanked out the last significant stands of bird-flocked, fish-breeding mangroves and replaced them with box hotels built by greed-sick developers from Denver. (This is true, in Baja—I know the guy—and in thousands of other places, too.) Even off of beaches where there used to be mackerel and tuna runs and now there are none, because they have all been fished out. Even then—and sometimes all these things are happening at once—the ocean heaves her inexorable breath and you feel humbled and renewed.

2.   Sometimes there are foxy chicks. They sit on a towel with a camera with a huge honking lens and take pictures of their semipro man who has been snaking your waves all morning; because he can. Lucky if they even nod as you walk by.

3.   Which brings us to Aloha Spirit, the greatest draw and the greatest misconception about surfing.

    Surfing is one of the fastest-growing sports in the world. Thousands of neophytes join the ranks of new American surfers every year. Worldwide, including surfwear and fashion, surfing is a billion-dollar industry. The cachet, the attraction, seems to be all about youth, strength, and that generous aloha spirit. The idea is that surfers have an easygoing, hang-loose relationship with violent hydraulic power and other people. Nothing much ruffles the laid-back surfer.

The problem is that the aloha spirit is generally a myth—surfers have always been aggressive, driven, and territorial. You have to be, temperamentally, to deal with waves of any size and to jostle for position with others. All the eager new surfers crowding the waves are exacerbating tensions and shortening fuses. Some California counties have actually enacted anti-surf-rage ordinances that ban aggressors from their local waves as part of the punishment for surf-related assaults.

4.   The prowess and grace are real. I wanted some of that.

5.   The machismo is real, too. As you shall see.

6.   Party—well, yeah. Not like beach blankets and camp-fires and volleyball, though that happens in rare fits of collective nostalgia, especially at big competitions. Especially in Mexico. Usually, though, it's a quick joint in the front seat of the car before bailing out into the dawn chill.

7.   Happy music: of course. Sometimes it's just in your head. One of the things I love most about surfing is all the time you have to yourself—long paddle-outs with the schooling fish and birds and breaking sets; sitting on your board away from the others with the whole ocean in front of you, looking for your own peak; catching that one long ride, when the music is acceleration, speed, thunder, and glide.

8.   The wave itself. It is the one thing that no one can exaggerate. As poetic as you wax, as thick as you lay it on, as

much as you magnify, you can never, ever encompass or describe the greatness of the wave. The wave that can be named is not the real Wave.

Nobody can be blamed for having all these wrong ideas about surfing. You read about how surfing started way back in the Polynesian kingdom of Hawaii, the first account recorded by British Lieutenant James King in 1779, who tacked into Kealakekua Bay on the Kona Coast of the North Island and witnessed the oddest thing: dozens of men riding wooden planks down the waves. You can see an artist's rendition in an engraving from the period: four Hawaiians dropping in on the same wave on what look like chunks of six-by lumber. Others show island women perched on boards, breasts bared, hair flowing behind them as they shred. One sailor reported that when a good swell came in, whole villages would abandon whatever they were doing and run down to the shore and surf. That was another version of Surf Eden. All myth is based on a rock foundation of truth. It is true that surfing began in the Pacific, probably in Hawaii or Tahiti, and that it sprang from a culture who lived in a place of such beauty and bounty that its people had generous bumpers of leisure time and an inclination toward laughter and play.

And maybe then there really was aloha spirit. Maybe the crowds of Hawaiians didn't get in each other's way on the wave, maybe they did not collide and crack each other's wiliwili-wood planks. Just maybe they didn't come up yelling, bruised, or lose control of their leaden, loglike boards, which then maybe didn't accelerate toward a whole clutch of little kids and mow them over like tenpins. Maybe they just stood on the front of their plank with the wave curlicuing behind and over them, feet together, hair flowing behind, perfectly balanced, perfectly spaced apart on the waves as in the engraving, Adonises and Aphrodites of Kealakekua, and the only thing you would hear from the beach aside from the sift and crash of surf was laughter and cries of innocent joy.

P.S.—WHY WE NEED STUFF LIKE SURFING

We are not a graceful species. We spend all day falling forward from one precarious step to the next; we bump, bumble, and teeter. Think of John and Jane Everyhuman walking down the street, chatting, sipping their Starbucks on the way to work. Think of them swiveling their bulbous heads on the stalks of their necks to look at something that catches an eye, their raw, hairless faces like blunt semaphores in the sunlight. Think of them stepping off a curb, wading to the other side, lifting their knees with some effort to gain the sidewalk, jostling Jocelyn Everyhuman, whose head is craned into her cell phone as she passes. Now think of a single minnow. Minnie. She turns like a bead of mercury. She is as at home in her firmament as an element. Water gains definition by her fluidity. Lightning can teach her nothing about moving from one place to another. When she idles, holding herself steady with a minute wavering of her tail, an invisible flutter of a fin, she is incomparable in her stillness, as poised with the potential for explosive movement as any loaded gun. She looks like she is thinking.

That's just one minnow. Look into the water off any seaside dock, and if the water is green and clear, you see a hundred minnows, a thousand, moving in liquid concert like a single thought, flashing back sunlight in a sudden turn as precise and effortless as a single swallow, as synchronized as a wave of wind moving through tall grass. That's minnows. We haven't even mentioned a big cat flowing down through rocks. Don't get me started.

We need surf—or dance or yoga—because it reconnects us with our animal bodies. For a little while we practice moving through the world with rhythm, with an intention of efficiency and power. Without it, we become just a bunch of walking heads.

THE SAINT

On that third day, our first stop was Huntington Surf and Sport, the large surf shop on the corner of Main Street and the PCH, just across the road from the pier. They served good coffee and blueberry muffins before anyone else in town. I loved coming in there when the cavernous store was empty and the few other cars on the street had boards on the roof. All surf shops smell the same—a fragrance of epoxy resin offgassing from the racks of surfboards, new neoprene, perfumed surf wax.

The dense overcast of the marine layer was burning off and the day was turning fine and warm. We got in the Chrysler van and rolled to the T of the Pacific Coast Highway. Across it I could see fast waves breaking either side of the pier. I winced. I turned to Andy.

"Maybe we could go someplace that's a little more gentle."

"We could try Seal Beach. It's only like fifteen minutes north."

We rolled up past the Cliffs, where there were already clusters of surfers floating off the bluff. From the hill we could see the low waves breaking all along the length of Bolsa Chica. We passed the big empty parking lots and drove through the strip of Sunset Beach, a tawdry jumble of fish restaurants and tattoo shops. Then the wasteland of the Navy ammo dump, miles of bunkers on flats of dead grass, ending at water's edge where a windowless destroyer was tied up to the dock waiting to be fed her load of torpedoes and shells.

Then quaint little Seal Beach. Palm trees and bungalows. Another tall pier, a curve of white beach. Away off to the northwest was the port of Long Beach, derricks and buildings. We pulled into the parking lot with a shirr of tires over sand, cut the engine, and while the engine ticked and the off-shore breeze rattled the palms behind us, we drank our coffee, looked through the windshield at the beach, and tried to get stoked.

I was forty-five. Andy was a year younger, but he had been a responsible corporate breadwinner and family man for many years and he was almost bald, so naturally I thought of him as a big brother. Also he had those little wire-rimmed glasses that made him seem at least twice as smart.

"Are we having a midlife crisis?" I said.

"Definitely."

"Is this what we are supposed to do?"

"That's not clear to me."

"It's cheaper than a Ferrari or a divorce, right?"

"You're not married."

"I'm just saying."

"Well, a lot of guys just build a shack in the backyard and then write a book about it. It's a genre of its own. I don't know exactly how much that would cost."

"Hmm."

We watched a pair of lanky teen boys head for the water with shortboards tucked under their arms. Heading for a before-school session. They were loose-jointed and carried the boards with the ease of Masai with their spears. I felt a twinge of envy. What if I had begun surfing when I was just a boy? Instead of the poker games and stoopball of my childhood in Brooklyn. I certainly wouldn't have had to wait until my seventeenth birthday to get laid.

Never too late, right? Wrong. You can't redo your first anything. Was this surfing thing about going backward or forward? Forward = brave, backward = pathetic. No, this surfing project would need to be about growth, about connecting with the earth and growing older with *grace*. I was thinking all this as I was trying to get my foot through the leg of the wetsuit and hopping along the side of the car and feeling every sore muscle. Just as I was teetering, a beat-up white van pulled in beside us.

A man of indeterminate age, with sun-bleached blond hair past his shoulders and a big round belly, got out of the driver's side. He saw us and smiled. He beamed beneficence, like some holy man. He stretched the wetsuit way up over his pink gut and reached back and pulled the zipper ribbon with a practiced grunt. Then he hobbled to the back—kind of shuffled over the pavement—and yanked open the rusty doors. He reminded me of someone. Santa Claus! Belly like a bowl full of jelly. He was pulling surfboards out of the back when a pretty surfer walked from her car and gave him a hug. Then a hulking blond guy with a handlebar mustache did the same thing. Santa couldn't get any work done; surfers kept angling over to give him a hug. Or rather receive one. There was something about the interaction that suggested bestowal. "Love you, too," I heard the man say in a hoarse, emphatic mumble.

I blinked. This was not the surf culture I'd witnessed so far. I don't think I'd heard a single surfer at Huntington Beach tell another he loved him. "Fuck you, too" was about as warm as it got.

The man's smile was beatific, broad. But there was something bullish and tough about him, too.

"Hey," I said to a freshly hugged mother in a wetsuit. "Who *is* that guy?"

"Don't you know? That's the Saint. The Saint of Seal Beach. Bless his heart."

Was I dreaming?

As if this weren't all strange enough, the driver's door popped open and out stepped a woman with bleached blond hair down over her shoulders and a round belly over which she, too, stretched a wetsuit. She was short, and looked something like a scale model of the man. A not-so-mini-me. She began to pull piles of wetsuits out of the side, while he hauled the big blue foam surfboards out of the back. I noticed that the dashboard of the van was covered—no, smothered—with plastic surf kitsch. Spring-loaded surfing Santas, hula girls, tiny woody station wagons. When the man had unloaded about fifteen soft boards, he unstrapped the high stack on the roof rack and slid them off and passed them out, too, to a gathering crowd of what appeared to be young mothers, teenage boys, pretty nurses, retired baseball players, and grandmothers. The whole gamut. The side of the van was painted with a Joe Cool pelican in shades holding a surfboard and the words M&M SURFING SCHOOL.

We watched all of this with growing interest. Then, at the same time, a lightning bolt of apprehension. We looked at each other with a wild surmise:

Surf school!

D'oh!

Why hadn't we thought of it?

We signed up on the spot. Saint Michael Pless said, "Sure, come on! Glad to have you!" He thought he would have a couple of extra boards.

"I've got my egg," I said proudly. He glanced at it with what I thought was less than an enthusiastic endorsement.

"Egg," he said, as if calling her by name. "Very nice. But I want you to use one of mine today. Here, take the one with the duct tape over there. You kids lay the nose of your boards on the wall there. Michael, Jr., has wax." Michael, Jr., waved. A handsome, broad-shouldered, curly-haired kid in his twenties. The Saint's wife, Helena, signed us up. She was as warm as her husband.

My board had a lot of tape on the nose. The front two feet of the foam board seemed to be held on by silver duct tape. And wax. There was a quarter-inch-thick smear of dirty gray, sand-embedded wax coating the entire deck. When I picked it up I realized I was dealing with a whole other animal than the fiberglass egg, as ungainly as she was. This thing was a barge. Must have weighed forty pounds.

Pless heaved two boards up onto his head—the man was a bear—and hitched and shuffled down to the water, following his stomach. I was now dubious about the whole enterprise. It always seemed to me that if you wanted to learn something athletic, learn it from an athlete. French from a Frenchman, carpentry from a carpenter. Surfing, it seemed, one would learn from a surfer. This guy did not look like a surfer. He could barely balance on the beach. He looked nothing like the lean guys who had been yelling at me for the past two days.

Pless had us lie down on the sand on our stomachs and practice popping up. He had us all do it in a line, grandma down to little boy. Chest up, eyes ahead, hands in push-up position, then Bang! Up to your feet. The most common mistake was to come up with feet together, or feet facing forward, or legs straight and body bent over at the waist like you were looking for a nickel. Those who couldn't manage the move from prone to standing in a single pop he had come up to their knees first. "Great!" he yelled. "You guys are naturals. Almost as good as Canadians! For some reason, Canadians, Asians, and doctors are the most natural surfers. Who knows why? Okay, again!" We drilled and drilled until we could go from chest in the sand to standing without thinking about it.

"That's all you have to do," Pless said. "And listen to my seven commands. How many? That's right, *seven*. Let's practice. Okay, lie back down on your pretend boards." Already this was much more fun than Andy and I had had surfing in days, and we weren't even in the water. Pless was giving us challenges, little benchmarks that we could practice and attain. With each came a sense of accomplishment. His encouragement flowed in a constant, good-humored stream. Everybody was smiling. The seven commands were: paddle forward, paddle back, slide forward, slide back, chest up, chest down, and stop. Then an eighth: you're up! We practiced them in a line, lying in the sand, paddling air like beached turtles.

"Okay, everybody in the water! Don't forget to watch out for people surfing in on your way out, and what did I say about your board? That's right, never let your board get between you and the wave. You don't want it getting shoved over you."

I looked at the break. The pier was a hundred yards to our left and there were a couple of real surfers there, catching lefts just off the pilings. The waves were about waist-high and seemed gentle. Pless waded in to where he was chest-deep and motioned a clutch of students over.

"Okay, Mr. Peter, hop on your board. Here comes your wave." I was on the board facing shore. He was standing, one hand on the waxed nose, facing the open ocean, studying the waves.

"Okay, scootch back, good, chest up, now—paddle!" I did. Then I felt a thrust of acceleration as Pless gave me a shove. I was matching the speed of the incoming wave. The swell came from behind and lifted me, I felt the nose tip forward, but I didn't wipe out as I had for the past two days. Because Pless had positioned me back a bit on the board and my chest was up, the front didn't dive and purl. I felt instead a rush of acceleration. The wave launched the board down the little face. Oh, man!

"You're up!" Pless's resonant shout cut through my reverie. I popped up. Instead of the weird crawl-and-stand I had been doing between near-fistfights, now I popped up as we had just practiced. The board sped forward and, miracle! I was standing.

Standing up on a rocketing surfboard.

My feet were apart, sideways to the board. Check. I was in a crouch, hands low. Check. I was speeding toward shore. Che— I was surfing! I saw green water at my feet. Then the wave broke around my knees and I rode the rough whitewater. I was frozen with amazement. I was yelling. I rode until the nose ground sand and the fins dug into the beach. A surge came behind and I toppled off into three inches of foamy water. I came up yelling, hands in the air. *Did anybody see that? Oh, my God! That was so cool! The sense of speed! I am officially a surfer! Yay!*

I was such a kook.

I was ecstatic.

I was not the only one. Andy surfed his first wave and

looked like he had just been hit on the head with a cow. The rest of the class was standing within half an hour.

Turns out that Pless is perhaps the best surf instructor in the country. He is so good, so warm and fun, that investment bankers fly in from Chicago for two mornings of lessons with him. Celebrities come down from L.A. Congresswomen and supermodels and star athletes have all been his students. Children with autism and cerebral palsy. An eighty-six-year-old lady. *Canadians.* Whole families from Manitoba who come back for a week year after year. A lot of people, too many, have actually quit their corporate jobs to take up surfing after taking lessons with the Saint. Nobody in the world is better at getting people surfing and having fun in so little time.

Midmorning we took a break. Pless told me that he had grown up in Orange County and had been an avid surfer his whole life. When he was in his twenties he fell in with a rough crowd. He rode with the Hells Angels as a young pledge. I watched him as he talked and I could see it. Beneath his jolly rotundity was a bull of a man. He seemed easygoing, but out in the surf he hustled students into the safe spots, shoved boards and bodies back up and into breaking surf if he didn't like the look of a wave, hauled people out of whitewater as easily as if they were drenched puppies. He kept everything in control and didn't miss a lick. He would have been hell in a bar fight.

One night when he was a biker he was late for a meet at the house of a drug dealer. The four Hells Angels who did show up were shot to death. Pless missed dying by minutes. He quit the gang.

Then one afternoon he was working at his job as a telephone lineman and he fell off a high pole. When he hit the ground he fractured every bone in his right lower leg. When the bones healed, they all fused together, so he had, essentially, a peg leg. He sustained other injuries, too, and the doctor said he'd be lucky to walk again unaided. Pless, being Pless, not only walked, albeit with a hitch, he learned to jog with a shuffle and completed a painful marathon. He refused to accept that he would no longer ride waves. But it is very hard to balance on a small pitching platform, even with feet and ankles that flex and roll. With a peg leg and scar-stiffened body, the job is much more daunting. Painfully, he retaught himself to surf. He figured that if he could teach himself to surf again, he could teach anybody, so he started taking students. He also found God and discovered that he was happiest being of service to others—as opposed to scaring the daylights out of them.

It seemed to me that his greatest gift as a teacher was his warmth and sense of fun. Gusts of laughter often came from the pod of boards floating around him. "The best surfer is the one having the most fun!" he'd yell. I didn't really believe that—I'd look over toward the pier where there were some shortboarders tearing it up, and I knew they were much better than me—but I was finally having a good time.

"Look at that!" Pless called as I paddled proudly back out. "Nice job! That's how it's done. Okay, c'mere, here comes your wave. C'mon, c'mon. Chest down, now paddle!"

I did it again. I caught a wave and hopped up and rode it until I couldn't ride it anymore, straight into the sand.

The world no longer looked the same. Part of it must have been chemical, adrenaline and endorphins. While we were surfing, a seal swam past the lineup and pelicans flew overhead. Gulls wheeled. The low swell rolled in from a bright sea, and Catalina Island lay dark and blue on the horizon like a sleeping animal. And Pless's encouragement and good cheer filled me with a rare magnanimity toward my fellow man.

Andy and I drove back to Main Street Huntington Beach and headed for the Sugar Shack. We walked up the sidewalk crowded with spring break tourists and young surfers carrying boards and I felt like a king. I *belonged*. All the surf kitsch— the surfboards in the windows of beachwear stores, the boards hanging over the fronts of restaurants, the surf-scene prints on the shirts of the passing visitors—I saw it all and thought, *Yeah, that's the culture everybody wants to be a part of. My culture. Cuz I'm a surfer now.*

You know what I did that afternoon? I bought a green rayon Hawaiian shirt with surfboards all over it. Like Andy's.

And then I wore it. In public.

Timmy Turner was our waiter at the Sugar Shack and I was all excited and I tried to tell him about catching my first wave while he took our order, and he flicked his eyes over me once and said, "Cool. Fruit salad or french fries?"

That night I called Kim. I said that I had discovered a new love, not a woman, and that it was the funnest thing I'd ever done aside from being in her company.

"That's right," she said. And added, "Get your butt home."

Andy and I took five more days of lessons with Pless. On the third day he let me use the egg and I caught my own waves without being pushed. I felt like a natural. I had had to work really hard at everything I had ever done in my life, from kayaking to writing, just to get the rudimentary skills. But this seemed easy. I was taking to it like an otter. I loved catching waves and I loved getting tumbled. I loved the violence of the break, and the stillness outside just sitting, waiting, watching the rolling swell all the way to the horizon; and the absolute quiet that descended when I caught one and zipped into the beach.

Back on land, all I could think about was when we would get back in the water. I was lit up. It was like a drug. I kept reliving the feeling of catching a wave. Andy and I walked into Huntington Surf and Sport to buy our own wetsuits; when you're on the water and you have to pee, you just let loose in a hot, groin-warming stream, then hold the neoprene away from your throat and slosh water into the suit and wash it through. I really liked the idea of having my own suit. I got so excited talking to the sales manager about surfing that at one breathless pause he put his arm around my shoulder and said, "Son, if you were a little younger, I'd say, *There goes college.*"

I had heard about a place in Baja where gray whales line up to surf a wave—wait in a queue, catch the wave in, ride the rip current back out like a chairlift, and do it again. Now I could see why.

When I got back to Denver all I wanted to do was return to the coast. In May I brought Kim to Seal Beach for a week of lessons with the Saint. I went back to Skip at Board n' Bean and bought my first board, an eight-foot-six-inch "funboard," meaning it had a rounded nose and a longboard shape, but was shorter. Sleeker and faster than the egg, and stable, too. Also it turned, which was an advantage. Michael began to teach me that real surfing is not simply about riding the wave straight in to the beach, but involves taking off at an angle and riding along the face of the wave, right to left or left to right.

That November, I got an assignment from *Outside* magazine to go down to Mexico and follow the Mexican National Masters Surfing champion around for three weeks, while he

competed and taught me what he could. His name was Leon
Pérez Yañez and he was my age. I got hammered everywhere
I went with him and had a grand time. I felt like the Karate
Kid. I'd paddle up to Leon and say, "Leon, what's my lesson
for the day?" and he'd think a second and say, "Today, watch
the peaks," and he'd paddle off. The next day he'd say, "When
you go for a wave, go like your life depends on it."

I returned to Denver and didn't surf much over the next
year. When I went back out to Seal Beach to surf again with
Andy, I found that I'd lost all my strength and timing and it
was almost like starting over. It was frustrating. I realized that
getting beyond the most basic level took a lot of power and
stamina and that would take time.

And then I took an assignment on an eco-pirate ship
in Antarctica that was trying to stop the Japanese whaling fleet from killing whales in a sanctuary, and the trip was
so epic it became another book. I learned a lot more about
the oceans on that voyage, and in the subsequent research.
What I learned drove me wild. How could an area twice the
size of the United States be bottom-trawled every year? The
weighted nets dragged the ocean floor and turned the benthic
community—the reefs and grass beds—into parking lots. Dr.
Sylvia Earle, the great oceanographer, likens it to bulldozing
the forest to get at some wild turkeys. And then, depending
on the target species, 20 to 80 percent of the catch is thrown
back overboard dead or dying. Twenty million tons a year of
"bycatch." This seemed to me more than negligence: it was a
sin. If overfishing didn't kill the oceans by shredding the web
of interdependent species, then warming and rising acidity
would. Half the coral reefs were dead or dying. They harbored
over a million species. The sequestration of atmospheric carbon has made the oceans more acidic now than they've been in

650,000 years, and by the end of the century scientists predict that they could be more acidic than they have been in millions of years, leading to the death of creatures that secrete skeletal structures, like coral, shellfish, and calciferous phytoplankton.

I found myself thinking about the sea all the time. Not just the waves, or the whales, or the fish, but the whole heaving expanse. As if she were a being, alive and entire. I longed to be rocked by the swell. To surf, to be buoyed and surrounded and engulfed.

I was now forty-eight. I got this idea that maybe, with total devotion, I could go from kook to riding a big, hollow wave in six months. I sensed intuitively that learning to surf could make me a better person. I thought that if I could take a solid chunk of time on the coast, head down the length of Mexico where there would be fewer crowds than in California, I'd have a real chance of learning, of making surfing a true path. Was it too late? To learn something this hard? It felt like the only thing to do. Just in case, I answered an ad in the *Denver Post* and bought an '85 VW Vanagon camper I quickly named the Beast.

And then I invited Kim. It was time to really give this woman a shot.

LOVE MEDICINE

Meet Kim.

Tall, long of limb, Chinese American, eyes of jet and rosebud lips. Thirty-something years old and pretty. Strong, too. Broad-shouldered. Trained as a ninja. Pretty good with twin short swords. Born in Denver to parents who spoke only Cantonese. Learned English from television, hence says "purchase" instead of "buy."

One of my friends calls her the Goddess of Stillness. Because she is slow and patient, very hard to ruffle. Wholesome in that she is cheerful, expects the best of people, and does not waste a lot of time in the past or the future. Stolidly present, she fears little on earth except mosquitoes.

Her hair cascades down her back like a waterfall of ebony. Her eyes are the eyes of a big cat who has eaten magic almonds.

I really didn't want to mess this one up. I figured that the surf trip would bring us closer, help us to get to know each other or— I couldn't think about what else might happen.

On a Saturday morning in late July we took a last look at the little ranch house in Denver; at the flower bed in front of the deep porch that was blooming in a riot of blues and reds; at the sweep of lake and mountains across the park; at our house sitter from Alabama, Terry Ann, who called, "Y'all be safe and call me!" and held her cat in one arm and waved her cigarette with the other. We scruffed the necks of our own cats, who knew we were leaving them for a big trip and were already huffy and pissed, and we climbed into the VW and roared the water-cooled 1.9-liter twenty-two-year-old engine and pulled away from the curb.

Kim is a model and actor who now works at the Denver Museum of Nature & Science as a performer; she puts on a NASA space suit and conducts experiments on the Mars-surface diorama. She also wears a white lab coat and dissects sheep hearts and brains under an overhead projector. She had gotten several months' leave. We were embarking on an epic road trip, leaving everything behind: jobs, bills, stuff.

I have been a traveler my whole life, and yet at moments like this I feel completely untethered. There is such a wave of loss it borders on grief. There is so much unknown just down the road I feel a disorientation bordering on vertigo. Part of me always wants to crawl back inside my house and curl up under the quilt with a gush of relief. Part of me never wants to go anywhere strange again. Wants to go to a movie for excitement and come home. Make tea like we always do at night before sleep. At least this time Kim was with me, which is not the usual way I leave home on a big adventure, so that lessened the poignancy a little. It's a wonder, given these powerful emotions, that I still don't live at home with my parents.

But there is the other part that cannot stay still for too long and needs to be out and away. That thrives on new topography and smells and rhythms, and wakes up and comes alive only when I travel.

We made it to Arizona before the brakes of the VW began to cry like a colicky infant. By Flagstaff they were screeching. By Kingman they sounded like a mile of ungreased freight train. I downshifted all I could, but there always came that moment in the gas station or at the stop sign when I just had to tap the brake pedal. Then all heads within a quarter mile would swing up. I saw people laugh, I saw them shake their heads and shove their fingers in their ears. After a day of this, just when I had tuned in NPR in Albuquerque and the digital clock showed four minutes to top-of-the-hour headlines, my favorite radio moment, the radio went dead.

"Dang. I hope that's not a sign."

"I was listening to that story. Cage fighting is *rough*."

We both stared at the radio. That night we pulled into a truck stop, backed into the end of a long line of eighteen-wheelers that would idle all night, popped the top, and dug out our toilet kits. The desert night pressed down on the rumbling diesels and the whine of the traffic passing on the interstate. We went into the brightly fluorescent convenience store to use the bathrooms. The place was crowded with Chinese tourists who had just piled out of a big bus and were crowding the shelves of Arizona cactus shot glasses and postcard racks.

"Excuse me," a middle-aged man in a clean white button-down said. "What is Route 6–6?" He held up a tin highway medallion. Three of his friends, each holding their own Route 66 souvenirs—a sign, an ashtray, a license plate—pressed around us.

"It's a road," I said, gesturing to the plate-glass windows and the highway.

"Ah, ah, I see." All four of them nodded and smiled. If I thought I'd gotten off that easy I was a fool.

"What signify?" the man asked.

"Well. It's a very important road to America." They nodded, waited. "It goes from Chicago to L.A.!" They smiled politely and digested this. It occurred to me that that's what roads do, generally speaking, go from one city to another. They looked at me with great expectation.

"It was made famous in a song."

I can't sing. I don't mean it the way other modest people mean it, I mean it with deadly seriousness. But I felt in that truck stop outside of Kingman that some scrap of national honor was at stake. These Chinese really wanted to understand Route 66. I got the sense that suddenly it was the most important element of their trip, their American Experience. They held their Route 66 mementos in their fists, as yet empty of meaning, and looked at me and waited for these souvenirs to be touched with significance, to shine with imparted spirit. I cleared my throat. I held up my toothbrush like a conductor's wand, snapped my fingers with the other hand. I snapped the intro and nodded to each of them, until they, hesitantly, began to snap along with me. They had perfect rhythm. Then I began to sing.

> Wont you get hip to this timely tip
> When you make that California trip
> Get your kicks on Route 66 . . .

I will never forget the expressions of those four Chinese tourists. Stunned. The snapping sputtered, died. It was like a star-spangled American Glory had just risen and blinded the sun, and the thing was God or devil, who knew? They blinked at me, their smiles frozen.

"See," I said, "Route 66 represents freedom. American freedom. To try, to fail, to seek, to live. You know, climb into a Cadillac convertible, hit the road to California, and remake yourself."

"Freedom," murmured the man. He said it like the name of a social disease. "Cadillac. I see." They all bowed. "Thank you."

They took their souvenirs to the counter, but it looked to me now dutiful, drained of excitement. I stepped into the men's room somehow deeply moved.

Back at the Vanagon, nestling under the flannel sleeping bags in our second-story pop-top, marinating in diesel exhaust, I said, "Those were your people in there. Chinese."

"Not my people. They were from Beijing. They spoke Mandarin."

"You can't understand Mandarin?"

"Completely different. Boy, they sure bought a lot of Route 66 stuff," she said, kissing my ear. "Good night."

We arrived on the afternoon of July 24, the week of the U.S. Open, the biggest surf event in the mainland USA and the biggest week all year in Huntington Beach for crowds and energy. Big shaded bleachers for spectators had been set up against the south side of the pier, with colored banners at the corners rippling and flowing, and behind them, acres of tents—surf industry stuff of every stripe, a circuslike half-pipe venue just for skateboarding, throngs of youths, shirtless, muscled, tattooed, girls with tiny short-shorts unbuttoned and partly unzipped along the fly in the new provocative style, sexy bikini models passing out free chilled cans of Red Bull, techno and hip-hop blasting from every quarter. You can just forget about parking or camping. But that first night in Huntington Beach we were given the key to the city. The head of Beach Safety at Huntington loaned it to us after hearing about our intensive learn-to-surf project. This was a literal key. It fit a small padlock that hooked through an eye that was welded to a bar gate that closed across the entrance to the beach parking lot just south of the Huntington Beach Pier. We had tried to get an RV spot at Bolsa Chica, one of the only public camping spots along this whole part of the coast, but they were booked up for a year in advance.

Anyone who has not been to Huntington cannot know what this means—to be able to open that gate. It means at ten p.m., when the lot is totally emptied of vehicles for the night, we are able to drive up to the gate, open it, and pull in to a spot by the sand and go to sleep. To the sound of surf. And drunk partiers. And the crackle of campfires. And megaphones from the lifeguard trucks and the sweep of their spotlights as they try to clear the beach. It was like Stalag 17.

Kim and I celebrated our first night on the coast with a cup of tea. This was really something. Our own private Idaho, except it was Southern California. Our party took about five minutes. We were whipped from our desert drive. We tried to sleep while revelers on the beach yelled for us to go back home to fucking Colorado. I guess they were jealous and could read the plates. Then we got feasted on by mosquitoes. Then, sometime in the small hours, the pavement-sweeping vehicles trundled by, yellow lights flashing, the broomed wheels getting louder and louder until it seemed they would vacuum us off the planet. Then they backed around us with glad beeps. Then the garbage truck announced itself with

a clashing of steel cans. Then it was daybreak. July 25. Exhausted, relieved, we climbed into the front seat and drove
up to Seal Beach for the first day of our new lives. We would
take lessons from Saint Michael until we were fit enough to
launch out on our own.

When we rolled down the ramp into the parking lot of
Seal Beach and saw the M&M Surfing van parked one row
back from the sand, and saw our round teacher hobbling
around the truck in a blue wetsuit, passing out boards and
hugs, and heard his hoarse laugh, I felt a little like the first
day of school. How often in our adult lives do we get to feel
we are on the verge of a new life? Exciting, demanding, shiny.
Scary. How often do we get butterflies and feel aquiver with
expectation and fear? When we date. When we marry. When
we have a child.

What I felt mostly was that this was not a lark. Surfing
was really hard. The surfers you see cutting it up on the waves
have been doing it their whole lives. The ocean is vast and
capricious and dangerous. We'd come all this way and now we
were committed.

BOOT CAMP

O cean. There isn't another word in the English language as strange and lovely and broad. Ocean. There is a trochaic swell moving through it, rising and falling, so that as I say it my spirit rises and falls, too, softly, like a boat, or board. If you look at it long enough, it is a word that opens and spreads out, makes a circle of a far horizon, a word on which rain can fall and dimple or sweep across in lashing gusts and leave unperturbed. A word that is calm enough to look at, almost lulling, but also hints at holding unreckonable power. The *O*, far off, where the tempest circles, the fearsome storms that beget the waves. And the *N*, I suppose, is the far shore, thousands of miles hence.

Ocean is, by levels of magnitude, our greatest wilderness. Her deeps, by metric measure alone, exceed the highest Himalaya. The mysteries there, in the most absolute darkness, rival those of outer space. The biodiversity puts a rain forest to shame.

As a kid, my absolute favorite television was Jacques Cousteau. The jaunty explorer took us to every corner of the sea, gray-scaled depths to reefs exploding with color, colors in combinations I had never seen before, with iridescences, phosphorescences, intensities of -escences that made my little head spin. The sharks, the eels, the whales, the jellyfish! *Ze humble anemone opening like a morning flower!* I loved his accent as he, like some orchestrating god himself, narrated the mysteries of our reticent world. I loved his Zodiacs and mini-subs, and the short black beards of his sons and crew, and the seriousness with which they gathered around the chart and plotted their approach. It was the grandest adventure ever. It was the reason that 90 percent of my woolly-headed generation, when asked what they wanted to be, would answer at some point, "Marine biologist." I doubt their seriousness. A data sample by definition demands repetition. I don't think they wanted to count thousands of microorganisms in samples of seawater or empty nets and catalog the contents along a grid of eighty characteristics, or conduct statistical analyses until their eyes blurred. Neither did Jacques. He wanted Philippe to prepare the Zodiac for departure. He wanted to immerse himself in beauty and mystery and adventure. And then pull into Monte Carlo or Nice and put on a tux and be the toast of the town. Who wouldn't?

But beauty, it turns out, is mostly hard work. It's hard work for a species that has to keep adapting, it's hard work for a marine biologist, and it's hard work for a surfer. And, it turns out, it is hard work for an ocean with human beings inhabiting the fringes. It was becoming ever more clear that the oceans may be on the verge of collapse. A study published in *Nature* in 2003 by an international team, studying fifty years of data, found that we have lost *90 percent* of our pelagic predator species—the deepwater game fish we all love to eat: the marlin and tuna and halibut and swordfish—90 percent of these stocks since 1950. The great sharks are functionally extinct, meaning that they don't occupy their niche in the ecosystem any longer, and the smaller predators, the littler sharks and rays, are multiplying and wreaking havoc on the benthic communities. Another, more recent study, published in *Science,* predicts that if current fishing trends continue, every fishery will collapse by 2048. It's hard to even think about. But as much as the ocean is struggling, she never fails to lift my spirits when I first catch sight of her, and there was no place else I wanted to be on that July morning.

I couldn't wait to try my new boards. Just before we got to Seal Beach, Bruno Troadec—a French surfboard shaper and a neighbor of Saint Michael—had begun to shape six custom boards for our trip. "Shaping" means he was sculpting the foam cores of what, once they were skinned with fiberglass, would become unique surfboards. I still had the 8–6 (eight-and-a-half-foot) funboard that Skip had sold me three years before. (Surfers just say the numbers and omit the "feet" and "inches.") But the first few days, the Saint wouldn't even let me use that. He had helped me patch it my first week. He had lifted the tail in his palm and run his expert eye down the rails, or edges, and proclaimed it an almost unadulterated blank. In other words, Skip had ordered inexpensive foam blanks, had someone shape them for maybe ten minutes, and then had them glassed—voilà, one cheap "custom" surfboard.

"Whose board are you waxing?" Michael asked me that first morning, eyes atwinkle.

He knew very well what board it was. He was messing with me.

"You know what board this is! This is Son of Egg."

"Why don't you put him back?" Michael winked. "I want you to use one of mine today."

"You mean a shortboard?"

"I mean that ten-foot foam board over there, mister. Go on."

The first few days, Michael, Jr., was trying to nudge me into actually learning to surf. This meant *not* heading straight for the sand on a carpet of whitewater. Straight-off Adolph. It meant taking off at an angle—at Seal most of the waves break left—and gliding in one direction down the face of the wave as it forms ahead, staying just ahead of the gnashing break. The first time I did it was a revelation. M, Jr., can get so excited he sputters. He's a former Navy medic who worked with Marine units. A torn-open torso will leave him cool, professional, efficient. But the sight of me thrashing around on my funboard, for some reason, excited him to hysteria.

"Okay, okay, okay, Pete, here comes your wave, get ready, get— Not that way! Left! Dummy! Chest up! No, I promise I won't push you, all yours—left! That's it, that's it, now paddle easy, paddle, wait for it, okay, go, go, go! *You're up! Yeah!*"

What had just happened was that a shoulder-high swell built up behind me and I angled left and paddled hard and it surged under me. Somehow, with M, Jr.'s urging, my trim was right, chest up, so I didn't dig the nose and flip—but not too far back on the board so that it stalled—and the wave picked me up. I was paddling like a madman, watching ahead of the board down the green berm of a building wave, and the

board tipped and accelerated and there was that blissful moment when the speed released us, me and the board. When I
knew that I had it. I was looking ahead at a world of sloping
green. This wasn't the spew of whitewater I'd been riding all
week, this was something entirely different. This was smooth
and fast. It had real angle, like the pitch of a steep ski slope.
I was rocketing along it. I popped up. Instinctively I edged. I
guess that meant flexing ankles, weighting my heels a little.
The board held its line and I coursed like a kid on a zipline
straight along the little face. Then the break, which had been
chasing, caught up and crashed around my knees and turned
the board straight to the beach and I managed to hang on and
ride the whitewater into the shallows and wipe out.

I stood up in the foam and pulled the board in by the leash
and took in the pier, the packed sand, the dazzling froth, the
yells, the sift and muffled crash of the next wave. I breathed
in the salt, wet sand, drying seaweed. I looked for Kim and
saw her lining up for a shove from M, Jr. I felt the board come
under my hand and steady like a just-galloped horse. I felt
somehow self-contained and open to the whole universe at
once, as if everything within the circle of the senses and I
were of a piece. It was euphoria, pure, sweet, unmediated, immediate.

Meanwhile, down at the Huntington Beach Pier, the pros
were battling it out at the U.S. Open. After surfing we'd go
down and watch them, and then go to the surf movie festival
at night. The pros were incredible. The horn would blow and
four of them in a heat would run into the water, hit their
boards, and paddle out through the surf without ever losing
momentum. That in itself awed me. They duck-dived under

breaking waves and came up like their boards were powered by twin Mercs. This was not a clean, regular wave—peaks cropped up and broke in sections—so the competitors fanned out and hunted the peaks. And then when they latched on to a good wave it was nothing like the wing-and-a-prayer rides of most other surfers. Even the best I'd seen, it was always a little touch-and-go: Will she make the drop? Can she pull off that cutback? Will she make it around the collapsing section of white in front of her? With the pros, there was never a question. If the wave sectioned out and collapsed in front of them, they floated the whitewater until they found the blue wall again. Or they jumped it. Or, if there really was no place to go, they performed acrobatic moves in the foam. The wave was a canvas and they painted it with whatever was in their imaginations and bodies to paint. They jumped the lip, caught air, and came down on one rail. They made fast, fluid figure eights in and out of the crashing pocket. We didn't even know the names for what they were doing, but we stood on the high pier, leaning over the railing, and cheered.

In the finals we watched C. J. Hobgood, a top pro from Florida, go head to head with Jeremy Flores from France. In competition, the horn blew and surfers had twenty minutes to charge into the surf, get out to the waves, and catch as many great rides and throw in as many great maneuvers as they could. The idea, basically, was to wow the judges. The Association of Surfing Professionals, which puts on these events, changed their scoring system in 2005 to foster ever more exciting moves. The new scoring criteria sound like a field manual for a superhero: "A surfer must perform radical controlled manoeuvres in the critical section of a wave with Speed, Power, and Flow to maximize scoring potential. Innovative/ Progressive surfing as well as Variety of Repertoire (manoeuvres) will be taken into consideration when rewarding points for waves ridden. The surfer who executes this criteria with the maximum Degree of Difficulty and Commitment on the waves shall be rewarded with the higher scores."

Hobgood had no problem with any of that, especially the radical and commitment parts—the man was like a wildcat, if a wildcat could surf. He would take off on a peak, make a fast smooth bottom turn, and charge back up the face for what everybody expected to be a classic "off the lip"—an aerial cutback. Instead he'd throw in a big reverse—a backward spinning 360—and land perfectly again in the pocket. He was agile and quick like a puma, and a total thrill. He just seemed unexpected and radical and he won the contest. But we loved watching the women the most. The two who got to the finals were top U.S. surfer Karina Petroni and top Australian surfer Stephanie Gilmore. Karina had spent so much time surfing in Australia since she was a kid, the two girls had been best friends since they were nine. They were both very tall for women surfers, about five-foot-eleven, and they both had fast, fluid, graceful styles that contrasted with the men's power and to me won hands-down for sheer beauty. Karina's board was a little 6–0 that seemed almost like a skateboard under her tall, willowy frame. She moved across the wave in big sweeping, carving turns and roundhouse cutbacks that were so smooth and swift she seemed like a dolphin. Stephanie won (would go on, we found out later, to become world champion), but to me they were equally stunning. When they paddled back in at the end of the heat they were mobbed at the pier by local surfer girls who wanted autographs.

Back at Seal, I had been eyeing our own pier for days. Facing the beach, it was off to our right. The unspoken agreement of the M&M Surfing School with the rest of the Seal Beach surfers was that the school would congregate and shoal a hundred or two hundred yards north of the pier. That gave room for real surfers to catch a decent long left off the pilings before running into students.

There is this moment in every beginning surfer's career. I was a little shy after the scene at Huntington Beach Pier. I was singed. I took a deep breath. It was time for me to paddle over there and sit in the lineup with the big kids.

THE SEAL BEACH LINEUP

This is how they were strung out from the pier:

Jack Hill. He ran the lineup when he was out there. Something like six-foot-two, one-ninety, square-jawed, curly hair almost to his shoulders. Ex-con, but the kind with a golden heart—jailed for something like beating the pulp out of a guy who offended his girlfriend. Looked like he stacked weights while he stacked time. Shaped beautiful epoxy boards in a garage. Competed and just missed going pro. Nice to me, for some reason, when I paddled up. Borrowed my longboard, said, "Just a sec," caught the next wave, and rode it in on his head.

Circus Man. Looked exactly like the strong man in a freak show. Little sinewy legs, brick-shithouse torso, handlebar mustache. Wore a Speedo. All tatted up, naked ladies and mermaids. Whizzed down a long wave with a cryptic half smile, Mona Lisa meets Ajax. Never said a word.

Eva. Supermodel. Swedish. So thin even her size-zero wetsuit hung off her butt. Had no butt. Huge eyes the green of the water when the sun is at its zenith. Surfed between photo shoots in Italy and Brazil. Painfully shy. Learned to surf from Michael and adored him because he treated her like a normal person. Whenever we chatted, I couldn't help but wonder what it would be like to make love to her—like hugging a fragile sculpture of sticks and leaves. Surprisingly strong, though—paddling out, she left me in the dust.

The Seal Beach Sistas. Actually a young mothers' club, very upscale, lot of pearl earrings and perfect coifs, even when wet. They surfed after dropping the kids off at school. In summer months they met when they could get away. This was not family-at-the-beach time, this was sitting out on their longboards, rising and falling easily on the swell, away from every tentacle of obligation—and talking trash. *Desperate Housewives* stuff. And laughing. And peeling off midsentence to catch a wave.

Bill Cartwright. Former CEO. Ran three multibillion-dollar health care companies. Made the mistake of taking a week-long surf class from Michael so he could be closer to his son who surfs. Became, like me, dazzled by the sea. Quit his job, found God, surfed every day. "I realized there are things that are a lot more important than making money." Really? Like what? Like he bought a house in Costa Rica so he and his son could go down and surf together. Became inarticulate when trying to describe the sensation of being out in the ocean on his board, with his friends, feeling close to God. A transfigured character.

Jill. A zaftig blonde, very sexy, mother of two, with a strong nose and stronger shoulders. No-nonsense. Got respect on the wave by being courteous and catching what she paddled for. A marine biologist by training, ran an innovative science program for home-schooled kids that included combo littoral biology and surfing clinics. That first day I headed toward the lineup, Jill was already there and she took me under her tan wing and surfed with me.

Willy. Another kind surfer. He was the only black man I have seen out on the waves. About twenty-two years old. Kind of shy, self-deprecating, but tenacious. Had to be. And brave as hell. Listen, surfers are rednecks with fins, generally. Lot of rough, lower-class, white toughsters out there, lot of tattoos and attitude. Some of it is racist. I couldn't admire Willy more for coming out to Seal every day off he could, driving the hour from the Valley where he lived and worked as an electrician's assistant. He had an eight-foot foam-top board, which was an inexpensive beginner's board, but he was not a beginner. He wanted to get a hard board when he could afford it. Very nice to me when I paddled up.

Rogue's Gallery. Assorted young hotheads on shortboards, who should really have been over at Huntington Pier and not terrorizing me. Why didn't they answer when I said, "Hi! How's it going?" One of them was French. He had a heavy accent like Bruno, and long, vain, curly locks. He hogged the waves. What was he doing here anyway? Go back to France.

Tykester. Tiny eight-year-old on the smallest shortboard on earth. Looked like a frigging skateboard. But the kid could rip. He was all freckles and confidence. On my second day in the lineup he was sitting inside of me by about ten feet. I was just on the spot, at the peak, and as the swell came in he turned to me and said earnestly, confiding, as if I'd be crazy to doubt him: "I got it." And then he took off. On my wave. I blinked at his diminutive retreating figure. "Okay," I said to the back of the wave.

It was a typical California crowd. Every segment of society now surfed. The culture used to be edgy and rebellious, and still thrived on that myth. Plenty of surfers still lived for almost nothing else, and they tended to be a breed apart. But most had families and a boss and drew a paycheck.

I had been talking to Jack Hill, the ex-con, on the beach. He operated heavy equipment when he wasn't surfing or shaping boards or seeing his parole officer. He liked the idea of our project and sold me a short spring wetsuit very cheap. When I paddled up to the dozen surfers at the pier, they slid their eyes over me in a way I would later learn to recognize—it meant: *Fucking kook. Not gonna let him get a single wave. If he gets in my way, gonna fuck him up. End of conversation.* Big Jack called out, "Hey, Pete! Come over here. Cool. You surf here before? Okay, this is a left, this is your wave." The rest of the surfers had been waiting for their own wave, many for a quarter of an hour. With one sentence, barely above speaking voice, and one sweeping glance over the lineup, he had made a proclamation to the tribe: *Back off, new kid gets the wave.*

"Thanks," I murmured, catching a quick glimpse of ten stony faces. "Hi, guys." I actually waved like a Miss America contestant. And then I prayed. *Pete, you better not, no way, kook out and miss this frigging wave. Or wipe out once you catch it.* I must have been living right. God granted me a reprieve from total kookiness. I paddled as hard as I could, angled left, and caught the wave. I stood up and rode it left. I rode it as far as I could. I almost fell to my knees in the foam and thanked heaven.

Two weeks into this first month I drove over to the French board-shaper Bruno's shop. It's a little garage-door unit a few miles from the beach in an industrial area of Huntington, up against the 405 freeway. It was evening. I called through the doorway and I heard the sander stop. Bruno came out covered in fine foam dust from the board he had been shaping. It stuck to his thinning unkempt hair and two-day stubble like snow.

He is short, about my height, five-eight, but he has shoulders as broad as a door and arms like Popeye. Sparkling blue eyes.

We pulled out two beat-up lawn chairs and opened them beneath a stunted little palm tree growing out of a chain-link fence at the corner of his building. We sat beneath the tree in the gathering cool and drank Perrier. I told him that I had gone out that morning to Bolsa Chica and caught a few rights beside some dolphins and longboarders.

"Oh, yah, those old guys," he said. "They spend all the morning in the parking lot talking about their boards. Afraid to surf, I think. Yah, yah. You see the little stands they have? Paw! They set up next to the truck and put the board on and talk, talk, talk. Surfing is not about talk. Paw!" He blinked foam out of his lashes. "Nice tree, eh? Good shade!"

I stared at him. "Bruno, the sun is down. It is all shade out here."

"Yah, well." He was unfazed. He said that the electric company had come by again today and told him to cut it down. "I had to—how you say?—bribe the fucking guy with a discount board or he cuts him down on the spot. *Tant pis.*" Bruno told me that he was going back to New Caledonia next week to shape boards for the locals and surf.

"*Bien,*" he said, screwing the cap on his Perrier. "You want to see your six-four?"

He meant a six-foot-four shortboard. I was beside myself with excitement. First custom surfboard. A shortboard, as I was learning every day out at the Cliffs, demanded a lot more effort than a longboard. They were harder to paddle out because they were a lot slower, they were harder to paddle into and catch a wave for the same reason, and you had to catch the wave right where it was breaking, which meant you had to have perfect timing and be super quick on the pop-up and takeoff. You couldn't, usually, sit way down on the easier shoulder and take off on the forming wall before the break even got to you, the way you could on a longboard. A shortboard was just too slow. The swelling wave just passed right under you. No, you had to get all up in there and look the dragon right between the toothy jaws. Because this is where the wave is steepest and fastest, and on a shortboard you need the speed. Shortboards are also a lot less stable. The payoff is that once you're up and riding the wave you have the maneuverability, the nimbleness of a swallow; when you get back on a longboard it can feel like a container ship. I was excited that Bruno thought I could handle it.

Bruno and I had become friends in the spring, just before Kim and I launched our big trip. Michael had introduced us and I told him about my project—kook to big fast wave in six months—and he agreed to sponsor me. Which made me probably the only sponsored kook in the history of surfing.

I had liked him right away. Bruno was from the harsh, stony North Atlantic coast of Brittany and he had been something of a legend in France. He opened the first surfboard factory and shop in the northwest of the country and organized the first competitions. Once he started making boards, they were all the rage. I liked him because he always surprised me. The first time we met, he wanted to talk less about surfing and more about the sustainable, floating, spherical house pods he wanted to build to help solve the housing shortage. They would be made of something like fiberglass, make their own energy and fresh water, and would be anchored to the seabed on long shock cords that could withstand hurricane seas.

Before he began shaping my boards, we thought it would be fun to get to know each other a little better and go surfing. In May, two months before Kim and I embarked for California, Bruno and I headed down to San Onofre, to a classic longboard break called Old Man's. A "longboard break" means the wave comes in soft and slow, ideal for beginners. I hadn't surfed in so long, but I was excited and eager to show Bruno that I could, well, stand up. We paddled out together and at the first waist-high wave I turned, popped up, and crashed straight down into another beginner. When I came up, the nose of the beautiful longboard Bruno had loaned me was cracked like an egg.

I was crushed. I paddled out to Bruno. "Hey! I broke your board."

"First ride? I don't know how many boards I will have to make for you for Mexico." I felt bad. "*Tant pis,* we can fix." Then a smile spread across his face. "Peter the *Destroyer.*" He grinned. "Every board I make for you will have a picture of a Navy destroyer on it."

Bruno agreed to supply us with six boards in all, an entire quiver. They included two shortboards and a 7–6 single-fin, old-style gun. Bruno told me that the short quad fin was for when I got strong enough and fast enough to take off right at the peak where the wave was breaking.

"You mean I will be a shortboarder?"

"Yah, why not?"

"Everybody says that if you start surfing after thirty, you will always be a longboarder." I was now forty-eight.

Bruno didn't deign to answer. He cocked an eyebrow. I knew he thought that most people, in general, were just too stupid. He was a Celt from Brittany and he even thought the French were stupid. "The gun," he said, "is for Mexico. If you get into some big waves. It will get you out of trouble fast." He smiled. Big waves—I couldn't imagine. I was having a hard enough time just getting up on the board.

Now, on this hot August evening, he disappeared inside his shop and came back out with a freshly glassed and sanded shortboard. It had four fins in the tail, a quad, for more responsiveness. It was beefy in the middle, a bit thick, and a hair wide, to give me a little more flotation and make it easier to paddle and ride than a pro's shortboard. He flipped it over and held it, deck up. There was the Bruno fleur-de-lis up near the nose, and down below the hip of the board was a blue rectangle in which was blazoned the stately menacing silhouette of a Navy destroyer; USS PH. Below it a torpedo held the words IN SURF WE TRUST.

I looked at the board and up at Bruno. He was grinning.

"The Destroyer, eh? Peter the Destroyer." When Bruno smiled it was all the more charming because he looked embarrassed to be doing it, to be breaking his Celtic reserve, and that gave it a goofy dissonance.

I was speechless. I couldn't believe my beautiful board. I had never had anything made just for me in my entire life. Not true. My father had written me poems, my artist mother had made me a dazzling sculpture, and my high school girlfriend had woven me a blanket. But this—this—this was a damn surfboard!

Bruno laid it across two sawhorses, vanished inside, and came out with a brick of base wax. He tore off the wrapper. "Here," he said. "You know how?"

"Not really. I just rub it on, right?"

He twisted his mouth with his usual contempt for a stupid idiot world.

"Why they don't teach this? Go in circles, *comme ça*? Light. Yah. You rub too hard and she creates heat, flattens the bumps. You want the bumps. Like so."

I laid the edge of the brick against the smooth glass and

rubbed overlapping circles. The wax caught and stuttered against my palm, moved on. Gradually, like the image in a developing photograph, the stuttered tracks of the brick collected more wax on each light pass and an even pattern of bumps appeared, a lovely rash of white on white, a nubby swirl of traction. The black destroyer now looked like it was sailing through a blizzard.

Can I tell you how much I loved surfing then? I was standing in a concrete jungle on an August night several miles from the shore. I could hear the thrum of the 405 highway somewhere nearby. I was waxing my first custom board and I was stricken with the beauty of surfing, the whole endeavor.

There is nothing you can say about a surfboard that you cannot say about a sailboat, an airplane, a ski. The artistry follows the function and the beauty is in the marriage. The grace of line is an expression of potential force. Motion holds its breath in every swelling curve. The trembling flank of a horse, warm under the palm, could not be more loaded with motion. But a board, if it is made by an old-school, traditional shaper like Bruno, is made just for you. He may ask where you like to surf and your skill level, but his assessment is mostly intuitive and is made in the first quick glance as you meet—the breadth of your shoulders, your animation, the length of your limbs, your quickness to laugh, all somehow as important as your height and weight and ability. One night at his town house, as Caroline, his six-foot-tall fashion-model wife, got her kit together for a shoot the next day, Bruno showed me schematics of specific boards on his laptop that he had been inputting for several years. These were all boards he had made, and the designs, drafted using a three-dimensional CAD program, each contained some two hundred measurements that precisely described thicknesses and curves, rockers and scoops. He could, if he wanted to follow the growing trend, take these designs to a computer-linked foam-carving machine and have a power tool shape the boards to spec. But he doesn't work that way. As many measurements as he records in his drawings, even a board out of his computer can't compare to what he shapes by hand from the foam blanks. Every board he creates is a unique animal with its own personality and potential for brilliance.

But usually, when someone like me comes in and asks for a board, a 6–5 pintail thruster, say, with a hard edge and loose tail, he will take one look at the person, ask a few questions, and then some board he made perhaps twenty years ago in France for someone of a similar size and ability will pop into his head. Along with some idea of how to modify it just a little, to be perfect for this surfer. And he will shape the board from memory, by feel.

I wonder where else in the world today this kind of crafts-manship survives. There must be tailors with this level of mastery. Or carpenters or chefs. Master board shapers are still doing it, tucked away in shops in Orange County and Ventura, Australia and Hawaii, but every year there are fewer of them. They can no longer compete with the cheap factory boards from Asia.

Now, in the gathering dusk outside of Bruno's shop, I picked up my waxed, perfect 6–4 and lay it inside the Beast like it was Excalibur.

MILITARY-INDUSTRIAL COMPLEX

For the next two weeks I sought waves where I could learn in peace. I liked Bolsa Chica, because the beach ran for miles and it was wilder. Sometimes my only audience were seals and dolphins. Usually, though, there was a Dawn Patrol of corporate guys who worked for Boeing and Lockheed Martin and Raytheon. They were reserved and single-minded. They needed x amount of waves to balance their day as weapons manufacturers. These men were all about metrics. The problem is that waves are a limited resource. Decent, rideable waves can come in bunches, or one may not show up for twenty minutes. And sets, the three or four waves that come in a group and are noticeably bigger, they may roll in only every half an hour. It's hard for a novice to understand, when you look out at the ocean and see wave following wave, that often only a small percentage of these are surfable. So the Dawn Patrol got surly if you took a wave from their plus column. They showered under the outdoor spigot and changed into suits in the parking lot. At first, I yielded to these Type A's. I figured they were on a much tighter time constraint than me, and if one paddled aggressively around me closer to a peak I'd been waiting for and took my wave, well, he needed it more than I did, and I could get the next. Also, since I was likely to wipe out anyway, best not to waste a wave. But after watching the same company men steal my wave again and again, I got surly myself. I held sustained interior dialogues. I looked to the ocean, saw three dolphins porpoising by, slipping through the long sunlight like glistening spirits; I breathed deep of the salt Pacific and praised the peaceful life of surf. Then I looked at the shaved neck and hundred-dollar haircut of the company man on a ten-foot longboard, a board designed to sit far out and take everyone else's wave. This guy had just caught a long right, and then paddled right past me into position for the next one. And I thought, *Fuck that.* What happened to courtesy? Why does the world bend for people in a hurry? Why doesn't the world bow to the ones who *aren't* in a hurry? Why are these guys in a hurry anyway? To make money. To make stealth destroyers. Destroyers! I looked down at my pulsing 6–4.

I am the Destroyer!

I said it to myself in the proper French accent. Fuck these Type A pricks. I looked straight at the guy and paddled around him, on the peak side. I could see the dude's blood pressure rise, could see it in his face. Insubordination! He was probably an executive. When one of these assholes scowled at me, I yelled, "I may kook out and miss this wave, but this board is double-glassed and I really don't give a shit if boards collide." In other words, if you drop in on me, cut me off when I catch this next wave, I will just keep going and listen for the crack of fiberglass. We sat eight feet apart for five minutes and I took the next good wave.

From then on, the rules were changed. Of course, sometimes, if the guy was really big, or was with his buddies, or looked more like a San Bernardino Mongol than a cryogenics engineer, I'd just swallow it and move off and find my own peak. It was tribal out there. I realized that the strain of the aloha spirit that surfing was bringing out in me was extremely aggressive. Like, *Aloha—now back the fuck off my wave.*

In my third week I had a revelation. I returned to Seal Beach, where Kim was still in school with the Michaels, and paddled straight out to the pier. I looked around and realized that the lineup was all kooks. In fact, I was the least kooky. I couldn't believe it. Where was the gang? Must have been Free Tattoo Day down at Harley's. I was on my Bruno 9–0 longboard, the one I had broken my first time out. He had patched it, with a large graphic of a whizzing torpedo on the nose—a warning,

I guess, to others. These others couldn't find the right position to sit in. They were waiting for the wave in the wrong place. Even I could see that. And they paddled like beached walruses. I could paddle straight out and catch every wave I wanted. Wow, this was what it must be like to be really good, how the experts were always getting all the waves and I just sat there. Then I caught a set wave left, probably shoulder-high, and I rode it swiftly down the line. I was whizzing north. I was a speeding bullet, or torpedo, of euphoria.

Just then, just in front of me, a balding dad shoved his daughter on a foam board straight into the beach. Straight into my path. I yelled. He hadn't even looked right, up the wave! In that instant I saw as if in freeze-frame both their faces: his was a mask of surprise and wide eyed horror; she just looked wonderstruck, like she was being washed with the colored lights of a close encounter. It was a close encounter. I collided with the girl and we both wiped out. I came up yelling.

"Jesus Christ!" I shouted. "You could have killed both of us! The surfer on the wave has the right-of-way! You got to look! Look up the wave before you just shove your daughter into a car wreck!"

They stared at me like I was completely crazy. Then the man remembered his role and started to yell back. Then he realized he had no case. He picked up his daughter's board. It was cracked. The man's shoulders slumped and I could see him deflate. "It's broken," he murmured. "I just got it for her." He looked up at me, eyes accusing. "You should go down to Huntington or somewhere. Or learn to control your board. This is a beginner beach."

Yeah, right, I thought. *You're in my house now, Little Man.* I breathed. I paddled back, still feeling righteous, out to my wave, the wave *I* owned for the first time, and as I sat and watched the man and his daughter get out of the water and carry their board back to the parking lot, the righteousness began to erode and I felt like a shit. Of course he was right. Jack Hill wouldn't have hit the girl, he had more control standing on his head. I hadn't even been here a month and I was already getting proprietary and aggro. Not even pitying the lesser kooks who waited while I rode wave after wave. Damn. I was acting just like the Military-Industrial Complex out at Bolsa Chica.

I called Andy, who had been transferred suddenly to Seattle. I told him the story. "Surfing is changing you," he said. "You were my most gentle friend."

Ouch. He laughed. "I remember kayaking, having to wait for you, because you were busy fishing some spider out of a pool and taking him to shore. Remember that?"

"I still do that," I said defensively. "Just yesterday I paddled a half-drowned pigeon in to the beach. She kept falling off the pier's seawall into the water."

"Yeah, well. Other surfers aren't as cuddly, huh?"

"No. Tell you the truth, I just want to kill most of them."

"You the man. Call me if you need a lawyer. I know a bunch of defense attorneys."

I didn't need an attorney, I needed backup. I noticed that when I went with Michael, Jr., or Bruno, out at the Cliffs, or some of the breaks south of the Huntington Beach Pier, the locals were less likely to mess with me. One guy I must have cut off—okay, I did; it was a split peak, meaning the wave humps up and one surfer can go one way off it, the other surfer can go the opposite direction. I thought this shaved-head fortyish longboarder was going right, so I took off left, but he changed his mind at the last minute and came down fast on me and wiped out. Honest mistake, I really didn't mean to get in his way. When he paddled past me he bumped me hard with his shoulder. I blinked. I couldn't believe it. M, Jr., saw it and it was like letting out the dogs. The chain broke. He lunged, paddled fast, halfway to the guy and started yelling.

"What was that? You better back off, man! You mess with him, you mess with me!" I was touched.

The guy started to splutter something about me dropping in on him and Michael went wild. "He's just a beginner. He was gonna split the peak with you, what's *wrong* with you? Whyn't pick on someone your own size? You mess with me, you mess with the U.S. *Marines*."

I felt like a pretty girl in the middle of a bar fight. Also I wanted to pummel the guy into a pulp for being such an asshole. He backed off. He went north and found his own peak.

With Bruno it was the same. We met at the Cliffs early in the morning. He was a dedicated believer in the medical properties of fine red wine, preferably French, so sometimes it wasn't that early. Whenever we went out there, though, we got respect. We'd sit on our boards a few feet apart and bob on the swell and watch the oil derricks up on the bluff nod their own rhythm and watch the light move down the steep bluffs and Bruno would tell me more about the composite spheres he wanted to build to solve the land shortage on the coasts.

THE SHACK. THE FORGE OF THE SEA

This felt, Huntington Beach in August, like the summer of our lives. Kim was still having a blast with M&M. She was starting to get strong enough to catch her own waves, and she had the balance of a ninja. Once she was up, nothing could knock her off. She loved Michael, Jr., and he would yell out his excited corrections. I could hear the call, "Kiim! What did I say? Is the beach between your feet? Where are you going to look?" She was still in the protective cocoon of the M&M Surfing School, hadn't had to deal yet with a real lineup. Where she was was like childhood, a good childhood. All of the play, none of the conflict.

Bodies humming from a whole morning of surfing, we'd make our way through the midday crowds. The animal beauty of so many of these young surfers—it was like moving through herds of delicately limbed ibex. Sleek, ripple-flanked, glossy.

The shell shops and T-shirt shops, the waxed cherry '57 Chevies rumbling in the street, the '48 woodie wagons, long-boards sticking out the back. Salty skin, lactic acid waning in the limbs, relaxed fatigue. Images of the morning session returned like slivers of a dream: the one long fast ride, the sheer luck of it. Edging through the doorway of the Shack, finding our little table against the wall.

I was happy. I can say that. Happiness like a tumbling of surprises. I loved Kim. Her simple appreciation of every day, how she applied herself to this process of learning—with laughter and gratitude, without fear. At night, parked now on a quiet backstreet of Seal Beach near the library, she even peed in a bucket.

"I'm always on four-wheel drive with you," she said with mild accusation. I winced. I knew that peeing in a bucket in the middle of a prosperous neighborhood had not been in her life plan.

"Where else are you going to pee? We're on a residential street and it's the middle of the night. Unless you want to go in someone's hedge."

Aggravated sigh. "Oh, all right, I'm going down. You better not jump into it in the morning."

We pushed our own limits every day and I think that was a big part of the joy. I was beginning to understand that what I loved most about learning to surf was the sheer beauty of wild ocean—turn from the shore and it was wild—wild, capricious, untamed. It might be dying by degrees, but the pelicans still plunged, the sardines still skipped the surface in panic, the wind still blew the spume off the breaking waves. It thundered and heaved and shuddered. The immense geologic force of the sea was undiminished. Every morning that I waded into the heavy whitewash and jumped onto the board and paddled out into the waves, I felt honored and humbled to take my place among the fishes and the birds.

Timmy took our order. Loose-limbed, thin, mid-twenties, boyish. There was a remarkable picture of him in a frame by the door. This was not a surfing picture; it was a close portrait. His shaved head turned, looking straight into the camera, calm, resolute, charged with a knowledge whose depths no normal person would plumb. He looked like he'd just come back from hell. Two feet away, level with his face across a polished surface that turned out to be the roof of a car, was a skull. His own.

I better explain.

Timmy never did anything like anybody else. He grew up surfing, biking down to the pier before school in the middle of winter to catch storm barrels with his buddies. When he was seventeen he went to Indonesia with brother Ryan and a friend and began to surf the fastest, biggest, cleanest barrels on earth. A few years later, he and two buddies got dropped off by some fishermen on a remote, deserted island in West Java with only the supplies they could carry in sacks on top of their surfboards. They ruined half of their provisions paddling through the shore break. The fishermen promised to return in a month. So for four weeks these kids from California camped in the jungle of this tiny island, spearfishing to supplement their meager rice, sleeping in hammocks, trying to keep their matches dry, catching fresh water from the rain. They suffered bouts of diarrhea and fever. They got cut and Timmy patched them up with Super Glue. They had no link to the outside world. No satellite phone or radio. They were on their own. This would be remarkable enough, a story of real survival for a few young guys from OC in a novel and alien world. But they weren't there to survive, they were there to surf.

Every morning, in the dark, they hiked along the shore for miles. They waded over reef, climbed through mangrove, shoved their boards through jungle, to arrive at a perfect, clean, powerful, sixty-second barrel. It jacked up and sucked the water off the reef, so that if they wiped out, they were hurled and battered in water three feet deep. Like the Banzai Pipeline but not—because there was no medical help for weeks.

They wore wetsuits and helmets for some protection and they surfed their asses off and managed to take off on these barrels with cameras in their hands. All morning. One private, double-overhead tube after another. One version of paradise.

Timmy made an award-winning movie of the epic called *Second Thoughts*. His narration of all this was straightforward, modest, and humble to an almost painful degree, and unsparing in the details of their trials. It reminded me of stories I'd heard from cowboys—real working cowboys, not the puffed-up, combed-mustache rhetoric of professional cowboy poets. And this narration was in contrast to the high-adrenaline, ecstatic footage of the wave.

When the tsunami hit, devastating many of the islands he had loved to surf, he immediately got a crew together—including a doctor and medical supplies—and flew over with tons of relief aid, chartered a boat, and set sail to see whom they could help. His mother Michelle accompanied him. Everywhere they landed, at villages wiped off the map, with stranded survivors injured and starving, his team brought the first help. He made a movie about the trip called *Tsunami Diaries,* which Kim and I watched on the laptop in the Beast.

Now in the Sugar Shack I studied again the portrait of Timmy and his skull. It was one of the most startling photographs I had ever seen. Timmy had contracted a staph infection while surfing in Indo or Huntington Beach, he wasn't sure. It had eaten into his skull and threatened his brain. He went into a coma. The doctors operated. They gave him almost no chance. Million-to-one, something like that. They took out portions of his skull and facial bones, replacing them with synthetic bone. He slept on.

Maybe it was his long-trained ability to relax and ride inside of devouring forces that saved him. One day at the lunch counter Timmy had described to us what it's like to be inside a big barrel. Dropping in, weighting back a little, slowing the board, waiting for it, getting covered up, the long tube forming ahead; accelerating, looking for the end, knowing you were going to make it, and blasting out the end before the whole thing closed out and collapsed.

"Yeah, you can feel the spit on your back. You're out in the sunlight. There's nothing like it. Coming out of it, not a better feeling."

On the hospital bed, inches from death, he was riding his own tunneling barrel. In a series of seven operations the doctors took out three-quarters of his skull. He had been in and out of a coma for weeks. His mother Michelle prayed. She prayed with the force of someone who has practiced prayer her whole life, who has made a discipline out of learning how to talk to God.

He listened. After three weeks Timmy Turner woke up.

You'd never know what he'd been through, watching him hustle out the orders, punch the keys of the register, call out to the kitchen. He was a handsome kid, no noticeable scars. As soon as he could, he got right back on his board. He went back to Indo and surfed the big fast waves.

Michelle and her daughter Holly sponsored me and Kim. I was so proud. We belonged in one of those photos up on the wall, with the middle schoolers, standing with our boards and a shy smile. Every day after surfing we went up to the café for a big lunch, salad to milkshake. And, of course, for a good dose of advice on what we should do next.

One topic that was always a source of conversation was what kind of board Kim should get next. Kim asked Bruno to make her a longboard, 9–0. The Michaels were skeptical. They were log-centric, meaning the bigger, the fatter, the better. Bruno scoffed. He took one look at Kim, his calibrated eye measuring her shoulders, the length of her limbs, gauging the easy way she moved, and said, "*Paw.*"

"Can you elaborate?"

"She needs a board she can grow into. If I make what Mike wants, in a month it will be no fun." He turned to Kim.

"Do you catch your own waves?"

"Yes. Starting this week."

"*Puis. Alors.* Something like this will be good." He pulled a shapely 9–0 off the rack. "You see, not too wide. The tail, it is a

squash tail, pulled in, so it will release, turn faster." He turned
the bottom outward. "You see the concave, the scoop in the
nose? That is so it won't purl. The nose will come up in the
drop. It forms like a bubble underneath. Yah, yah, something
like this."

Kim was thrilled. Her own Bruno board. It was like being
given permission to get better.

We were collecting surfboards. We now had:

1. *6–4 quad.* My slightly fat shortboard with four fins in
the tail, placed like so: The evolution of fin placement
is a book in itself. The condensed version goes like this:
The first boards in the U.S. had no fins. They were long
and heavy and surfing was mostly about taking off down
the wave and going straight. Then somebody attached
the first keel-like single fin to the back. Depending on
who you talk to, this pioneer may have been Tom Blake
in 1934, who got the idea from talking to a speedboat
skipper about the skeg on his boat; or it may have been
invented in the mid-Forties by Woody Brown, who was
a glider pilot and sailor in Hawaii and knew a lot about
fins and wings and fluid dynamics; or it may have been
his friend, surf legend Bob Simmons. In any case, the
evolving fin revolutionized surfing. Suddenly you could
make a fast bottom turn, with the fin both stabilizing
and propelling the arc. You could go down the line and
turn. The thing about a single fin is that to turn fast you
need a lot of speed, and thus bigger waves. Then in the
late seventies a competitive Australian surfer named
Mark Richards began to use a twin-fin setup—a fin on
each side—and blew away the surfing world by winning four world championships between '79 and '82.
The twin fin makes a lot of sense: when you weight

one rail of the board, one fin digs deeper on the inside, encouraging the turn, while the other lifts out of the water and frees up the outside edge. Turns now could happen really fast, and surfers could have fun turning on a small two- to four-foot swell, because the fin on the side would prompt a turn at much lower speeds. A variation of this setup that became popular in the eighties and is lately experiencing a resurgence is the quad fin. Two fins on each side, the inner pair a bit back of the outer pair. This allowed for even looser turns on smaller waves, because with twice the fin you could get the same turning power with shorter fin length. Thus, to dig in the fins on one side, and get the outer fins out of the water, the surfer needed less input, less muscle, less speed. Now you could rip on your average SoCal knee-high swell.

Then came the Great Change. The fin development that was like giving fire to a caveman: the three-fin thruster. Two side fins, and a center fin the same size and set back. The problem with the twin-fin setup was that while it was awesome for turning quickly on small to medium waves, on big, steep, fast waves it was subject to instability, a sort of "speed wobble" like you'd experience on a skateboard with loose trucks, or short, fast-turning skis when you really start to haul ass. The twin fins were so sensitive to inputs that at speed they exaggerated the slightest shift and got squirrelly. It could make for a wild ride. Simon Anderson, a surfer and shaper from Australia, decided to solve this problem by building the first production thrusters in 1980. The third fin stabilized the ride without sacrificing nimbleness. Now boards could be fast *and* incredibly loose.

Surfers could drop in on giant barrels with a light, fast shortboard that fit in the hollowest part of the wave, and still have stability and still turn like a bat. Surfers haven't looked back. Well, that's wrong; surfers are a very nostalgic bunch, and they love to go retro. The quad setup, especially as coupled with the stable but fast fish board design, is popular again, as are single-fin longboards—for those who miss the sheer speed and the big, sweeping, classic turns.

2. *7–6 egg, single fin.* Bruno wanted my quiver to march me through the natural history of surfboards. So he included a 7–6 single-fin egg. That's right, egg. This was nothing like Egg, sweet hapless ivy-covered Egg. This was a mini-longboard, good for days with smaller, slower waves when shortboarding would be frustrating. Also, oddly, good on very big, fast, hollow waves. Rounded on both ends, stable, could hold a straight line and zoom away from the apocalyptic explosion.

3. *7–6 gun, single fin.* A big-wave machine. Narrow, arrow-fast; one fin for going fast and straight. Straight rails for holding hard to the curved face. Turned only with a will. A little rocket for getting yours truly straight out of trouble. Bruno told me that this was for really big waves. I noticed the defensive emphasis—get the Destroyer (me) up, make the drop, then get him the hell out of there. Struck me that this was like giving a cavalryman a really fast horse—for running away. Again, I was touched.

4. *Aforementioned 9–0 longboard thruster, three fins.* The one I cracked at San Onofre, first ride. Bruno patched the nose with a large graphic of a screaming torpedo, a warning to other surfers. Always in surfing there has

been a tendency toward retro, a yearning backward, a nostalgia. Fin configurations come in and out of fashion like bell-bottoms and short skirts. In the nineties, as the first generation of shortboarders paddled into middle age, there was a resurgence of the old longboard. But young surfers with a flair for classic styles also love longboards. Mine was made originally for Bruno's twenty-something son, who is a billboard underwear model in France. Rounded and buoyant in the nose for ease in making the steep drop, and pulled into a pintail for easier release, easier turning. I loved this board. It was very easy and fast to paddle, the nose rode up on the drop, and it was quick to turn for a board its length, but also stable in a straight line.

5.   *6–7 shortboard.* Standard three-fin thruster, tapering quickly to a sharply pointed nose, thin enough, and narrow. Low volume for its length, quick turning, made to tear it up on the wave.

6.   *5–8 fish.* Short, fat, thick, ugly. Quad. A design made popular in the eighties and one of Bruno's specialties. This is the board that can do everything—though short, it had enough volume in its other dimensions to float high and paddle fast. Turned easily. Stable. Good on smaller, slower waves, but could handle big waves, too. This board was all Bruno used when he went to New Caledonia to surf big hollow waves. Many advantages of a shortboard, but didn't require the same crisp quickness. Used by surfers young and old. On the wave, driven by someone who knows what she's doing, the fish does possess a certain charm. It is like a fat woman dancing salsa. I didn't get it. I tried it once at the Cliffs and found that while it did catch waves easily, turning

required a heavier weighting of the back foot and then the board skidded rather than carved. Being a kook, I was not the best board tester, but I knew what I liked. I liked beautiful things.

We had all these, plus Kim's new longboard and the old, chunky 8–6 funboard I'd bought from Skip. Eight boards. I felt rich. It was way too many.

Veteran surfers said, "Take them all. Boards break in Mexico. You'll be glad you did." It was good advice, but it meant that we had to put the four longer boards on the roof, and the others inside the van in our living space. The four boards on the roof made the top heavy. At night, to pop the top for sleeping, we had to simultaneously lift up on the roof and shove a hinged bar forward and up until it locked into place. It required a weight lifter's jerk, but with a vulnerable, arched posture, and day after day it killed our backs. Finally we went to Home Depot. We bought two construction-worker black Velcro back belts with shoulder straps. Kim and I pulled into a dark spot near the Seal Beach Library, looked around to make sure no one was watching us, then suited up with our weight belts. We cinched the belts tight as tourniquets.

"You look great in a corset."

"Yeah? You look like a mover from Brooklyn."

"Ready?"

"Ready."

"Uno, dos, tres—!" Ugh.

Philosophically, with regard to material things, there are two ways of moving through the world: Light or heavy. Swift or bogged down. The absolute happiest times in my life were when I was responsible for the least amount of things. Backpacking, with home and food in one compact fifty-pound bundle. A long bike trip, when all I carried in the world was a tent roll and two panniers. A month-long horse trip from Colorado into Wyoming leading a single packhorse with light packs. I spent most of my twenties in a blue Toyota pickup with a cap on the back, two kayaks on the roof, and everything I owned in the back, under the plywood bed. That was living life close to the blood-beat of Now. What I *did* back then was everything.

One of the things that appealed most to me about the Beast was that she reminded me of those days. Not an inch of space had been left to its own devices; everything doubled itself, had two uses at least. Nobody can do this better than a German. The lower bed was a seat, a car trunk, a chest lid. The driver's captain's chair was a front seat facing forward, a dinner chair facing backward, and a recliner when dinner was done and you wanted to stretch out and read. The stove top was a drying rack when it was time to do dishes.

What is so appealing about this kind of efficiency? I think people spaz out and buy RVs and yachts just because they see all the cabinetry, the ingenious tucking away of every element of daily life, the whole thing fitting together like a puzzle, compact and hidden; some atavistic neuron group at the base of the brain begins firing, some nesting-lizard response.

As our time in Huntington Beach began to tick down, I became focused on outfitting the Beast for everything she needed to survive the long trip into Mexico. The first thing I did was shod her with aggressive Hakkapeliitta triple-ply, on/ off-road tires. I Cloroxed and rinsed her ten-gallon water tank and filled it with fresh water; topped off her underslung pro- pane tank. I had the mechanic change the oil and check her all through: fluids, brakes, clutch, alignment. After the tires, I put screens in all the windows. Kim had bad reactions to bug bites, so I also fitted a net over the upper bed and got some twelve-volt fans.

The next problem I had to tackle was how to carry surfboards securely. Bruno and others who had surfed a lot in Mexico said to always sleep with the boards *inside* the van, no matter what. It's not difficult to cut one strap and slide a board off a roof. Bruno said that at La Fonda, where we planned to stop first, just inside the border, boards were stolen all the time. He said that a friend of his left her car there for lunch and came back and her car was gone. Another surfer got killed right in the parking lot. Dang.

We had heard a lot of these stories, and they had begun to mount up and produce a toxic gas of fear. Everyone we talked to said, *Never ever drive at night.* Bandidos, drunk drivers, animals in the road. Mostly killer thieves. Experienced Baja travelers recommended that we find a place to camp several hours before sunset. Sounded like a trip to Transylvania.

Given what we had heard about Mexico, how could we prevent our boards from getting ripped off when we wandered across the beach to look at a break, or stopped for a meal? Online I found a company called Inno that made a slick locking rack. All my life, carrying kayaks on the roof, I had been a simple tie-down man, proud of my tight trucker's hitch. This rack dazzled me. It looked a little like a ski rack. I ordered one for each side of the roof and two extra-long crossbars to support them. No throwing ropes over the top here: two stiff rubber arms rose from the inside of the rack, at the center of the roof, and angled over the crossbar like cranes. You slipped the boards onto the padded crosspieces and pulled out a loop of steel cable from a roller on the outside. You caught the end of the rubber crane arm with the loop, then turned the knob on the roller, reeling back in the cable with a ratcheting

click until the arms and the cables were snugged down tight
over your boards. Then you turned a key in a small silver lock
and nothing would release the boards but a pair of stout side-
cutters.

Wire cutters are not uncommon, even outside of America.
Well, the main thing was that no barefoot surfer could just
walk past the van and lift a surfboard. If thieves wanted the
boards badly enough to carry specialized equipment, there
probably wasn't much we could do about it.

Some of the boards would go inside. It was a real chore
stacking all the boards on the roof, and then there was no way
to lift it for sleeping, so I figured we could keep the boards we
used every day down below. The nine-footers fit easily. I got an
industrial version of an adjustable shower rod, a steel bar that
extended itself by twisting, and fit it behind the front seats,
above the level of the stove and cabinets. That way we could
rest the longboards across the rear bench seat and the bar up
front and still get into the little fridge and closets beneath
them.

With all the extra security, the Beast sat up on top of her
big tires like a warhorse. She was so unabashedly rough. She
looked exactly like 318,000 miles of bad road. She was the
color of sand and mud. The sand was the once-yellow paint
roughened to the texture of peeling skin. The mud was the
scraped patches of rust, the veins of it between body panels.
The headlights, though as old as dirt, were as round and trust-
ing as the eyes of a child. The grille gave off a cryptic smile,
like a dog's. The sliding side door growled open and barked
closed. Between her frame and the ground were hand-spans
of daylight, nine honest inches, as much as a four-by-four
pickup. She just looked tough and true. You knew she wasn't
concerned with frivolous things.

We were feeling pretty proud of ourselves. At least I was. Kim watched me unload my purchases and took daily tours of the Beast with cheerful encouragement, but I could tell that she was leaving the details of this odyssey to me. I got the sense that she was coming to support me, but in truth, she did not like relentless sun. She would really rather go somewhere without bugs and sun, like San Francisco.

Next I got plastic cans for water and gas. Blue and red, so nobody would mix them up. I lashed them neatly into an indented storage pocket in the front of the roof.

Extra water, extra gas—what else? Something for flat tires.

The heavy off-road tires I had gotten on the advice of other Baja travelers. It was important to have an extra ply of steel in the part of the tire that hit the road, and in the sidewall. There was usually only one paved road in Baja, and that was the main road. I'd heard about potholes that could swallow a truck. The rest of the roads were dirt, rock, sand. Every other plant had a thorn or a spike. Flats were endemic. Most veterans advised carrying two spares. Our one spare was slung under the frame up front. I couldn't bring myself to carry another; I'd have to make a mountain out of the stuff on the roof. Instead, I tried to prepare for two flats in the most desolate place by getting a patch kit—the kind with the plug you twist through the hole—and several cans of Fix-A-Flat. The stuff actually works, I've used it in the city: screw the nozzle onto the tire stem and reinflate with a spray of thick glue that fills the hole, then drive to spread the goo around the inside of the tire. I also got a cute little tire inflator that runs off the car battery because people told me I wouldn't be able to get the tire up to pressure with a bicycle pump.

It is always this possibility of breakdown that looms in the mind of a Baja traveler. A lot of people travel down the length of the peninsula in convoys of two or more vehicles. It makes a lot of sense and eases the threat of being stranded alone and without help in the desert. If you look at a map, you can see that much of the Pacific coast of mainland Mexico is strung like a rosary with cities and towns and *pueblitos*. There is some form of coastal highway all the way down. It's not like that in Baja. There is one road mostly down the middle like the vein of a habanero, a narrow, shoulderless highway that in places staggers east and west, reeling from one coast to the other, and that's it. Except for a few spots, the only way to get to the Pacific coast is on a branch road, usually dirt.

I sailed that coast once, helping a friend deliver a sailboat from San Diego to Mazatlán, and I was struck every day by the total desolation. A hundred miles would go by without sign of a harbor or a town. The rest was sere hills and cliffs every color of hide and blood. It was intimidating, is what it was.

On August 19 we slipped all the boards into their zipped Cordura bags, loaded them on and into the van, and headed for the border.

THE OCEAN AS A SECOND LANGUAGE

Interstate 5 passes through San Diego in a blizzard of billboards and fast-food strips. You wouldn't know you were near the ocean but for an occasional slice of gray water in the distance and a glimpse of the port itself as you pass over an estuary. Then the highway shoots straight for the border. The exits get sparse. There are signs for Mexican auto insurance. There's a sense that this part of the wide interstate was built for one thing only: to expel you. To deliver you into the arms of another county. The sun was lowering over the palm and scrub hills on our right and I began to feel we were being funneled toward our fate. I thought that cows must feel like this as they are herded into the last turning chutes.

That the last exit before the border was a town called San Ysidro reinforced the sense of imminent foreignness. And that all the signs were in Spanish, and everybody in the streets looked Mexican. We pulled into a gas station advertising *se-*

guros and bought a year's policy on the van for $200. I didn't even know what it was for except that I was told not to be stopped by the police without it. The closest food was a taco joint with orange plastic tables. We ordered tacos.

"Ready?" I said to Kim. She looked a little nervous. What was wrong with us? This was supposed to be fun. We were both world travelers. This was Mexico, for chrissakes. We were going surfing, not to the front lines. We had prepared for this moment for months. "It's already four-thirty, do you think we should go?" I thought about the crossing, how they might pull us over and go through all our stuff, make us sign a customs declaration, how we might have to bribe some official not to charge us for importing surfboards. All this had happened to me and my friend Larry when we'd brought in a bunch of equipment for his sailboat. And by then, after filling out forms in triplicate, the capricious sun would be down and we would have twenty minutes to scramble for our camp before darkness settled and the vampires came out.

Do not get caught out on the highway at night . . . The admonition sang in my head with a ghoulish vibrato.

"Lista," Kim said. "I don't really want to camp around here."

"Okay."

We climbed into the Beast and thundered her up the ramp.

We needn't have worried about the border. There was a gate like a toll station and a green light that blinked on as we approached. We never even stopped. Not an official in sight. Our lane funneled into a highway and we joined the other cars going southward at sixty miles an hour. We climbed a long hill with the Tijuana barrios on our left—narrow streets and beat-up concrete houses, mechanic shops—and the barren DMZ on our right—the high steel wall topped with wire, the big arc lights, the bulldozed swath of open ground just inside the U.S. where a white INS patrol truck idled under its bar lights. Poor Beast. She struggled up the grade in third gear and then we topped out and saw the sea. At last. What we came for. Relief swept through me. The ocean is the ocean is the ocean. We forked onto the toll road. The sun hung orange over the water. As far south as we could see was a continuous jumble of buildings on the sea side of the road. Mostly white stucco condos, strips of adjoining units, walled in and gated; or garish hotels with Moorish towers of concrete, metastasizing at the edge of the sea cliffs. Tall billboards staggered up the highway, THE GOOD LIFE AT MAR Y SOL CONDOMINIUMS AND RESORT, always a swimming pool and a blond chick in a beach wrap smiling as if her life depended on it. A huge development being built by Trump. Older barrios of gringo vacation houses crammed wall to wall at the edge of the bluff, flaying the breeze with TV antennas and satellite dishes. Even the fancy stuff looked a little like a slum, cramped between the highway and the cliffs. And up to our left, on the scrub hills, bulldozers scoured out more paradise, unpainted blocks of concrete bristled with rebar, thousands of units under construction, waiting for subcontractors.

We passed Rosarito, where the cops were supposed to be predatory and where a four-stack *Titanic* gleamed at her pier—the life-sized mockup used in the movie. We passed Puerto Nuevo, an enclave of wall-to-wall restaurants by the water, famous for being mobbed up and for lobster. A little farther south a hundred-foot concrete Jesus, blue-robed, gestured at the ocean from a hilltop with a stiff, inward expression as if His last meal wasn't sitting right. Under His hands we turned off and joined the local traffic on the bumpy coast road. A cluster of low buildings held the famous K45 Surf

Shop. We pulled in. The owner, who spoke perfect English, didn't seem to care whether we put our boards in the water or not. I told him we were beginners and showed him my map and asked him where we should surf. His expression said, *No place.* "Quatro Casas," he said. "But this time of year . . ." He shrugged. "La Fonda is a good idea. You wanna go to Todos Santos? Going south . . ." He traced the pen along the one main road and marked the long interior stretch between Guerrero Negro and Constitution. "Fill up with gas. Don't drive this part at night." He sold me a little K45 sticker with a VW bus carrying a surfboard and we went outside and I put the sticker on backward—it was supposed to go on the inside of the window glass.

"The Mexican surf community sure is welcoming," Kim said in a rare gust of sarcasm.

I shrugged. "Must be cuz we're so close to the border."

We drove a few more miles. The sun hung over the water. From a rise in the road we looked down a rugged coast of steep hills and cliffs and points fading southward in an ocean haze. The clefts and folds were shadowed purple and the rock faces blazed back the orange sun. Right below us, on the top of a bluff, behind a string of motels and restaurants, was a jammed crowd of tents, campers, trucks. Surfboards everywhere.

"That's it?" Kim said.

"Yep, we just passed kilometer fifty."

"It's not what I imagined."

"What did you imagine?"

"I thought it might have, you know, less people. Baja."

I was starting to wonder if any beginner surfers ever took long road trips. The guy in the surf shop thought long and hard when I said we were kooks. He couldn't really think of anyplace good for us between La Fonda and Todos Santos eight hundred miles to the south. Or maybe he didn't want to. He did mention a famous spot called Scorpion Bay, but he said there had to be a decent swell from the right direction and it was a long way off the main highway.

I was getting the idea that most of the well-known spots would be over our heads, breaking too fast or breaking on rocks and reef. And the less threatening breaks like this would be as packed as California. We drove down to the bluff and through an arched concrete gate and a man in a straw hat came out of a house with a ticket book and took $18 for the night. Eighteen dollars! For that we better get a view. The campers were mostly Californians. Music spilled out of the Jeeps and RVs. Coolers everywhere crammed with beer. We rattled past a giant white water tank with rows of shower heads sticking off of pipes beneath it. Surfers were stripping off shorty wet-suits and sudsing up in the long warm evening sunlight. We rattled to the edge of the cliff, which was lined with campers, and I asked a Mexican family if they could move a couple of lawn chairs. We wedged in on the precipice under the blast of techno from a bar across the lot.

We looked at each other. Mexico. Time to make this car a home. We dug out the weight belts and strapped them on and jerked up the top. The sun balanced on the wide water. Well, we had made camp before dark like good boys and girls. There was no wind, and all along the line of the break below us knots of surfers gathered at the peaks.

THE END OF SOMETHING

La Fonda was harder than we were used to. The waves broke farther out, so it was a longer paddle, and they broke faster.

But we had each gotten a couple of good rides and we were tired in the way one can only be after a day of being battered by waves. We rinsed off the salt under the tank, and every cell of my skin felt alive to the breeze. Muscles relaxed, fatigued, happy, the wash of adrenaline ebbing away like a tide. The rhythm of rising and falling water still moved through our bodies like music.

It was Monday night and mercifully quiet. Kim and I had endured two nights of blazing party. The techno had gotten really enthusiastic after midnight and when it finally died down we had been treated to an hour of fireworks by some boys from San Diego; that was Saturday night. Sunday night there was a loud fight. The waves were crowded. Shower water ran in algae-chocked rivulets past the campsites. Cigarette butts and wrappers littered the packed dirt. A lot of campers pulled out early Monday morning, evidently on their way back to work in California. It had not been exactly relaxing.

But now the crowds were gone. I had the nose of my 8–6 up on a chunk of wood and was patching a small ding. I glanced over at the couple in the campsite next to us. A pretty girl poked forlornly at a smoky fire. On the dirt beside her lay the red plastic tie from the bundle of split firewood sold at the gate for five bucks. She wore a sorority sweatshirt and a blue ribbon in her blond hair. The boy, a little older, dug a pack of hot dogs out of a travel cooler in the back of his compact pickup. He was tall, lean, broad, and moved with the erect, shoulders back balance of a lifetime surfer. He opened a can of beans and set it inside the ring of rocks beside the fire. He put a hot dog on a fork and tried to roast it. Didn't look like the brightest idea.

"*Fuck*. Damn." He dropped the dog in the dirt, sucked his

fingers. The girl rolled her eyes. He pulled the sleeve of his long T over his hand and grabbed the fork again, knocked off the ashes, thought better of it. He went back to the truck. He found a roll of aluminum foil, wrapped up four new dogs, and lay it in the fire.

She crossed her legs in the low camp chair and swung her beach sandal back and forth at the end of her toes, looked around the camp.

"Matt."

"Huh?"

"Do we have any beer?"

He got up, shuffled back to the truck in his flattened flip-flops. "They're not real cold," he said over his shoulder. I noticed there was only one surfboard on his roof rack.

"Whatever. Set the cooler down. Why do you keep getting up?" She huffed out an impatient breath. He handed her a warm beer and I heard the two tabs spit. He sat back down next to her in a low camp chair.

"Matt."

"Yeah?"

"This beer is not 'not real cold.' It's fucking hot. Don't they sell ice up there?"

He puffed his cheeks, blew. "I dunno. Not really worth it for the last two beers."

She looked at him, exasperated. And then she smiled; from a distance. It was tender and I saw tears in her eyes, which she blinked away. "It's okay," she said. "I guess the English or somebody drink it like this."

The sun hit the water and a breeze sprang up as it often does just at sunset and blew their fire into scraggly flames.

"Fuck." He set down his beer, reached forward quickly, and with two forks managed to grip the edge of the boiling tin can and slide it away from the flames. The girl opened her mouth to speak, stuffed it. She threw a longing glance over her shoulder at the restaurants up behind us, then looked away, out at the water, swung her foot. I smelled burned beans.

I thought I could read the whole scene and it made me a little sad. I blew away the fiberglass dust I had just sanded, and squeezed out a dollop of Solarez liquid patch, scraped it flat over the ding with an old VingCard, spread a piece of Saran Wrap over the curing fiberglass, and stretched it taut and smooth. Probably still enough sun to kick off the resin. I got up. We had stacked the shorter boards against the front of the van and now, in our expansive parlor, we emptied a can of corned beef hash into a frying pan. I fried four eggs on the other burner. Kim sat on the rear seat and cut up an avocado and a tomato on a plastic plate. While the eggs spat, we watched the night pour an amber syrup over the darkening sea. Right now, almost everything made me think of food. We were starving.

We had surfed about three hours today, two in the morning and another when the wind dropped in the afternoon. I was so proud of us. The wave was slow enough, with a nice sand bottom, and Kim had caught one long ride straight into the beach. She paddled for it and I yelled and miraculously she caught it. Her snow-white Bruno board catapulted down the face—these waves were about shoulder-high—and miraculously again she didn't purl the nose or somersault. She popped up, stance wide. Once she's up that's usually all she wrote, almost nothing can budge her from her determination to get to the beach. I saw the back of her head and her long black braid over the back of the wave, receding, and her signature victory stance: back hand held up high behind her like a fencer, left held out ahead gesturing at the shore. I could see her hands shaking the air with excitement and I knew she was yelling.

The next morning I woke early, with the silent camp still in the shadow of the hills. I nudged Kim.

"Hey, Gidget."

"Huh?" She curled up and snuggled more deeply under the flannel sleeping bag. All I saw was a spray of dark hair. She was not a morning person.

"Maybe we oughta get out early before the crowd. Give ourselves a chance."

"Uhghuuh."

"Okay, cool."

I swung down. I glugged water out of our blue can into the old-style enamel coffeepot, shook a handful of grounds out of a Peet's bag, and put it on to boil. Cowboy coffee. From way up here the ocean looked almost flat. The lighter blues moved in what seemed rivers of color and the slightest breeze sanded across them and darkened them back to a near-cobalt. At the fringe, along the beach, the waves ripped the blue into a blazing feathery white. While the coffee water heated, I watched them. They threw up mist that hazed the break and I could hear the overlapping impacts rise and drift like a battle smoke of sound and I knew that the waves were bigger than they seemed from up here. They were unraveling in both directions. I searched for the peaks: where the swell pushed up the highest and broke first. Many were split peaks, with a snowy line coming off both sides of the hump. Some broke left and some right. A surfer could go in either direction. In many places the sections curled over themselves in a simultaneous dump. In those cases, even the best surfer in the world would have no place to go.

I moved a lawn chair out to the front of the van on the cliff edge and just watched the waves breaking. I was less interested in the surfers than the waves. Somebody once famously said that a tennis player wouldn't sit and watch the tennis court for hours but that a surfer could watch waves all morning and be happy. It was true.

I smelled coffee. Hopped up, made it just in time to see the upwelling water crack the floating grounds and boil through like lava. I twisted the flame off and got our bowls and mugs out of the cupboard under the sink.

I'd been on too many long wilderness trips with just a backpack or a kayak to worry about keeping food cold; it wasn't a habit, so our little fridge was stuffed with surf wax and Kim's contact lenses, and the red camping cooler was full of cereal boxes, cans of hash, and powdered milk. It cut a lot of complexity out of our lives, not having to worry about cold milk and ice.

I poured the two mugs, added milk powder and a teaspoon of honey to each, snugged on the lids, and raised one hand up to the second floor. Coffee in bed is about the nicest little thing we can do for anyone.

"Room service." With the other fist I knocked against the bottom of the bed.

"Uraghur." I felt a warm hand fumble over mine, take the mug, and retreat. It was like feeding bats.

I went back out to the chair. I liked sitting and watching and drinking coffee in the quiet.

Waves work on the spirit. They have a sound that we mimic in the blood: throb and drum of contraction and collapse, the rush and hiss around it in constant surge and recession. Up and down the shore the surf is a congress of overlapping percussions that swell like cicada song in the trees.

I wanted to learn to read waves. Waves were a new language. They had a lexicon and a syntax.

Sitting in my lawn chair, watching the shadow of the cliff retreat to the edge of the sand, I reflected that my best attempts at benefiting from the acquired knowledge of surf culture consisted of paddling up to some surfer and saying, "Hey, I'm pretty much a kook"—this was to disarm him so he treated me tenderly—"is this a left or a right?"

I mean, I couldn't really tell. Seemed like surfers from near this spot were going either way. This question elicited one of two responses. It was a good litmus test for potential friends. Nice people, people secure in themselves, people with generous hearts and a sense of humor, these people laughed or grinned and said, "It's a left. Pretty fast takeoff. On that board you might wanna move down the shoulder a little." The other response was to look at me with wolf eyes, the wolf expression that says, *Is this fool worth eating or not?* These guys said nothing, and took off on the next wave.

Everywhere we went I tried to mix with the locals and pick up valuable surf knowledge. In this way I would make up for decades of not having grown up surfing, not having a surfing dad and a surfing older brother.

So I did not just sit and drink coffee as I watched the waves. I bent myself to studying them.

I watched the peaks, but they seemed to shift around. As soon as I decided exactly where I would sit in the water, a bigger, better wave would form up twenty yards away. Was the tide going up or down? That should be easy. There was a broad line of damp sand at the edge of the beach that must have been left by a retreating tide, so I figured the tide was on the ebb. I was feeling proud of myself for gathering this one nut of fact when a set wave barreled through and washed foam up and past my wet sand line. Okay, needed more study. I looked at the wind. Not strong enough to blow off the tops of the waves either way, so I wet a finger in my mouth and held it up and it got cool faster on . . . all sides at once. Well, I was blocked by the van. Let's just assume the breeze was off-shore, since it was morning. (A simplified explanation of this relationship is that in the morning, the sea is usually warmer than the land because the mass of water holds the heat better and the land has been cooling off all night. The warm air over the ocean rises and creates a vacuum that pulls in cooler air from land, thus creating an offshore wind. In the afternoon, the whole process is reversed.) Tide, wind, peaks—what else? Riptides. Was there a riptide? Of course there was a riptide. You can find them by looking for currents or plumes of cloudy, sandy water between the sections. They often ran from the beach right out through the break. When you were on one, sitting on your board, you sometimes didn't notice until you turned around and saw that every other surfer was sitting way, way inside of you and the beach was receding into a thin line and you were heading inexorably to Seoul. Whoops. Then the thing to do was to paddle sideways down the beach—parallel to it—until you were out of the plume.

Kim and I had both been in many rips in the last month. None of them were really scary, but we learned fast that it was useless and dangerous to try to paddle straight in against them. We quickly tired. We could paddle ten or twenty feet to the side and the force would quickly dissipate. So I looked for rips. There seemed to be one river of sandy water up the beach, but I couldn't really tell. So much for my reading lesson.

When I got back to the Beast, Kim's feet were hanging

down from the top, which was a good sign. The couple next door was also stirring. They came out of their dome tent blinking. He went to his truck and came back with their breakfast of granola bars. She stood with her hands in the pockets of her sorority sweatshirt and looked at the sea with a joyless abiding. I got two enamel mugs and the coffeepot and stepped over to their cold fire ring. I offered them each a hot cup. I was surprised at how fast they said yes.

They were from San Diego. They were high school sweethearts, dating since their senior year. He had been the best surfer in the school. After graduation and a summer of parties, she went to UCSD to study hotel management—she loved to travel. He did not go to college. He wanted to pursue his surfing, go pro. He worked on and off as an electrician's assistant. He had hoped to get on the World Qualifying Series and travel, but it was extremely competitive. He struggled to make ends meet and to surf as much as he could.

She had just gotten an internship at a five-star hotel in Italy. This was their last interlude before she came back next summer.

It was the end of something. Written in their every action. She declined the granola bar he offered her with near-disgust, and then put her arm around his waist and rested her head against his shoulder. He held himself like a tree as she leaned. It was his role now, he had been frozen into it. She was breaking it off and there was nothing he could do. But when Matt stretched on the light neoprene shirt and took his board off the roof, his body recovered its elasticity and animation. In that one movement he gained his strength, like Popeye eating spinach. I always loved that: how people got bigger than themselves when they reentered their world of mastery. This was something he understood. Whatever else happened in the world, whatever pain and confusion, he could get on his surf-board and paddle out into the waves where his dance partner waited with breathless power. The girl saw it, too, and in a moment of relief came alive to him, and I saw her smile for the first time, a genuine smile that gathered light, and saw in an instant why he had loved her.

He stepped over to the Beast, said to me kindly, "You want to come out with me? Maybe I can give you some tips." I had told him about my project.

"Oh, yeah. Thanks. Just a sec."

I threw all the shorter boards into the bus, told Kim to come down and find us when she was ready, jumped into a shorty wetsuit, and picked up my 8–6 where it was leaning against a chunk of wood. I never used sunscreen unless Kim was watching.

"I've got some wax," he said, and we tucked our boards under our arms and walked barefoot down the steep track.

Matt watched the wave as we walked and steered us down to the water's edge. We crunched over a line of dead seaweed. Small crabs skittered over the damp sand and disappeared into tiny holes. Long strands of wet kelp glistened on the beach. Their ends were tailed with rubbery bulbs of air. Matt's board was a 5–10 and seemed tiny for his height. He had a half bar of wax in his fist that he'd been clutching to soften it up. The morning was still cool. He tipped his board up over his left thigh and ran the wax over it cursorily, glancing at the wave. He handed me the wax.

I set my board on the sand and made light passes back and forth, and then broad circles, over the places where my feet would land. One long session could wear off fresh wax and my landing spot had worn thin. Also two smooth holes where my bony ribs set when I paddled. I loved the stuttery scrape in my fingertips as the wax passed over the old bumps, the squeak when it hit virgin board. It sounded like some wood-slide percussion. Usually I just waxed the hell out of the whole board, but I didn't want to be a kook right away in front of Matt. Either the way he'd done it was the way pros waxed, or he was running out of the stuff. I handed him back a sliver and he stuck it in the pocket of his board shorts.

He squatted, Velcroed the leash to his ankle, gave me a half nod, and jogged into the water. He hit the whitewater, dove onto his board, and began paddling in one fluid accelerating motion. When he met the first wash of incoming foam, he arched his back and let it pass beneath his body without loss of speed, and at the next, bigger push, a two-foot-high wall of whitewater, he buried his nose and himself in a duck-dive, let the wash pass over, and came up on the other side paddling, with an undiminished slug of forward momentum. He moved through the water like an otter.

I won't talk about how I moved. Duck-diving was not an option because (a) my board was too big to shove underwater, and (b) I didn't know how to do it. A longboarder has a couple of options when paddling into a breaking wave. You can turtle—grasp the board near the front in both hands and flip upside down, letting the avalanche of whitewater pass over, then flip back again and keep paddling—or you can keep paddling forward if you think you can punch through the barely breaking peak, or you can ride up and over the steepening shoulder. Another alternative, of course, is to do what I often did without meaning to—get caught off guard and do the kook-a-matic. Yell, get knocked off the board, lose your grip, and roar inshore at high speed in an antipersonnel projectile of tumbling kook and leash and board. Slab of board, knife of fins. Hanging rope of leash. *Destroyer.*

This is a very irresponsible way to surf. One should never ever let go of the board. Sometimes in a big wipeout it can't be helped, but as a rule this is verboten. I met one kid who said that his surf coach in grade school used to make them all surf without leashes so that they had control of their boards at all times and reflexively grabbed them when they wiped out. It's a bad feeling to be in a big wave and have your board heading to the beach without you, so they learned fast. In any event, I was a lot slower getting out than Matt. He had already caught a long right and was up again beside me by the time I got past the break and was sitting near the peak. It was nice to watch, his ride. He did that thing that good surfers do—the crouch, the aggressive leaning forward into the next move as if breasting a stiff wind, the legs and board almost acting independently of the torso, working the wave as the head and shoulders fare forward as if driven under sail like a figurehead. The effect is dynamic and graceful.

When Matt sat on his board he was in the water up to past his waist. Not much flotation on that little thing. Still, the board, being mostly foam, wanted to surface, so when he spun to take off he let it rocket up from between his legs like a watermelon seed. At the same time he grabbed it and got a boost of speed. Like grabbing on to a bolting horse.

I wanted to straddle my board in one smooth motion like Matt, so I shoved it down and under me and widened my legs so I could leap into the saddle like an Arapaho, and I overshot. The board squirted back behind me and I landed on my face in the water.

There is no smooth way to recover from a move like that. You come up beside your board, blink the water out of your eyes, get on it again, reach down and back to free a loop of leash from your right foot, and do all this while looking far

out to sea, scanning for the big tuna run, or the signs of a tropical storm. Because by then you cannot even look at the other
guy—or worse, girl. When you kook out and pull a move like
I just had with Matt, well, it is very hard to be on the same
ocean, much less act like an individual who is entitled to hold
up one end of a mutual, collegial conversation.

I did sneak a look at Matt. He was smiling, unperturbed. "I
used to do that, too, when I was learning."

"How old were you?"

"Five."

We rode the swell. I thought how easygoing he seemed
for a guy who was spending his last day or two with his high
school lover.

"I noticed when you were paddling out," he said, "get forward on your board a little. You wanna have the nose kinda
just clear of the water. When you lie back it stalls the board
and slows you down."

"Okay, cool. Thanks."

We talked quietly and I asked Matt, who had nearly been a
pro, if the great champion Kelly Slater was really that good, or
if it was hype. The guy had won eight world championships.

"He's special," Matt said. "People say he has a special relationship with the ocean, and it's true. He goes for places in the
wave other people are scared of, and he makes it look easy."

"Yeah?"

"Yeah. His body is like made for surfing." Matt was getting excited. "He's got these giant flat feet, kind of like suction
cups. Like newt feet. They just stick to the board. And he has
this low center of gravity. Short legs. When you watch him
he's like a dolphin or something. He's that at home."

When Kim paddled out, the three of us sat in the lineup.
I swung my toes in the cool water. Down past them the sun

sprayed into the green depths. A flight of minnows skipped over the surface. I could see the Beast at the top of the cliff, her roof jacked at an angle, and our little bedroom window, the four surfboards clinging to the rack. Kim paddled hard and caught a long ride to the beach. I thought, *This is how it's supposed to be. Fun.*

THE TORTOISE AND THE HARE

Conejo means rabbit. Punta Conejo, Rabbit Point. We heard about it from an excitable Italian in the La Fonda parking lot. He slept curled up in the backseat of his car. He had a flamboyant accent full of flourishes. He lived in San Diego, did some vague business where a sense of style was mandatory. Never stopped moving. I mean, I had the sense he was always in motion, even when talking to me. He talked and untied his seven-foot board. Talked and climbed into his wetsuit. Talked as he jogged away toward the beach. Didn't make a lot of money, but it seemed that with that accent, and with never stopping, any difficulty in life could be surmounted, endured, talked through, and walked around. He was one of those people I couldn't imagine ever getting down in the dumps. Or if he did, he would wear it in such a charming, dramatic way, his despair would look a lot better than most people's happiness. A long silk scarf tossed around the neck. Ah, Italians.

I got the sense he wasn't a very good surfer, though he caught a lot of waves and cut a lot of turns. He was capable, but I was just learning that to be good required something else I couldn't yet articulate. It was something to do with grace and working with the wave. A surfer could stick a fast wave and cut dozens of turns, but the best swooped with the natural rhythms of a water creature. Anyway, in the parking lot, reaching into his backseat and shoving aside his sleeping bag and pillow, he told me that if we really wanted to go to a place that was not crowded, that had a long, long left that was easy to catch, we should go to Conejo. Where was it? Way in the south, Baja Sur, just this side of La Paz on the Pacific coast. Worth the drive. He said that sometimes when he knew there was a good swell coming he would go there straight from his house, something like eighteen hours driving fast and all night.

He asked to see my map, traced the highway through Constitution, slipped his finger down a dotted branch road, tapped on a jutting of the coast. In the middle of nowhere. No village on either side, no nothing.

"Ah, *sí,* right here. The Rabbit. I brought my wife here in May. The wave, it is a left off the point, long, you can get on it anywhere. She is a beginner and she got very long rides."

That was it, the image was enough. The prospect of long, easy waves sounded like the ticket for both of us.

We packed up in minutes, jostled past the big water tank where surfers were showering, turned onto the highway, and headed south. An hour to Ensenada, a crowded city where we got our passports stamped, and then we navigated back out to the two-lane blacktop. The Beast snorted and roared, vibrated, shuddered, made a great show of power, and crawled up a long hill. Sweet Beast. We fled civilization. Civilization obliged us by vanishing minutes out of Ensenada. A few miles south and we were in the Baja desert, the one I had seen in my sleep for months, the one that lays itself out under the sun and couldn't care less. The one that shrugs off the bones of travelers and horses, that rolls over in its dreamless, star-singed sleep and pierces you with a thousand thorns. Where after an hour you wish that beyond the shoulderless road there was just a little sign of civilization here and there.

Oven-hot air poured through the windows. Could not speak over the roar. The road shot arrow-straight across the flats, through plains of tufty tree yuccas green from recent rains; it squiggled over the steep hills in tight switchbacking loops decorated with shrines to the dead.

It was a good road. Travelers complain about the terrible Baja Highway, the potholes and cracks, but this was a proud, mostly smooth, well-maintained highway. It was just, well, skinny. Your lane is bordered on the outside by oblivion (cliff) and on the inside by death (oncoming semis). The outside has no shoulder, just a sharp edge of broken pavement and a dropoff of anywhere from a foot—enough to roll us—and a tenth of a mile off some cliff. The steering in the Beast was a bit loose, and we did not under any circumstances wish to lose concentration and drift a few inches to the outside on a left curve. The person who did that now has a miniature chapel shaded by a thorny mesquite where the only sermon ever heard is the wind whistling along the little concrete eaves and the only listeners are the ever-mute Jesus, the plaster Virgin, the photograph of a young man in a cracked frame, a fallen bouquet of faded pink plastic orchids. The ones that really got to me were the shrines that held two or three pictures, a brother and sister or husband and wife, or cousins, or toddler siblings, protected by a Calvary of three somber crosses in a line. Half a family obliterated in one instant of inattention.

The sandy arroyos were littered with the weather-stripped and rusted hulks that still held a memory of their original colors. What did the living think these memorials did for the dead anyway? Some were obviously well tended—freshly painted, laid with fresh artificial flowers—and the relatives must have driven long distances to get here. Or maybe they had been dropped off the side of the road by some express bus, carrying their bag of paint, new glass picture frames, a bottle of water, chicken tortillas wrapped in a towel. What a strange vocation, repainting a little chapel high above a gully in the empty afternoon. While the sun and wind who care about nothing push and pull at you, your only company the shadow of the rock mountains to the east, a frayed vulture, some silent stones. Mother of God, everything reminds us of our mortality. And the memories, of course, to keep you company, of the child or spouse, not even memory anymore, just a stone in the gut like a calcifying pearl.

Grief is the thing we run from and toward our whole lives. Judging by all the shrines, Mexicans are much better at it than we are. It struck me, driving down the road past all these crosses, that a midlife crisis, maybe even a surf trip, was just another response to grief. Grief this time at my own flash-in-the-pan brevity. Suddenly realize I am only here for a short, very short while, getting shorter by the minute. What do I do? Surfing seemed like a reasonable if immature response, maybe a bit outworn, but better than buying a convertible. My less aquatic, forty-something friends were becoming Buddhists in droves. Which was all about acceptance. They meditated for weeks, months. I really respected them. They were not running pell-mell from mortality, death. They were not the figure in *The Scream*.

The figure in *The Scream* with a surfboard under its wavery arm.

Me, I just couldn't sit that still.

The Baja Highway keeps itself a safe distance from the sea, from the jaws and horns of the coast. The road, challenged enough in the desolation of the desert tries to stick to the longitudinal valleys that run beneath the cordillera. Now, in late August, the rainy season was in session. Rainy season is a grandiose moniker. It means that now and then the rock peaks are shrouded in black thunderstorms. The rain rings off the stones, thickens, beats into the crevices, pries open the seams, burrows into the gullies. The rain sweeps over the thirsty silent basins of yucca and mesquite and cardón cactus, over the slopes of ocotillo and acacia. The friable soil sucks it up with an almost audible hiss. The flinty scarps shrug it off. It braids and twines and tumbles into the wash and the wash swells with a muscular torrent that gathers speed with the un-hurried inexorability of a freight train that blows no warning whistle when it crosses—and takes out—the road.

At 5:15 p.m., past our curfew, we pulled into Guerrero Negro, about halfway down the Pacific coast. The sleepy main street was lined with motels and restaurants all named Ballena this, Ballena that. Whale town. Laguna Ojo de Liebre, or Scammons Lagoon, one of only three breeding spots in the world for the California gray whale, is just outside of the city. We didn't see any whales, but on the sea side of town we saw miles of industrial salt flats and we saw dogs. There were dogs in the street and on the low rooftops. Dogs under the cars. We went into Pollo Loco for some crazy chicken and the matron had an air rifle in the corner to shoot chicken-hungry dogs. At the RV parking spot behind the Las Ballenas Motel there was a shepherd puppy under a picnic table, who looked at me over its shoulder with a pleading, dire hope, and thwomped its scrawny rat tail so hard in the dirt it made a little dust cloud of endearment. I wanted to adopt her more than anything. She squirmed and wriggled under my hand in such an ecstasy, and her odds of survival here seemed so short that I tried in my mind to play out every way to keep the thing and couldn't make it work. To get home in October for two months we were planning to fly, and then what? Our house sitter couldn't keep her when we returned to Mexico to surf again. Kim and I had our hands full just trying to get on friendly terms with this harsh country and with the sea, which we really knew little about. Which was true. But I wish we'd taken her aboard still.

Dogs and whales. Whales fascinated me. For the past few years I had been learning about them. How so many species are on the verge of extinction, how they embody the plight of the ocean itself. And if you've ever surfed with dolphins you know that cetaceans are the original surfers.

Dogs and whales are supposed to share a common ancestor. Some sixty million years ago this four-legged progenitor took one last look at the flinty ground, at the stingy hills, and said, *Screw it,* and went back into the sea. I imagine that the transformation from sea dog to whale did not take place in one afternoon. But I can also imagine the dog's relief as she felt herself lighten in the water. The burden of carrying around this heavy carcass, of falling forward foot to foot, was relieved. She wriggled her hind end, *dog*-paddled, and shimmied forward. Her limbs shrank, her vertebral column became cabled with muscle and got stronger and stronger and more flexible, and she grew flukes to harness this new power. Food was everywhere. Every other hour she swam through breakfast, lunch, and dinner. The food came at her like weather fronts. The best protein on earth. If she was a toothed whale, like dolphins, orcas, sperm and pilot whales, she was besieged by fish, the bait balls rolled by like those dim-sum carts laden with treats. If she was a baleen whale, like blues, fins, humpbacks, minkes, and the local Mexican gray, then she only had to open wide as she swam through clouds of krill and plankton, sifting the bucketloads with her sieve of baleen. Hunting had never been this easy on land. Why hadn't she thought of this sooner, coming home to the ocean? And a curious thing began to happen. Maybe it was the easy availability of all this high-protein food. Maybe it was that she had always been a bayer, a cryer, a barker, a singer, and now the delight of song carried so easily and far underwater and prompted pitched and echoing answers from so far away—her dog brain got bigger. It grew and grew. It got massive. To accommodate it, and the mouth to catch all that food, too, her head, her front end, became gargantuan. But her brain did more than increase in size. I imagine it self-delighted. The gift of song, the auditory cornucopia, the ease and grace and speed of movement in the buoying sea, the freedom from all but a couple of predators, this was a true, green, light-diffusing paradise. Her brain evolved with the speed of euphoria. It folded in on itself. It wrinkled, got convoluted, it's crenellations multiplied. It increased its surface area like the Maine coast. These folds are thought to signify intelligence—more equals smarter. The brain of a whale is the only animal brain that has more sulci, or convolutions, than a human's. The whales also developed spindle neurons—specialized brain cells once thought only to exist in humans and some higher primates. It welcomed complexity and divided into four lobes. (Humans have three.) It grew some more.

Thirty million years ago, when human ancestors were still hopping around in trees, screeching over a fruit, the whales were communicating over vast distances, calling each other by name, referring to a third whale by name (these behaviors all well documented), and singing songs of unplumbed complexity.

Cetaceans today, with their demonstrated capacity to experience emotions and to be self-aware (there is an objective test for this, using a paint spot on a whale and a mirror), must be feeling levels of grief and bewilderment unknown to their preindustrial ancestors. Their home has changed radically. Abandoned fishing gear—ghosting drift nets tens of miles long, lobster traps, longlines—entangle and drown upward of three hundred thousand sea mammals every year. Ship engines and props mangle the quiet depths and turn the sea into a cacophony in which the old, long-distant whale songs are lost. Midfrequency active sonar used by the U.S. Navy, the loudest underwater sound produced by man, ruptures the delicate hearing mechanisms of whales and wrecks their navigation systems, and they wash up on shore hemorrhaging from their ears and disoriented. Pollution—especially mercury, PCPs, and other heavy metals that are a by product of industry—precipitates into the sea and is absorbed by krill and plankton. Baleen whales eat so much of the stuff that their tissue is often too toxic to eat. Other small organisms are eaten by fish, and the pollutants concentrate up the food chain so that the toothed whales at the top are so poisoned that when a bowhead washes up on the shores of the St. Lawrence it is treated as toxic waste. Fishing and warming are wiping out food resources. Last year, when the gray whales returned to Mexico from their wintering grounds in the Bering and Chukchi Seas, scientists were alarmed that many were emaciated.

And as if all this weren't enough, every year the Japanese outright slaughter twenty-two thousand small cetaceans along their coasts. Dolphins, pilot whales, false killer whales, porpoises. The Japanese also send a commercial whaling fleet each year to Antarctica, in brazen violation of a 1986 world-wide moratorium on commercial whaling, to kill over a thousand whales, including endangered fin whales.

New studies suggest that present-day great whale populations are 1 to 3 percent of what they once were before man really began messing with the oceans.

Gnawing on my Crazy Chicken leg, I was thinking that if the water dog way back then knew what was coming, she might have kept her legs. But then, mammals on land aren't faring that well, either. A few weeks earlier I had read about the big IUCN census report that found almost one-quarter of all mammals on the planet are in grave danger of going extinct. Because of yours truly. It was a mess whichever way you looked.

Us humans are certainly crackerjack smart. I mean, who else could think up mortgage derivatives? But if you measure intelligence as an ability to survive millions and millions of years as a species in harmony with one's environment, then whales have it all over us. They make us look like crazy chickens.

One bright spot in all this was the drug gang in Consti-tution, the town to the south that we would drive through tomorrow. They were called the Tomates. I told you how the California gray whale was born in only three lagoons on the Baja. (The Western Pacific gray whale, at last count, consisted of just over a hundred individuals.) Well, Mexicans therefore consider the cetaceans Mexican citizens and are very proud of their whales. A Baja whale expert told me that the leader of this drug gang gave a significant amount of money to gray whale protection. Whenever I feel that the world is going to total hell thanks to *Homo sapiens* I think of this cartel protecting its whales and it cheers me up.

Since we were heading to Punta Conejo, we were also becoming aware of rabbits. We knew there were rabbits because Kim and I had seen them. Darting off through the cacti at dawn. Frozen in the shadow of an acacia. Munching sparse grass at the edge of the RV parking lot. We also knew there were gray foxes, opossums, coyotes, deer mice and cactus mice, wood rats, hoary bats, bobcats and mountain lions and desert shrews and ground squirrels, mule deer, jackrabbits— because the guidebook said there were. We marveled. We were still supposedly in the rainy season and it was so dry and hot. Not a spring anywhere. Not a lake. The rivers were rivers for a few hours: the flash floods steamrolled down the gullies and within a day the arroyo was mute sand and gravel reflecting back the glare of the sun. Stuttered with the tracks of these animals. How did they live?

We suspected it was the dew. It came from somewhere every night, and every morning before the sun had any heat it clung to the tips of thorns, the feathery leaves of the mesquite.

Kim said, "Maybe the foxes go plant to plant like hummingbirds, you know, tonguing up each crystal of water."

"That is so frigging poetic. Hummingbirds with fluffy tails. Write that down, write that down."

"Oh, really." She smiled, unabashedly proud, erect in the passenger seat.

For some reason, Kim and I still had some of that formality you find in new couples, though we had been together for a couple of years. I think it was maybe because she is Asian, and I have noticed that her family, her culture, is much more formal than my own. I liked it. Formality is one way of not taking something for granted.

As we drove south, I marveled at her as I did at the water-gathering mammals. She was never afraid to show her appreciation outright. Either at others, at something in her day, at herself. Her attention went leaf to leaf, gratefully, like the desert fox-bird at dawn. It seemed at once childlike and more mature than anyone I knew. She was very easy to please, because she took joy in the smallest things, but exacting, too, because that small thing must be authentic, and wondrous in its small self, and not any kind of bullshit. She could detect bullshit from a hillside away. But then she took people at face value and expected the best of them until proven otherwise. Which is a great talent. She was very complicated. Very simple, really. She awed me a little. As we drove south, as she covered her window-side arm with a towel and insisted I do the same, and made me a peanut butter sandwich, I was filled with a gratitude that almost scared me, and I realized that I was a lucky man. When we got to La Paz, after Conejo, I was thinking of asking her if she wanted to get married. You know, elope.

The metal sign for Punta Conejo was hard to read, the black letters faded and almost obscured with surf stickers. It was late afternoon when we turned off the highway onto a rough dirt road that the guidebook said was twelve miles long. It cut off through the acacia scrub and paloverdes. This track was so rugged—who knew how often anyone came down here? When we turned onto it we were committing ourselves in a way we hadn't yet.

"Our first remote camp in Baja, huh, Ting?" (Oh, that's what we called each other. Cute, I know. You don't really want to know the etymology, do you? Okay, it's because I used to call my tiny niece Little Thing, or just Thing, and one day I entered the room and she was clinging to the top of the playpen and she yelled the greeting, "Uncle Ting!" Hey, you asked.)

"It's kind of scary."

"Road's good." It was. Sand, deep in spots, and pretty smooth. I downshifted into a garrulous second gear and we trundled up the road nice and slow. I stopped once and Kim got out and cleared a branch covered in thorns. We swooped down around a right bend, climbed steeply, and topped out with a broad view of the sea. The coast curved in a shallow arc to the north and that, below, us, must be the point of the rabbit. We stopped the Beast, got out, and looked. An onshore wind shredded through the thorny scrub and I thought I heard the beat of surf beneath it. I was excited. The way you are when you double up a hundred dollars on eleven and say, *Hit me.* This was what we came for. All this way. To camp down by the Baja sea and catch waves few other people would come so far to ride. Wasn't it?

The washboard road ended at a navigation light on a steel tower commanding a low bluff. On the north side was a curving beach, empty, and on the south was a dry sand wash banked on the far side by a high dune. A handful of fishermen's shacks huddled against a hill above the beach. No people that we could see. Just below, barnacle-covered rocks tumbled into a seething rip. A dry wind came flat off the water and tore at a wave that shattered on the reef.

Not the benign scene I'd imagined. A forlorn whitewashed ranch house sat back under the scraggly shade of an old live oak, away from the beach and the brunt of the wind. We stood beneath the steel tower.

"There's the left," I said.

"Huh," Kim said.

I was a little nervous, but I didn't want to infect her. I started to sing "Little Joe the Wrangler," which is a cheerful song about a kid who goes out on a cattle drive and gets run over by about a thousand stampeding cattle. I sang it now because I *was* worried, more than anything about bringing Kim into this harsh world of desert and backbreaking surf and wayward souls. It was harsh and it was real, and it was no joke. If I were a pro surfer, or a desert survival expert, or some former Navy SEAL, like George Hayduke, it would be a different story. But in truth, Kim knew just about as much as me about any of this. We would have to protect each other. So I started to sing. And Kim, who had been looking at the heavy, thundering wave, turned and said:

"You a little nervous?"

I laughed nervously. "Yeah."

"Me, too."

She didn't offer any *Everything is going to be fine,* any lie. Because how could she know? She was in this with me all the way and she was my best friend.

The wave did not look easy. There was a man surfing it, only one. Below us, on the near side of the arroyo, was a big pickup with a cab-over camper. Out in the middle of the wash was a green Volvo wagon. The hatch was up and a pink umbrella was planted in the sand, and a man sat on a low camp chair beneath it. On the far side, on the top of a dune, was a giant pop-up trailer, kind of a canvas mansion. That was it.

I swallowed. Conejo. Up the track from the ranch house came a lone figure. He came slowly, stopping often. He held something to his chest. He wore a red shirt, white cowboy hat. We watched, fascinated, the way we would watch the slow progression of a snake. He crossed the arroyo and came up out of the brush. He was a blade-faced scrawny man in a bright red snap shirt who walked stiffly, cradling his sharpened machete like a dead child. He moved a few feet at a time, then paused, looked out at the sea under his fraying hat. The ocean was still foaming with whitecaps. It hadn't changed since a few steps before. He wore narrow wraparound sunglasses. His skin was taut over his cheekbones, burnished there like wood. When he grimaced he showed a few teeth. A few steps, stop, a few more steps. He ended up fifteen feet from where we stood, still without a word, and looked out at the sea. This close, we could see his shirt was stained. He didn't say anything, just let the wind play with the loose straws of his hat. It occurred to me that he moved exactly like a predator. Kind of circling in. So slowly that its prey didn't notice the growing proximity.

I called out. Introduced myself. The head turned.

"Victor." Pause. "*Todo*"—he waved an arm—"*este rancho es mio.*" All this land was his. "*No problema, no problema. Muy tranquilo. No bandidos.*" He patted his machete, spread his mouth into an unsettling rictus. Then he waited. Didn't move closer or away, waited with the stillness of a wolf.

"Ahh," I said finally. "*Cuanto por un noche de encampamento?*"

"*No problema*" Victor said. "*Treinta pesos, no problema.*"

I gave him a hundred. "*Cuatro noches, me falta veinte.*"

"Okay, okay, *no problema. Muy tranquilo.*" He must have been half drunk. His face, even with the impenetrable glasses, was at once sharp and blurry.

El rancho. There were no cattle, no fields. Not many surfers. Kim and I walked down to the pickup. Two lawn chairs, a stone fire ring, a fishing rod corded to the side of the camper, a board rack above it holding two shortish boards. This guy must have been here for a while.

His name was Jamie. We hailed his truck from fifty feet away, which is good camp etiquette, and he came out of the camper blinking from his nap. He was in his early fifties, a master electrician from San Clemente. He had been here six weeks. He did it every summer. Cleared his schedule of jobs, drove down here, camped, and surfed every day, with the wave mostly to himself. He was built like Tarzan, had curly blond hair down over his collar, eyes mineral-blue. Deliberate and kind.

"Yeah, Victor," he told us, pulling another chair out, opening it for Kim. "He's harmless. Collects the camping fee. A remittance man, I guess. His family didn't know what to do with him, so they sent him out here. Strange cat, but he won't bother you." Jamie's speech came to a halt and he looked out at the sun-dazzled water. I realized that he didn't carry on many conversations out here and wasn't in the habit of keeping one rolling. No need. There was plenty of time to communicate anything that needed saying. I laughed. Couldn't help it. Everyone out here seemed to be on stop-and-go time. It was a little like the pacing in a dream. Jamie turned his leonine, handsome head. Misinterpreted my laugh, smiled, said, "Victor keeps the *bandidos* away with his machete." Jamie took a neoprene shirt off a short clothesline and folded it, put it on the step of the camper. He had the fastidiousness of people who live alone for long periods of time. "Do you all want a Coke? Or a beer? It's cold."

I saw that the man out in the middle of the sandy arroyo under the umbrella was Asian. "That's Eddie," Jamie said. "They're camped on that dune way to the north. That's his cousin Freddie out on the wave. No kidding." The man was reading a book. Occasionally he looked up to remark his cousin's progress. Jamie was watching the surfer, too. So was I. So was Kim. He was the only thing, really, to look at. Compact, tearing it up on the fast overhead left in a full wetsuit and booties. "He's been surfing for hours. A little too windy for me."

I'll say. Felt like a gale. The wave, though, jacked up hard against the point and was strong enough to hold its shape even with the wind pressing on its back like a hand.

"How long have they been here?" I asked.

"Almost a month."

I looked at the man reading his book in the wind-shivered pool of shadow in the middle of the dry arroyo at the edge of an empty ranch in the remote Baja desert. The lone surfer. Jamie and his truck. The wind. Victor the remittance man collecting the fees. Only something as crazy as surfing could have brought them all together. Brought *us* together.

The half dozen meager fishermen's shacks up against the dune to the north must have been temporary. Not much more than some planks and scraps of corrugated metal for a roof. It was all a bit surreal.

We camped right under the lighthouse on hard ground and surfed for four days. Well, I did. It was too strong and fast for Kim. There was nothing friendly about this break. There was a terrific rip just off the shore, and it swept over an ankle-deep shelf of sharp reef. You had to carry your board and walk over it. Hard enough to walk at all in that current. It was hairy.

Out at Conejo, nobody woke up too early. It wasn't like you had to get out at first light ahead of the crowd. The second morning, about nine, Kim and I paddled out together. She was being very brave. The wave was just too fast and heavy. After a few minutes of fighting the current and getting shoved back in, she called, "I'm getting out!"

"Okay, be careful," I yelled. "The rocks are sharp."

I watched her. She tried to get out where we'd gotten in, and stood unsteadily on the razor-edged rocks in the strong current. She tried to pick up her board, and got knocked down, lost her grip. She struggled to standing in the lull of the out-wash and I saw blood on her hand. Jesus. She was standing, half bent over, unbalanced, trying to hold her board again and scared. I saw her face dissolve in tears. I saw it and paddled as hard as I could, then ran over the rocks, slipping, trying to keep from breaking my own board, grabbed hers too, said loudly, too loudly, "It's okay, it's okay, you're all right! You're okay, sweet, just undo your leash, I've got your board."

I didn't know if I did. We braced together against the next push of foam. "Okay, now you can walk, wait for this white-water to go through. Okay, okay, now walk carefully, good, you're all right."

It freaked me out probably more than it scared her. To see her so vulnerable. Simply unable, for all her effort, to get in safely. Things can happen out here, they can happen fast and spin out of control. It changed me.

We talked about it and decided we'd stay a couple of days because we'd come all this way and the wave was perfect for me to learn on. Jamie was a good coach and he told me where to sit and when to take off, and I made some hard fast drops down some waves that were over head, and managed to ride a few out along the left face. I used the 6–4 a few times, because the wave was certainly fast enough. I missed a lot of waves and wiped out a lot. It's just very very hard to catch a wave. The strength it takes—that burst off the blocks—and the timing are unforgiving. They can't be fudged. Their effect—moving for a split second at the speed of the wave, in just the right place—cannot be gotten at in some other way. You are exactly here, right now, with that burst of power, or you aren't, and mostly I wasn't.

At night, Jamie made a fire and the three close camps gathered around it and drank beer and pop. The big trailer on top of the dune was occupied by a clean-cut blond couple from San Diego. They had been camping on the dune for a few days. He had a nice shiny new four-door pickup. He surfed a little with the rest of us, was pretty good. And helpful, encouraging. He said he was a mortgage broker. She said she was a boogie boarder, but I never saw her go out onto the waves. Pretty, blond, chatty. I remember having wondered, the second day, that if they weren't on the waves much, what were they doing here with their rig that looked like a house? The point was windy and hot and dry and worried by the constant tearing and thundering of the surf, and there were prettier places. It seemed to me like solely an outpost of surf.

Waves have personalities. You can quantify a wave, say how tall it is, describe the interval between it and the next in seconds, say whether it is hollow and fast or mushy and slow. And on different days at the same break, with a different wind, a different swell coming from a different angle with more or less force, these measures may be very different. But every break has a spirit beyond the metrics and standard characterizations. Every spot where a wave forms. So that Seal Beach, for instance, may be knee-high and gentle as a rabbit one day, and twelve feet and rubbing its back against the underside of the pier's high deck the next, actually shaking the ground with its weight, but its underlying spirit is cheerful, accommodating. It radiates goodwill. It may get drunk with the power of the Pacific, but it is not a mean drunk. It may wrestle you to the ground and thump your chest, but the next moment it will be helping you up, grinning with irrepressible cheer, buying you a drink. With salt on the rim.

Conejo was not like that. Conejo was a misnomer. If it had been named by a surfer it would have been called Punta Lobo. Conejo came at you lean and hungry. It came at you straight, long-legged, locking eyes. When the wind blew against it you could see its ribs. It came with one fixed idea: to eat or die. To grab you by the neck and shake you. That Italian, the one who had sent us here with his description of it as accommodating and sweet, he must've been high.

Sitting beside Jamie on the 6–4, which I was determined to ride if not master, we watched the wolves come. With the wind on our backs. Here was a beauty, tall, regal, an alpha wave. As we sank into the trough ahead of it I said, "Can I get this?"

"It's yours. You've got it."

I rocked back on the tail, bringing the nose out of the water. I reached for the rail with my right hand and pivoted. Looked back once over my shoulder at the looming thing, took two strokes, and was gone. Lifted and dropped. Rocketing in a free fall that left me somehow standing. I may have shouted. I probably did, I'm such a kook. I crouched, pressured the left rail against the face, and swooped back, all the way back up to the lip, the propulsion like a jet engine. For a moment I felt like a bird. And then I hit the lip where it was already folding. Instead of getting out ahead of the pocket, doing this move a few feet farther into my own future as a surfer, I had boomeranged back right into the snapping jaws. I flew airborne. The wave landed on top of me and drove me to the rocky bottom. Tumbled me along it. In this state, tucked and rolling, several thoughts occurred to me.

One, *I hope I breathe soon. That would be good.*

Two, *I am as helpless as a rock in a landslide.* Three, *My board, the one with the extra sharp, shortboard spear of a nose, the one that has the destroyer on it, is attached to me on a short leash, and if I am being tumbled, it is, too. Somewhere really close by. Way too close.* I tucked tighter and covered my head with my forearms.

Four, *I really hope I breathe any second.*

The wolf released. Made his point. I flailed for the brightness, for the sun coming through all the champagne. And popped up. Yay! Big breath. But oh, shit! Just seaward and right on top of me was a four-foot flash-flood wall of whitewash from the wave behind mine, which must have been even bigger. Somebody had told me, "Hey, don't ever take the first wave in a set. Sets come in three or more. If you fuck up on the first one, bro, you'll get hammered by the next ones. Right in the impact zone. Right there, where it's all fucked up!"

The guy who had told me this seemed really enlivened by the prospect. Happily, he said, "And if you get caught inside, and worse comes to worst, just turn around, belly the back of your board straight in. Don't be no hero. Run!"

That was the first time I'd heard the phrase "caught inside." Sounded like bank-heist lingo. Now, for the first time, I knew what that was about. Ride a wave all the way along the face, kick out over the backside, and you finish at the end of the line, down where the wave has exhausted itself. The wave is spent, you are spent, everybody is happy. But screw up and wipe out right in the heart of the wave as I had just done, and you are bobbing right at ground zero. You are right where everything is happening. Impact zone. Where all the energy is loosing itself. You are this little head in a soup of white, looking up at a collapsing building. It's like jumping off the bow of a fast frigate, as opposed to the stern. I had barely enough time for one breath, and then I was run over, tumbled again, shoved down. Didn't last as long. When I came up I was converted. I believed. There *is* a Wave. I was so happy to live. I gasped. I bellied onto my board like it was a life ring and paddled it feebly toward shore, then let the rip carry me north, north to where the wave petered out. Away from the thoughtless violence. Away from the terror and the madness.

Taking several gulping lungfuls, I shook the salt burn out of my eyes, then turned and paddled back out into the surf. One stroke at a time.

I think that's what it takes. To learn to surf. Just plain idiot doggedness. If you have that, you don't have to be smart, quick, strong, or good looking. All of that will come. At least the strength will come.

"How was that?" said Jamie when I got there. His handsome, creased face, his blue eyes like some kind of tourmaline. He'd caught two more waves since I'd been gone.

"Interesting," I said.

On the fourth night we made popcorn and watched a surf movie on the laptop called *North Shore* and crawled up into the top to sleep.

Wind. All night snapping the canvas walls. Groaning the Beast on her frame. She sounded like a boat. Heaving into the seas and the wind. Which was what she was doing, parked beneath the lighthouse on a rise too small to call a bluff, facing the sea and the weather head-on. The light, unprosaic on a steel tower, washed our bed every twelve seconds. The flapping canvas muted it, but in the passing illumination I could see Kim's face as she slept. The planes of her high cheeks framed by a sweep of her night-dark hair, her bowed lips, her large eyes, beautiful even closed and dreaming. Her colors were ruddy and warm and dark. Mystery.

That is what I feel when I am with her. More than anybody I have ever known. Odd, because she is so open a person. She hides little; I would say she hides nothing, but we all know nobody hides nothing. If she is hiding, it is her own bafflement at her parents, who did not treat her as she saw other parents treat their children in this new country. She, the first child born in the States. They, her parents, speaking no English, working fifteen hours a day at the Chinese restaurants they started, Kim translating for them and working in the restaurants beginning when she was six. There wasn't much time in her family for affection.

The wonder of this lovely person, I thought, as I watched the navigation light play with the delicate shadows of her eyelashes, was that she expected the best of everybody, and that she could love me at all with such a sparse upbringing. Much less this steady, warm current. Where did she learn it?

I met her in a coffee shop near my house in Denver. I had just been through a terrible breakup. When I finally got up off the floor, I borrowed my buddy Sascha's electric clippers, popped on an eighth-inch jig, and shaved my head.

Some guys look fine bald. Not me. I've hit my head too

many times. It was midwinter and I swore I would never date again, and I almost guaranteed it with my lumpy scalp. When summer came, I felt a little more like myself, and began to write in the local café. One August Sunday morning I was there early working on a magazine story. I was unshaven, in an old T-shirt, had a cap pulled down over my eyes, and was not paying attention to anything but the screen on my laptop. I was at a small table facing the front door with my back tucked up against the counter where people lined up to get their drinks. In my reverie I heard the little bell on the front door jingle and the hinges yaw and I glanced up.

She was standing tall just inside the café looking over the tables. It was as if there were lights playing around her. She had this *energy,* sort of wholesome and pure. Happy. Clear. Her black hair fell softly around her neck as she turned to scan the room. She saw her girlfriend at a table by the front windows and smiled. Wow. It was like turning a bulb to the highest wattage. And she was so pretty, too. Her lovely, deep, gorgeous eyes. They were knowing and calm and terrifically sexy all at once. Her shapely legs. I felt a stab of pain and desire. More than that, I felt a sudden kinship, I'm not sure why. I knew right then that more than anything in the world I wanted to take this woman on a date.

I am not smooth. I have never been able to pick up a girl. My girlfriends always got to know me because they were forced to be in close proximity over long periods, like in college seminars or extended field trips when my great charm and wit would slowly become evident, sort of surprising like the sprouting of potatoes in the fridge.

Now, after nine months of not even talking to a woman, I knew that I was way beyond not-smooth. I knew that if I walked up to her table and tried to introduce myself in some

suave way I would twitch, look at my feet, say some gratu-
itously stupid thing, and go home and weep.

I thought, *Get it together, Pedro. Do what you do best.*

I pulled the clean napkin from under my cup, dug a pen
out of my pocket, and wrote:

> *Hi,*
>
> *I'm an adventure writer. I write for a lot of top magazines.*
> *I have a lot of great stories, but I'm kind of shy though. I would*
> *love to take you to dinner. If you think that's a good idea, you can*
> *just give me a thumbs up.*
>
> *Peter*

It's true, I wrote that. I folded up the napkin, and when she
got up and passed me on the way to the counter to order her
coffee, I said in what was barely a whisper:

"Excuse me, I have a note for you."

She paused, cocked her lovely oval face, looked down at
me, smiled. "Oh, my very own note."

I was gone. I fell in love with her right then. She was so
good-natured and gracious. She didn't recoil in suspicion, or
appraise my clothes, she didn't shoot any angles at all, she took
the thing at face value with a positive sweetness.

She got her coffee and returned to her table and opened
the napkin. She leaned over it. Then I saw a furrow form in
her brow. She frowned. She passed the note to her friend, who
read it, glanced at me, read it again with an equally puzzled
look, and passed it back. Oh, man. My heart hammered, head
flushed, and I shrank down below the laptop screen. But I
couldn't help peering over. They passed my note back and
forth.

In a flash I realized that they couldn't read the thing! I

write like a doctor, in a fast careless scrawl, and they couldn't read it.

There was still a chance. *Don't blow this. Now or never. You don't act fast, she's gone forever.* Crisis made me bold. There was another square napkin on my table. I slid it to me. I looked at her again. So beautiful. Clearly Asian. Okay, okay. Asian genre, Asian motif. For once in my life I did not ponder. I wrote:

Extended Haiku
Sudden Sunday invitation
How should I answer?
Beauty caught breathless
like a blossom blown off a limb.

I wrote it in all caps, the kind architects use, and I stood and brought it to her table and set it down in front of her. The two women, startled now, watched me as if it were some kind of weird pageant. I went back to my table and sat down, tall and straight. She picked up the note in her long, tapered fingers and read, and then turned to me and smiled and gave me a thumbs-up.

What woke us up beneath the lighthouse on the windy night must have been the sound of motors, of boats. We came awake and instantly the canvas sides of the pop-top were rinsed in red light. A flare. Then another.

"Put on something," I said. "Get down."

I had heard a rumor just before we left about a couple along the Baja coast who had witnessed a drug deal and been killed and buried in their car. I didn't know if it was true and

I didn't know if Kim had heard it. Either way, I didn't want to be that couple. We clambered down fast, slid open the sliding door quietly, and stepped out barefoot onto the cold dust of the ground. Gingerly, we tiptoed over broken shells and peered around the front of the van. Another flare. It arced from the high dune on the south side of the arroyo that ran right down into the water. That's where the friendly, clean-cut couple from San Diego was camped.

It must have been late, because the wind had backed around and was coming from the land. We stood close to the Beast and peered across. A crimson streak arced over the water and crumbled into the darkness. A moment later a halogen spotlight cut down to the arroyo and swiveled south in jerks. From the top of the dune. Our little yuppie friends were having a serious rendezvous party. *Respondez-vous, s'il vous plaît.* Whoever was RSVPing was doing it on the other side of the hill and the point, beyond our sight. The light dropped down to that side, to where a long beach curved away. I was glad. You can't be a witness if you don't see anything.

The next morning I was pulling my board out from under the lean-to tarp on the back side of the Beast, when lo and behold, Barbie and Ken swung up from the arroyo in their fancy pickup. They rolled down the window, grinned, said they were going to Cabo for a few days for some R&R. I thought this *was* R&R, but I didn't say anything. They looked wholesome and happy, expectant, like a couple off on their honeymoon. I guess the prospect of stacks of crisp greenbacks might do that to a couple. He told me to take off at a hard angle on waves like these. He said, "You're doing great. I saw you catch a couple of honkers yesterday." He smiled his white even teeth and I wished them well. I *did* wish them well. I can never separate my personal warmth for someone—the guy had been

really encouraging to me out on the wave—with my indigna-
tion at this same person's politics or career choice or moral
deficiencies.

An hour later Kim squatted with our breakfast dishes
down on the barnacle-covered rocks in the little flushing
tidal pool at water's edge, when I heard the throb of a diesel engine. An armored amphibious boat charged around
the point. Must have been doing thirty knots. It was army-
green, heavily plated, shaped like an angular beetle. Two
fifty-caliber machine guns were mounted forward and aft,
and helmeted, very serious soldiers trained them on the
shore. The boat went past us, north, until it was in line with
the fishermen's shacks, made a tight turn, threw up a wave,
then chopped back across its own wake as it skimmed just
off the beach and the rocks. They seemed to be aiming their
guns at Kim. I yelled to her, "Come up here! Hey, get up
here, now!" I was doing a lot of urgent yelling lately. She
was wearing her big straw hat, which made her look more
Southeast Asian. I was from that sad era, and I couldn't help
an unwanted association with Vietnam and her villagers.
She gathered up the pans and hustled up to the light tower
and the van. The patrol made one more pass. What could
they be looking for that hadn't already vanished in the night?
I could see the mother ship offshore, a large gunboat, just a
shadow, about five miles out.

We left. Enough of rabbits and remittance men. Kim
couldn't surf here anyway. We packed up in half an hour. We
left the van untended and walked down to say good-bye to
Jamie. (He said he would stay another two weeks, he was
stuck to this spot like a limpet.) We were gone from the Beast
for five minutes. We rattled up the road. It wasn't until we got
to La Paz a couple of hours later that we realized that in that

time someone had stolen my fancy altimeter watch (hanging from the metal push-up bar of the pop-top), a Leatherman multitool, and a nice folding knife (kitchen drawer), Kim's sunglasses (between front seats). Where we had parked, our open side door faced the shacks. Every afternoon I had taken off my watch and hung it up on the bar. I had opened the drawer, taken out the tool and the knife. Whoever had robbed us—either one of the fishermen, who had just passed with a sack of mussels, or Victor, who was lingering around up there—must have had binoculars. Must have been watching us. That was unsettling, more than the theft.

After half an hour of washboard road we turned the Beast back onto the smooth central highway and aimed for La Paz. A city of soft-spoken, almost unreal beauty. I was relieved and happy.

"Want to take a few days off?" I said over the glad roar of the Beast.

"Yes!"

"We could go snorkeling. That place I told you about, with the sea lions."

"Yes!"

She was in a Yes frame of mind.

"We could get married."

"Yes!"

I beamed. She beamed. La Paz doesn't have any surf waves and I wasn't sure if she was so pleased by the prospect of a few days without the labor of surfing or a lifetime of marriage to me. I figured both.

"Tomorrow is the full lunar eclipse," she said. "I think that's auspicious. Let's get married tomorrow."

I was happy. The Chinese are always concerned about being auspicious. Better, I thought, to have an auspicious bride than a—an inauspicious one. I knew that Kim would get online tonight at the hotel and check the astrology of the eclipse and the numerology of the date. If the numbers added up to four, eclipse or no, I knew we would not get married tomorrow. In Chinese, four is the number owned by death.

LUNA DE MIEL

The Hotel Los Arcos looks out over the promenade of the Malecón and the bay of La Paz. Across the shallow inner bite scattered with sailboats at their moorings, to the long sand spit of El Mogote, and beyond it to the Sea of Cortez. El Mogote is edged with rich mangroves, some of the last in the bay. Something about the evaporative breath of the sea and the clarity of the desert around it combines to make the softest, most dramatic sunsets I have ever seen. Like an Impressionist painting a massacre. If there are clouds in the sky they are flayed, bloodied, bruised in a spectacular, celebratory nubicide that is lovingly muted by marine haze. The water-clear bowl of sky above remains an unperturbed luminous blue. The highest blues pulse the hardest just before dying into night and a rich blackness that is alive to stars. There are desert nights and then there are nights on the Sea of Cortez. This is not hyperbole. Couples come here just for this spectacle.

Reflecting back the firmament is the liquid desert of the sea herself, sparking with phosphorescence. It's the bioluminescent plankton that glow when agitated. Once I sailed in here with friends on a small sloop. Every night, at anchor, I hung over the rail and watched the light show like submerged fireworks. In a black sea slick as a lake, big fish chasing little fish painted branching trees of panic and fire. There were flaming arrows of light, big enough to give a swimmer pause. Playful darts. There were calligraphies of what may have been love. Large rays flew through the water and trailed wakes of luminescence like divine starships. When they leapt into air and crashed down, soft explosions of light preceded the percussion.

The Sea of Cortez is one of the richest marine zones in the world. A third of the world's whale and dolphin species hang out here. Sea lions breed and bark on the skirts of the numerous rock islands. Blue whales, our largest cousins, swim up into the Sea and breed. At least scientists think they do. So little is known about the biggest mammal. Most of what they do and where they go, even how many actually exist, is a mystery. Most recent estimates put their numbers between five thousand and twelve thousand, but it's a hazard and a guess. Common and Pacific white-sided dolphins are also here. Fin whales, second in size to the blue, critically endangered. Humpbacks, gray whales, sperm whales. Whale sharks, which aren't a whale at all. Elephant seals and harbor seals. Even orcas.

There is an island off of La Paz, just to the north, called Espiritu Santo. Big, about the size of Manhattan. Except for a small fishing camp on the channel that separates the island's two halves, the place is completely wild. On that trip on the sloop a few years ago a couple of buddies and I sailed up the shore of Espiritu Santo to a rock islet on its northern end. There's a voluble sea lion rookery here beneath black cliffs painted with the guano of blue-footed boobies. We could hear the barking two miles out. We anchored close, put on snorkels and masks, and dove. I'd heard that the lions were used to snorkelers, would swim by but would never let you touch them. You weren't supposed to get too close anyway, that was harassment.

I swam around in wonder. The sleek females jetted by, spun as they passed, and held me with their dark eyes. I could almost feel their whiskers. Hulking black bulls with heads like cannonballs glided past, bit down on fish in an explosion of flesh. I felt very aware that I was a tolerated guest, that this was their house. Then I saw two youngsters roughhousing. They must have been adolescents. They were playing tug-of-war and tag with a shock cord dropped from some boat. I wanted to play, too.

I dove down and performed a double somersault, triple lutz, as I went to the bottom. Very awkward in the flippers. It caught their attention. *What the hell was that?* They looked incredulous. They whizzed over and around me, and as they did they executed streamlined barrel rolls and loop de loops. *Oh, yeah? Watch this!* I took the biggest breath I could and went to the bottom performing every turn and twist I could think of, then added a kind of Peggy Fleming flourish with my hands. They were floored, if a teenage sea lion can be floored. They went nuts. They roared around me like the Blue Angels. Then suddenly I felt a tugging on my right flipper. I looked back and the littler one had the fin firmly in her teeth, pulling and pulling. Okay, two can play this game. If you can dish it out . . . I arched slowly around and pinched her two rubbery back flippers in my two hands. She didn't give up. We circled in an antic donut. Then she broke away and described a fluid arc and came straight at me. I held my hand, my fist, straight out and she glided up and took it in her needle teeth. She had grabbed the flipper hard, but she knew the difference. Ever so gently she mouthed my hand and stared at me, straight into me with her large liquid eyes. I thought I could see humor there, something like the delight I was feeling. She broke again, and again circled back. We played and played. I held her torso and she pulled me through the water. We hung upside down a few feet apart and just looked at each other. I forgot my name. I forgot to breathe and came to the surface gasping. When finally I was blue with cold and the crew was calling me and I swam back toward the boat, she swam around and around me in fast figure eights. It was the most euphoric moment of my life. I had been an invited guest in a wild place.

Marriage is an act of faith and of great hope. I wanted to take Kim to this place on the day we promised each other our lives.

After over a month living inside the Beast, the Hotel Los Arcos was paradise. All the sweeter because we knew that after two nights we'd be on the road surfing again. The polished Saltillo tiles of the lobby were so glossy they reflected the slow-turning ceiling fans. The breeze from the fans ruffled the potted palms and were barely heard over the bubbling of a central fountain. I could have wept. We were dirty, we carried one baby-blue and one pink gym bag, all stained with dirt and grease. And four longboards off the roof rack. In the States, the staff would have been snotty. Not here. They treated us as if we were arriving Ambassadors of Adventure. The surfboards were whisked away by young men in uniform tunics with brass buttons. We declined a porter for our little bags. In the room, overlooking the bay, we fell on the king-sized bed in an ecstasy of creature comfort. We were just as thrilled with the crisp ironed sheets as we were with each other. We laughed. We were getting married! A sense of deliverance and relief overtook us. Part of it was all this—the little sign above the sink that said the water was potable, the hot gush from the shower head, the cold Cokes in the bar fridge. I didn't really realize how much we had been on full alert over the past two weeks—for the safety of our stuff in the camps, for our lives on the highway and in the surf. Always keeping track of who was coming in and out of the rough access roads, what the tide and the waves were doing, how we were fixed for water, gas. Now we dropped our guard with a sigh of relief. But part of it was this sense of deliverance into each other's care.

We strolled down the Malecón. Bronze statues of dolphins, throngs of travelers. We ate homemade gelato under palm trees whose trunks had been painted playfully with polka dots. The sun lowered and turned us ruddy. We stopped in at a store with a folding sign on the sidewalk that advertised boat tours and booked an Espiritu Santo sea lion trip for the next morning. We ate Chinese food, Kim's favorite, and she spoke Cantonese to the staff, and they gave us extra plates of vegetables. We slept. Free of wind and worry, with visions of eggs and bacon in our heads.

The Jeep picked us up outside the Los Arcos at seven-thirty. Drove out to the headland north of town. The cactus hills, Balandra. A protected cove on our left thick with mangroves and a beach at the head of it. Some of the last mangroves around La Paz, and a consortium of developers planned to yank out the mangroves and construct a resort. The city, the local people, the fishermen, were fed up, though. One after another they had watched their local beaches get overrun by fancy developments that cater to gringos and rich Mexicans. All the favorite spots for swimming and weekend family picnics had been placed out of reach. Tecolote and Pichilingue. They no longer felt welcome there. This was one of the last, a green paradise of littoral richness in the tawny desert, a breeding ground and hatchery for countless marine animals. The locals had drawn a line in the sand. Last night as we walked the streets, all over town, posted on doorways and in the grillwork of windows, were posters that read BALANDRA NUESTRA. Our Beach.

At Pichilingue Beach we climbed into a *panga*. It's the twenty-six-foot open boat used by Mexican fishermen everywhere. Classic paint scheme is white hull outside, Boston Whaler blue inside. This was no different. Faded lettering identified her as the *Tecolote*, or *The Owl*. Our captain was a young fisherman named Christian. On the tour today we would be joined by a cheerful gay couple from Montreal, a lone middle-aged traveler from Santa Barbara who never looked at us when he spoke, and a book salesman from Paris. A sufficient wedding party.

Christian may have sensed something was up. He ran the boat across the strait, a few miles out to Espiritu Santo Island. The straits are dangerous, cut with wicked currents that can get rubbed the wrong way by afternoon winds and raise hackles of helacious chop. But this morning the sea was dark glass. The wingtips of a vast ray sliced the surface like twin fins. A family of dolphins swam fast to the east, gleaming like polished metal. The long mountainous island of Cerralvo lay beyond them in haze. And ahead of us, the island of the Holy

Ghost rose steeply out of the sea, cut with cliffs on all sides, banded and striped with the colors of fire and coal. Christian ran us up along the sea cliffs. He did all the things a good ecotour guide should do.

"*Mira,* the cave," he said.

"What do they call it?"

He seemed uncomfortable. "They call that the La Vagina." We could see why, it was a geologic puss twenty feet high, perfectly rendered down to the color of the labia. He ran us through a tight rock arch, gunning the outboard in time with a sloshing surge of swell. We coasted the strips of sand, drifted into the coves, passed under steep slopes prickered with cardón and saltbush, craned our necks up at burned rock towers splashed with guano and crowned with the stick nests of osprey. We could see the fluffy heads of chicks and hear the sharp, single keen of their mother. The island herself was immune to our attentions. She had been conducting herself in the same manner for millions of years, presiding over an ancient argument between land and sea, bird and fish, wind and tide and stars, and the buzzing of our boat left her indifferent. I was not used to being a tourist. Sitting on my duff being shown the sights. It made me tired, like walking through an art museum. I wanted to jump out and swim into it, climb the hills, take Kim's hand.

I got really excited when we rounded the north end of the island and saw the black rock islets of Los Islotes and heard the sea lions barking. Kim got to snorkel close to giant bulls and jetting youngsters. Some lay sleeping on the surface, arched, their smooth, whiskered heads and rubbery black rear flippers sticking out of the water. Then we motored down the west side of the island and entered a big deep turquoise cove with a sand beach at its head. Ensenada Grande. We snorkeled along shallow coral banks while Christian cut mangoes for lunch. We followed a small octopus who flowed over the rocks and changed color until he squeezed his amorphous body into a crack the width of a Popsicle stick. Anemones bloomed and retracted. Needlefish, almost transparent, right at the surface, seemed a distillation of both water and air.

We waded out onto the warm sand and asked Christian, as captain of his boat, if he would marry us.

He put down the knife and blinked. He wiped his hands. Straightened up. "Of course," he said.

We made one of the gay guys the ring bearer and the other the photographer. The two older men were the wedding party. We all waded thigh-deep into the water. Kim and I stood in the sun facing each other, holding hands, and exchanged the vows that came to us. Mostly they were songs of appreciation. She began to cry as she talked. "I am so happy with you," she said. It shot into me like an arrow. Mostly I had made my girlfriends miserable. Nobody had ever said that to me after the first month.

"Me, too!" I answered. "You have soothed me. You are a light. I love being with you."

This couldn't hold a candle to the eloquent vows my friends had spoken to each other at big weddings, vows they'd written themselves and wrestled with for months and pronounced in front of scores of family and friends. But, hell, we were standing in the water. Tiny fish were nibbling at the hairs on my legs.

And then Christian did something very beautiful. He stepped between us and held each of our hands. He joined our hands together. He cupped his own and poured seawater over our clasped palms. He was a fisherman. The sea was his life, the arbiter of his own survival. That simple gesture. As the water poured from his hands and covered our fingers, our new rings, I felt the depth of what we were enacting. The sea had borne us all. She was as close to God as I would know in my own life. Christian reached up and poured water over each of our heads. I guess he thought we might as well get baptized while we were at it.

He stepped back. He looked at each of us. He looked at the ocean. He seemed overwhelmed. I wondered what he was going to say. He said, "By the lights of this island, Espiritu Santo, and by the power invested in me by these two people, and by their love, I pronounce you man and wife."

That simple. We kissed, the wedding party cheered, and then we ate ceviche and mangoes. For a wedding present Christian gave us the bottle of chili powder he'd sprinkled over the fruit. We went back into the water to snorkel and everywhere we looked it seemed as if the fish and anemones were congratulating us.

PROGRESS

It was time to surf again. Back to work. We loaded up the
dented Beast in front of the fancy Los Arcos. Put on our
shades and drove. Back across the bottom of the peninsula to
Todos Santos. A church on a hill overlooking the sea. Streets
crowded with art galleries, crafts. Gringos with the smug look
of Californians everywhere. We parked the Beast and went
into a surf shop. The kid had heavily moussed hair and dress
pants, didn't know anything about surfing. Handed us a surf
map. Here, just a few miles south of town, beside a hamlet
called Pescadero, was Cerritos. Okay, we'd heard of that, we'd
go. They taught lessons there, so it couldn't be too rough. Kim
needed a spot where she could surf. We headed back to the
Beast. About to climb in. Looked up at the sign over the gal-
lery-covered sidewalk.

HOTEL CALIFORNIA. Hmm. Walked into a lobby that felt
more like an art gallery. Each wall was a different bold color.

On them were paintings. A giant ceramic vase in the corner. Slow-turning, wood-bladed ceiling fans.

"Is this *the* Hotel California?" I asked the man at the front desk.

"*Original,*" said the man.

"The song? Pink champagne on ice?"

"*Claro.*"

"Can we check in *and* leave?"

"I'm sorry. *No entiendo.*"

I turn to Kim. "Is this our honeymoon? I mean, technically."

"Definitely."

Back to the man. "We'll take a room."

There were no mirrors on the ceiling, but the halls were cool and covered with paintings. Sculptures looked down on the courtyard from the surrounding rooftops. Huge vases bloomed with feathers and rushes. At night, standing candelabra lit the passages with scores of candles that melted with grotesque abandon and threw intricate patterns of grillwork on the ceilings. It was like sleeping inside an art collector's dream. The art collector, it turned out, was named John Stewart. His wife, Debbie, the hotel's proprietor, met us for a drink that evening. A brisk, slender Canadian, about fifty, with long uncompliant brown hair. She said people were fascinated with the place, came from around the world.

She said, "This was John's vision. He picked all the colors, the art, decorated every room. He was very bold, had a real sense." She took a deep breath. "When he passed, I just decided to carry on."

How long ago was that?

A year ago, last August.

Her lips pressed together. She had pronounced cheekbones, shadows under her eyes. She didn't look like she slept much. "Well. We're doing an overhaul now. The first rooms I'm decorating myself. I've picked all the material, the colors. It's rather exciting."

Her eyes were moist. She didn't look that excited. I got the sense of someone very frail. Every day she would have to summon her strength and run this place. It was prospering, she was doing it.

Kim and I had been married a day. I looked across the table at my bride and it struck me that we, the two of us and Debbie, were bookends. This was what it meant, this thing we had signed up for. Planning a life together. Most likely one of us would outlive the other and go through this same grief and the struggle to survive it.

Debbie motioned to the young waiter for another round, and I saw in the way he bowed his head with tenderness that her staff were devoted to her and protective.

We were excited to surf again. We drove away early, down the cactus highway to Pescadero. Only took twenty minutes. Asked someone where was Cerritos. Through the village, took the dirt road on the right. Down a two-mile sand road. A high rock point on the right, the north. Crawling with workers, trucks, heavy construction equipment. Hazy beach curving for miles to the south. A restaurant, umbrella tables on the sand. In front: surf. Peaky beach break and some sort of heaving at the point, but not clean. I was beside myself. Finally we were far enough south to ditch the short wetsuits. In a flurry I unsheathed the two 9–0 longboards from their bags, waxed them, changed into board shorts and rash guard. Rash guards are skin-tight nylon or lycra shirts that protect your chest from rubbing raw on the board.

"Sunscreen," Kim said.

Couldn't be bothered. She was braiding her hair slowly, taking her time.

"C'mon, c'mon. Don't you wanna get out there before anyone else?"

"Ting. I've gotta do my hair, lather up."

Heavy sigh. Impatience like a physical pressure. "Go!" she said. "I'll be out."

Dog off a leash, I grabbed my board. Relief. Over my shoulder, trotting onto the sand: "I waxed your board. Don't forget to lock up." I jogged past a picturesque little shack with a shaded veranda on the sand, a palm thatch roof called a *palapa*. A stack of patio tables and chairs.

One thing every surf teacher has ever told me is: watch.

Do not just run out at a new break. Look. Look for half an hour. Study the peaks, the rips, the wind, etc.

Are you kidding me? I am going to show up at a popular wave before every other surfer, with the day's virgins uncurling and stretching in front of me, and wait for the crowd to show up? Never happen.

I jumped on the board and paddled straight into the surf and was carried south by the current, hammered by every incoming wave, pushed back in a tide of froth, carried farther south, then I flailed, paddled, tumbled, bellied on again, sprinted, got buried, and got shoved down the beach as the sun rose over the dry Sierra. I paddled back into the surf, nearly crying with frustration, and the next set wave rose straight up in front of me. There was a crumbling shoulder on my left; maybe I could make it over in time before the whole thing collapsed. I angled, sprinted, and the thing fell. In the aerated foam, tumbling back all those yards I had just painfully gained, I yelled into the bubbles. I hadn't been out half an hour and I was already exhausted, whipped. Surfing could be like trench warfare. Gain a foot, lose three.

Finally raised the white flag. I turned my board around and bellied on the foam back to the shore. Crawled up onto the sand. Kim was just crossing the beach, board on head. I could always identify her from a mile off—the girl in the starch-white rash guard who carried the longboard on her head.

"Hi, Ting," she said brightly. "How are the waves?"

"Grrmps hurf in frmp," I mumbled.

"What?"

"I don't know."

By now a handful of surfers had shown up and we watched them walk straight to the northern corner of the beach, right where the rock point met the sand. They launched and a riptide right along the rocks took them out with zero effort like a moving sidewalk.

"I guess that's where we go out," Kim said cheerfully. "Look, Ting, they're not even paddling! How cool."

"Fringshpumf."

She caught a wave right away, rode it right, down the line, all the way to the beach. Another girl was out there, a short-boarder from Canada, and they sat together and talked. *Okay*, I thought, *we'll stay here for a while*. One thing I was discovering about surfing, my surfing, was that at this stage I could expect one good ride all morning. And to be honest, I should be grateful for that one. So much has to go right that even this ride is a great boon.

A flock of royal terns wheeled just past the point, feeding on a bait ball. The sun was up, whitened, warming the morning and spangling the crests. Squads of pelicans flew in single-file, wingtips just off the swell. I sat on my board and wondered: *So is surfing a giddy escape, skipping over the surface*

*of a great suffering, or is it a triumph of courage? To find joy in
an always-painful world?* I wanted to say: *The wave howls. It
is cathartic release. When I surf I accept the full brunt, the chaos,
the devastation and death and transform it into a kind of flight.*

Was that our job here? To take flight? To create joy? In
ourselves and others? To love?

Hell if I knew. A set wave unreeled off the point and I
turned and caught it left toward the rocks.

As we were loading up in the sandlot beside the restaurant, a
Jeep pulled in full of surfboards and kids, gringos and Mexicans. One, a curly-headed white boy, about twenty, said, "Hey,
you guys got any wax I can use?"

I tossed him half a brick. "Keep it."

"Hey, *thanks.*" He walked toward the Jeep, then turned
back. "Where are you from?"

"Colorado."

He grinned. "Not too much surf there, huh?"

"Not much."

We chatted for a minute. I told him what we were up to.
Kook to big and hollow. He thought it was cool. He said, "You
ought to run up and see my dad. Just a mile up the road. He
runs the Pescadero Surf Camp. I'm sure he'd put you up. Ask
for Jaime." He said *Hymay,* the Spanish pronunciation.

"Hey," I said. "What's going on up there?" I pointed to all
the construction up on the rock point.

"It's part of all this," he said. "A rich guy from Mexico City.
He's building like a twenty-thousand-square-foot mansion
up there. This restaurant. Gonna be a resort. Maybe a marina.
Cerritos." He looked around. "Everything changing."

"What's that?" I pointed to the *palapa* shack on the sand.

"That's Rosa's. She makes great tacos and stuff. Been there for years."

I nodded, waved.

The Pescadero Surf Camp was just up the hill from the beach, on the way into the village. It's an elegant little compound with a limpid swimming pool surrounded by small tables, a *palapa* bar at one end, an open-air common kitchen area, and a bunch of sweet thatch huts nicely appointed with queen beds, fans, sinks. A larger one for tents. A few common hot showers. The place was designed for the dedicated surfer. He could roll out of bed, make coffee, drive five minutes to the wave—or ten minutes to another, faster wave just north—surf all morning, and come back to a comfortable scene somewhere between camping and the Ritz. But the best feature of all was its proprietor. Jaime unfolded himself from a chair in the little store at the front of the camp. He stood up and just kept going, higher, like a wave jacking on a reef. Must have been six-foot-five. He wore a goofy white golf visor that seems to be the stylistic signature of all guys from San Diego. Plaid shorts. Swaybacked with a bit of a belly, but the strong, set-back shoulders of a lifelong surfer.

"Nice to meet you," he said, holding out a hand. "Take the *palapa* over there. Nice van. Colorado, huh? Did you get blown off course?" His bluish eyes were full of mischief. A little sausage of a dachshund wagged his curly rat tail and bumped in and out of our legs.

"That's security," Jaime said. "Cholo."

I shook his hand. The man's, not the dog's. It was the beginning of a strange and beautiful friendship.

Our second morning at Cerritos, the swell formed a breaking wave more from impacting the shallower water of the beach than from meeting the rocks of the point. So I got in position fifty yards from the point and the takeoff surprised me with its speed, and the ride was bumpy and fast, and I took it left into the white froth at the bottom of the escalator. Just fell into the water at the end, climbed back on the board, and was tugged out again on the rip. Dang. There is this great internal grin when you catch a good wave. This Old Faithful of glee that for me gushes forth with a rebel yell. I have been told that this is the ultimate badge of kookdom. This morning it was compounded by being carried back outside on a riptide like a ski lift. How much better can it get?

Jaime came out, as he did every morning, and coached me, which I appreciated. He told me to place my palms on the nose and straighten out my arms and shove the front of the board down just before the pop-up, and explained that the extra slug of weight up front would help accelerate the board to make the drop over onto the face of the wave. Like most beginners I was having the hardest time just catching the wave. Time after time I'd paddle like a maniac, think I had it, and then the hump of the peak would roll under me and on into shore. Jaime's tip seemed to work. Kim caught a couple of waves and after surfing we had coffee with Jaime back at the surf camp and then he drove us around town in his pickup, showing us the big skateboard park he helped build for the local kids, and the fields of organic vegetables, and the site of the new "tequila ranch," a fancy resort where they would grow their own agave and distill their own tequila. Jaime explained that progress was coming to Pescadero in an inexorable wave. It was one of only a handful of natural oases in all of Baja— thus the groves of palms down by the water—and the organic farming center of the peninsula. And several world-class surf breaks (too fast for us) were within minutes. Americans were discovering it and beginning to buy lots and build houses all over the hills that rose just back of the beaches. Jaime got excited talking about it. He said the local people were trying to adapt. If he had his way, he would help them: though not native-born, he would one day like to be elected as mayor of Pescadero. He seemed to be halfway there. As we jounced up and down the dirt roads of the town, he yelled greetings and encouragement out his window and everybody waved. His enthusiasm was infectious. Kim and I loved this guy.

On our fifth morning we were putting on sunscreen, waxing boards in the sandlot below the high point. Still early, before eight, but power marimba was pounding out of the restaurant and the chuffs of diesel machinery and screeching of steel-tracked dozers was coming down from the top of the bluff. Overnight they had planted a row of full-grown palms up there. Workers with bandanna masks were crawling over a high rock-faced stem wall they were building along the cliff edge. Fancy arched doorways and stone steps. Down here, the waiters already seemed hepped up on something, moving a little too fast in and out of the tables, giving each other props, banging fists, gold earrings twinkling. There was juice here, the juice of progress.

Not at Rosa's taco stand. The shack looked like Cannery Row. On the sand, under the deep shade of the thatch, four local men took their ease and shared a bottle next to the stacked patio tables. They might have slept there.

A breeze, still cool, stirred the frayed ends of the palm roof and the waves crashed and thumped with a reassuring rhythm. A bulldozer coughed to life in the parking lot. As we watched, a beefy gringo in a Ralph Lauren powder-blue polo shirt and safari hat walked toward us. He wore a gold watch. He half nodded, flaring his sunburned nostrils as if we were tolerable riffraff, then turned and waved the driver to the beach. I think the white guy was the architect and project manager for the rich Mexican. I'd heard him bragging at the bar about some fish he'd caught and he had an Australian accent. Maybe South African, I don't know. He walked ahead of the dozer onto the sand. Then he spoke to the driver, pointed to the taco shack. We watched with horrified fascination. He wasn't. Unh-unh. No way.

Two of the loungers seemed to be asleep. The dozer driver chunked the machine into low gear, lowered his blade, and came at the shack. The two others, the ones still drinking, startled themselves to standing and backed out into the sunlight blinking, not even a peep of protest. The blade hit a corner post of the *palapa* awning and it creaked and collapsed. The driver lowered the blade and slowly shoved the roof in on itself. A few seconds later the sleepers flushed like two quail. Unfriggingbelievable.

Kim's mouth hung open. They could have really hurt those guys. This was like the South African townships, apartheid era. Maybe that's where the architect learned it from. It was like Israelis vs. Palestinians. Except this was just a taco shack that had been there for years. A local lady from Pescadero.

I trotted over to the architect. "You could have killed those guys! What the hell?"

He looked at me like I was a bug. "They had time. I've told them for days. No more squatting. That roof is just palm thatch."

"Jesus."

I asked Jaime about it later and he pushed his visor back and said, "It's sad, Peter. Rosa has been there forever. Has all her permits. It's progress." I couldn't tell if that was an endorsement, an objection, or just acceptance. Some local surfers, kids from Pescadero and Todos, told me out on the waves that they hated this guy and his resort. They said locals from the area used to love to come to Cerritos and picnic with their large extended families. Rosa sold her food. Now, though the beach is still technically public, the locals don't feel welcome. I could see why. In fact, all the Mexican coastline is public up to twenty meters past the mean high tide line, open by law to all citizens, but of course it doesn't work out that way. Private owners and resorts are very good at blocking access and running people off. As witnessed.

Later I was sitting in the lineup, looking for another fast left, and a local kid named Rolo, an engineering student wearing a thin gold chain, about twenty-three, told me that the local surfers don't feel welcome here anymore, either. The break is usually crowded with gringos. He said the gringo surfers from California were not respectful. Damn. While we were sitting there, we saw a new four-door blue pickup charge up and down the beach.

"You see that?" he said. "That's El Jefe's boys. They are not supposed to drive on the beach. They crush the turtle eggs. They don't care."

Kim got a couple of good rides, which made both of us happy. The swell was pretty mellow, the waves about shoulder-high, and she loved the escalator ride back out. If she turned straight and rode the whitewater all the way to the beach, which she loved to do, she just got out, put the board on her head, and walked back up to the corner of the point and took the riptide express.

So in the bright sun blare of midmorning it was with a happy body fatigue and mixed emotions that I zipped our boards into their bags and shoved them into the van and we drove back up the sand road. Cerritos was leaving a bad taste in my mouth. The surf was fun, the "progress" pretty rough. The same drama was happening all along the coasts of Mexico, had been happening for decades. Had been happening, for that matter, on coasts all around the world for the last fifty years. Mangroves yanked out, marinas trenched, wetlands drained and filled, resorts built, local people displaced. It's exactly what was happening back in La Paz, where the people who lived there had finally put their collective foot down.

We had stayed with Jaime for ten days. We could hardly bring ourselves to leave. In the morning, early, I made us instant coffee at the outdoor stove and watched a faint blue radiance wash over the stars the way a tide covers rocks. We had cereal with powdered milk. We rolled five minutes down to Cerritos and nosed up to the sand. Surfed for a few hours. Drove back to Jaime's, jumped in the pool, took a hot shower. The little dachshund greeted us like royalty, licking our shins.

"Security!" we called him. His best buddies were two pit bulls from the hood. All three of them showed up like a gang in the gateway. Jaime yelled, "You two get out of here! Cholo! Sic 'em!" Security wagged his little tail, then wheeled like a dervish kielbasa and yapped at his bros, who shrugged and loped off. Kim and I clapped. Jamie drove us around on errands, told us again that one day he'd like to be mayor of Pescadero.

For our big, second breakfast we drove a mile into town and had plates of *machaca,* salted shredded beef, all mixed up with scrambled eggs. Hand-patted tortillas that tasted almost like crepes, and big mugs of *café con leche.* And that was our day. That was all we really had to do. The rest was elective. We read, went for walks, got Jaime to show us more beaches. We were in some kind of Baja trance. I never wanted anything to change, except to get better at surfing. And then the south swell thundered in like a herd of buffalo.

THE SCORPION'S TAIL

O n our eighth morning at Cerritos—which we were loving, except for the music and attitude emanating like a
toxic smoke from the restaurant—we drove up to the new tall
chain-link fence that had been erected across the road with
a sign that said PUBLIC WELCOME. The gate was open, but its
very existence implied that it could be shut. Since when do
you have to tell the public they are welcome on their own
public beach?

We trotted down to the water and gazed out at a different Cerritos than the one we knew. It was marine mayhem.
There were no surfers on the water. Was it because it was so
early? No. It *was* early, but the waves were breaking out past
the point. They were making sounds we'd never heard, angry
sounds, sounds like gods at war, and they were whiter than
we'd ever seen before—and the whole inner bite, where the
escalator had been along the shore, was one churning wash-

ing machine of confused foam. Did I mention that the waves were big? Really, really big.

This was our conversation:

Kim: There's nobody out there, Ting.
Me: That's because it's early yet.
Kim: I dunno, Ting. Those waves look big. It looks really rough.

We both fell silent to watch a wave like a floundering freighter tear itself open on the point and dump its cargo of foaming snow. It sounded like muffled artillery. Like charging elephants, if the elephants were albino and exploded just before they crushed you.

Me: Am I tough enough?
Kim: I'm serious. I'm not going out there. No way.
Me (pulling out my shortboard): I'm going. Just to check it out. Look at that one. There was a shoulder. There! You could ride that . . . sort of.

Just then, Jaime's pickup pulled in, throwing dust. His longboard stuck out the back, but he never touched it. He looked at the water for three seconds from his front seat, shoved the stick on the wheel up to park, cut the engine. He got out, swaybacked, adjusting his visor, smiling to himself and waving to us.

"What are you doing with that board, Peter? Giving it a tan?"

"Uh, well, I was just gonna check out, you know, the swell."

Jaime shook his head. "Nobody can say you don't have rocks for brains. That right there is worse than a waste of time. Did you notice there was nobody surfing, Peter? No locals?"

"Well, I—"

"Yeah, Ting. You never listen to me."

"You should definitely listen to her."

"You should listen to Jaime. *And* me."

I was putting the board back.

Jaime said, "I have an idea for you guys. You guys should drive up to Scorpion Bay. This swell is perfect for the Scorp."

"It's like seven hours, isn't it?"

"About five—" He looked at the Beast. "Yeah, seven. Or eight. What do you care, you've got, what, another month down here? What's seven hours? You can take the boards you want and leave the rest in my shop, and whatever else you don't want to carry. I'm telling you, it's a great wave. Kim will love it. C'mon, Peter, listen to your elders for once."

I looked at them, back and forth. Kim had her hands on her hips.

"Great. Great idea!" I said.

"Follow me back to the camp, I'll help you guys move your boards."

Why was he being so sweet to us? We weren't even citizens of Pescadero; we couldn't vote. He was walking back to his truck. I said, "Jaime?"

"Yes, Peter?"

"Even if you don't become mayor for a while, to me you are mayor."

"Thanks, Peter. That means a lot to me."

Scorpion Bay is maybe the most famous surf spot in Baja. The name lifts heads, invites comments. The place lives in most surfers' minds as a legend, as a perfect wave. A ten. Most surfers have never been there for the same reason Kim and I passed it up on our way south: the hooked bay is thirty miles down a rough dirt road that fords two rivers. And when you get there, there has to be a decent swell to excite it, and the swell has to be just right—surging in like a gift from the south-southwest, muscling out of a narrow arc of 180 to 215 degrees on the compass rose. With a good forecast on Wetsand.com, with a powerful stoke to surf a perfect wave, and a good strong vehicle with big tires and some lame excuse to your boss, you might load up in San Diego and drive sixteen hours south and however many hours it takes to negotiate the dirt road, and then you get there and the swell has shifted a bit, or dropped off, and you are surfing a knee-high bump. You coulda had a V8. You could have gone to Disney World, ridden the log flume.

But if the stars are lined up and everything is right, there's no rush quite like the Scorp.

We drove back up the main Baja highway, and then thirty miles through the most jarring washboard dirt I had ever experienced. There was no speed or part of the road where I could find relief. The boards, the windows, our teeth rattled painfully. I had pulled over and let fifteen pounds of air out of the tires. It helped, but not enough. After two hours, I thought all of us—Kim, me, the Beast—would vibrate apart at the seams.

It was evening when we hit smooth blacktop. The sudden silence, the tarmac hum, was almost a shock to the system. Bones, teeth settled back into their sockets. The Beast pulled herself back together with audible creaks—springs, bearings, joints. Smell of tar still hot from a sun now setting. We could see the ocean down a cactus draw, stone-blue and still. I could see the moon, soft, rising. That was strange, too. It was *rising* over the Pacific.

"Kim."

"Huh?" She was half conscious. Either she had fallen asleep or she had washboard PTSD.

"Kim."

"Huh?" She pushed the towel back off her head.

"Where is the sun setting?"

"That's silly, where it always sets, over the w—" She craned her neck out the window. "Behind us. Weird. It's setting over the land."

"Look at the moon. Rising over the Pacific."

Disorienting. Of course, it was because the coast made a big hook here, like a scorpion's tail.

We followed the road into a small town called San Juanico with one dirt main street. We asked some kids where to go, and they pointed us out of town through the other side. *"El faro,"* they shouted after us. The lighthouse. We wound past a hill of what must have been gringo houses, fancy bungalows with *palapa*-thatched palm roofs. We snaked in and out of a draw, following the sand road through the brush. The sun was low, burnishing the road, the cacti, the bark of the small scraggly trees, with a ruddy warmth. We broke out of the mesquite and Mormon tea and then we saw it: the bay. It was enormous, hooking around to our left and running out along a coast that marched into a shadowy distance of headlands and ridges.

We followed the road out along the edge of a bluff, the sea on our left, the cliffs getting higher as we climbed toward the lighthouse point. On our right, a thatch-roofed restaurant, a few cabins. Campers scattered in their rigs all up the bluff. We pulled into a gap in the mesquite between a travel trailer with Christmas lights strung around the awning and a Volvo wagon presiding over two dome tents. A bald guy stirred a pot on a folding table next to the car. He lifted his spoon and waved. Beyond the Volvo was a fancy pickup with a cab-over camper and a custom surfboard rack at the back. A tall, dark, handsome man and a petite, blond, pretty woman sat in lawn chairs beside the pickup drinking cocktails in plastic tumblers and watching the moon over the water, looking just like a Cialis commercial. The man sported a white tennis visor, so I figured they were from San Diego.

We climbed out and stretched. The air was soft and warm like brushed flannel. It smelled like creosote and flowers and the tang of some sagey herb, and there was a damp scent of recent rain. The ground was fine dust and dry, but in this desert the ground can be dry minutes after a shower. We walked to the edge of the cliff and peered over; we were high enough up that a tumble over the edge would mean certain death. There was the sea, oddly unfamiliar. She felt at the moment like a girl you have known for a while but see in makeup for the first time. I don't know why. And right below us was the wave. One of the waves. We had heard there were several. On our right, the cliff jutted out to a shallow point. Dark rocks tumbled out into the water, forming a reef. That's where it started breaking. As it pushed in, it shaped itself into a wall. A perfect slate-blue wall. Straight as a chalk line. And long. Mother of God, how long it was. The break ripped white along the face of it as evenly as the tear tab on a FedEx pack.

I grabbed Kim's hand, the way people do in the movies when they're struck by the beam of the alien spaceship.

"That's a ten. That's like a perfect wave. That's, that's un-friggingbelievable."

There was the moon rising over it, shinier now, like a peso.

Behind us, the sun blazed, firing the clouds over the sea, streaming colors, unrepentant. That's what it was: the sun and moon were reversed, they each occupied the other's gate, and the sea, everything really, seemed somehow off, touched with strangeness. I felt the soft wind at the back of my neck, the breeze that always stirs just as the sun hits the horizon, and realized that it, too, had flipped. The evening wind flowed off the desert instead of the other way. It shouldered up against the wall of the wave, standing her up nicely, brushing her hair back. I'll be damned.

"We need to look at a map." I felt as if we had gone to heaven, one of those heavens that imitates life, but doesn't get it exactly right.

Kim swatted her leg. "Damn! I thought there might be just one beach, just one."

"Look." I pointed below us. A large pale bird flapped slowly, coming in off the water. Rose on a vestigial thermal. Lifted up over the cliff edge, right over our heads. Snowy breast caught the blood light. Carrying a fish in talons. An osprey, winging home to a stick nest somewhere. She carried the fish headfirst like a missile. The tail moved. The fish was alive. I wondered if it could see. What a strange last sight for a tuna.

The Cialis couple, it turned out, *was* from San Diego. I walked over while Kim armored herself in her bug shirt, bug pants, and big stylish hat.

"Hi."

"Hi." They smiled and lifted their tumblers. When they smiled they showed their teeth.

"Nice camper." I nodded to the cab-over pop-top in the back of their white Toyota Tundra.

"We were just going to say the same thing about yours," he said. "We had one just like it. 'Eighty-six?"

"'Eighty-five."

"Sweet!"

I noticed that they had stowed their boards under a drum-skin green tarp extended off the side, to keep the harsh sun from breaking down the fiberglass. My tarp shed off the Beast always flapped and luffed and I held it out with rocks, but theirs was staked out with little stakes. From a corner of their camper a clothesline stretched to a pole, guyed out and staked as well. Hanging on it were her green bikini, his black board shorts. Her pink rash guard. Was it envy I felt? I usually threw my wet shorts over the driver's-side mirror. They seemed to dry just fine.

Dave was a sport-fishing captain and Leesa was a Realtor and interior designer. They looked to be in their forties, and had been surfing since grade school. They came down here to the bay as often as there was a swell and they could get away.

"Pretty good front porch," I said, gesturing at the burning pink layered over a fading blue. "What a color."

"That's Pittsburgh 2247," Leesa said.

"Huh?"

"Pittsburgh Paints. That's the number of the paint chip. Perfect match." She said it without a trace of irony. The colors over the ocean had now deepened. They were spectacular.

I stared at her. She was smiling like a winning contestant. "Wow."

She closed both her eyes in a double wink. "I've been doing interiors for a long time."

I felt like I had just levered myself over a mountain ledge and discovered a guru in a loincloth. These two had something I would never, ever have.

Standing there on the soft dust, between Dave and Leesa and a whole sky full of 2247, probably muted now to something like 2234, I thought, *Damn, Self. What has all your fancy education got you? That finely honed critical sense, that overdeveloped sense of irony? Huh? You will never have what these two have: the ability to take things literally, at face value. The sunset, the wave, the gin and tonic. The tight tarp. The simple limpid contentment that clearly brings.*

I thought, *You don't tighten your tarp to the tautness of a drum, because you are telling yourself,* What does it matter in the end, existentially? *Well, maybe it does matter.*

Kim had it. Every day she carefully put on sunscreen. She took doctors' orders literally. Every day after surfing she lathered herself with moisturizing cream. She stopped at all stop signs. She was not worried about anything. Once, on your first camping date, you took her fishing up a mountain creek during the height of fall colors in western Colorado. You took a couple of bikes, and on the second day you biked up a winding dirt road to the top of a pass, and there were ridge after ridge of rocky peaks skirted with blazing yellow aspen forests. The sky arched over it like blue enamel. Kim's breath made a sound, an involuntary bleat. She said, "Oh. That's pretty as a postcard."

And you, you big idiot, looked at her sideways with the harshest judgment, and considered right there, as you were swamped with beauty, both hers and nature's, whether you should be seeing a woman who said something so unsophisticated.

Well, it was exactly like a postcard. You didn't consider that she grew up in a family that did not speak at meals, that had no real conversation. That as a toddler she learned her English from television because her parents couldn't speak it. She did not have the verbal arsenal you have, buddy. She never learned the rhetorical hijinx of sarcasm, irony.

And Dave and Leesa were *nice*. They listened when I told them the sum total of our surfing experience and they said that if we came out early in the morning, they would line us out on the wave. They said that this, in front, was Third Point, and that Kim might enjoy Second Point more—still a very long wave, but smaller, gentler.

I thanked them. I was all shook up. I passed the balding guy at the Volvo. He held up his spoon again. He, too, smiled, but with closed lips, with something held back, maybe a hint of self-mockery, for his own protection. I recognized one of my own. I veered in like it was a pit stop.

"Hey."

"Hey." He put down the spoon. "You from Colorado?"

"Yeah. We spent a few weeks in Huntington. We're just learning, making our way south, hitting the best spots."

"Cool. Want a beer?"

"Don't do it."

"You a friend of Bill W.?" That's code. It's the Alcoholics Anonymous secret handshake.

"Yeah. You?"

"Nah, but my last girlfriend was. Here." He reached into a cooler, tossed me a Sprite. I liked this guy right away. "Pull up a chair." He pushed an aluminum-framed folding chair with his foot.

"Okay, for a second."

He covered the pot and turned off the burner, came around with another chair, and set it beside me. "Fuckin' L," he said, lifting his can of Dos Equis to the sky.

"Fuckin' L."

I sipped my Sprite and I felt happy. This guy was my instant friend. This was one of the most beautiful damned places I had ever been. Not just the view, the cliffs, the bay, the desert behind, the coast across the water marching away into territories of the lifting moon, but also the gentle air, the fragrance, a lucid quality to the light. And I felt an immediate kinship with this guy, Jay, though we had traded only a dozen words.

Kim walked over in her long sleeves and loose pants and Jay got her another chair and a pop. We sat in a line as before a film. It was dusk. Sharp-winged birds flitted and veered in the half-light, peeping softly. Nighthawks. Their white wing bars blinked. Vespertine. We heard the waves breaking along· the cliff. It rose in a long ever-renewing hush. Without saying a word, we were reduced to silence, the way a certain church will command it. The colors faded and darkness rose around the swollen barge of the moon like a swift tide and floated her higher.

"Where are your buddies?" I said finally.

"Still surfing at Second Point. They are beginners and they've caught the fever. With this moon, no telling how long they'll be down there."

Dawn. I stood on the top of the cliff with my instant coffee in the half-light and I believed. In the perfect wave. Dave and Leesa were already out, the only ones. The waves arrived in that flawless long rip. I watched Dave's shadow rock back on his funboard, spin, nose in the grainy air, lunge forward, and hook onto a wall of water that stretched across the cove and looked like it was smoothed with a mason's trowel. A bat flitted over me. His leathery wings made the softest flutter on the sharpest cutbacks. He was surfing, too. Then Leesa took off. I timed her. For half a minute husband and wife, shadows only, sledded in tandem down the two waves. Sliding across to my left, about thirty yards apart. She made graceful swooping arcs to the lip and back down to the bottom. Ahead of her, he made sharper, almost slashing cutbacks. Like the bat. They moved, one behind the other, like the elaborations of a single thought. Maybe that's how they knew what the other was about to say about my camper. Forty seconds. That's how long her ride was. *Forty seconds.* Count it, with the full Mississippis between, it's a hellacious long time to be at peak ecstasy. My longest ride so far had probably been about ten.

At the end, way down to my left, almost to the beach, the wave subsided until it was swishing against her knees. In the wrung-out shoulder wash, she just sat down on her board. Like stepping off a magic carpet. Meanwhile, the ocean was in a quiet labor. Her voice was in the gulls who whimpered and cried. The bloody sun crowded and breached the surface of the sea like a birth. Hit me full in the face with a wail of light.

Time, time to go. Before the crowd. Three more surfers were already paddling out.

This is where Kim drives me crazy. If I was going to have a religious experience today I had to beat all the others to it.

I trotted across the packed dust to the van. Her bare feet hung down from the top, rubbed against each other. I could tell by the rhythm she was putting in her contacts. She was humming. She still had to braid her hair. Cover every inch of exposed skin with sunscreen. Stretch on her rash guard. Meanwhile, every minute she dallied, another surfer launched from the beach. I could feel them behind me. A steady trickle of barefoot surfers walking up the bluff, boards in hand, hopping over the edge onto the slippery-smooth ladder of broken rock. I could feel the knot of surfers at the takeoff zone growing into a flock, then a crowd.

"Ting."

Break in hum. "Hi, Ting!"

"Ting, we gotta get moving. It's already getting crowded. The wave—the wave is like incredible."

Taut silence. No hum, no foot movement, not even a twitching toe. The sense that my very survival was at stake. I mean that if I didn't get down that cliff and out into the water right now I may miss my salvation. It was that critical.

Finally, a world-weary sigh floated down. A rare sound from my new wife. Low-register, kinda scary: "Go. Just go. I still have to eat something. Lather up."

"But . . . but . . . I need to help you down the cliff. It's pretty steep."

"Go! Come back in forty-five minutes and help me. Okay?"

"You sure?"

"Go! I'll wave from the cliff. Scram."

"Okay, okay. I love you so much!"

"Whatever. Jeez."

I could tell by the tone of that last exclamation that she had forgiven me whatever it was that I needed forgiving—maybe just being self-centered and compulsive—and I was suddenly gleeful again. I shucked the two 9–0 longboards from their bags, waxed them fast, leaned Kim's against the wheels, waxed side away from the new sun, grabbed my rash guard from the backseat, and ran to the edge of the cliff trail where I joined three others—and over we went like lemmings.

BIG BILL

It was the first time I'd ever seen a surfer hit another. They were yelling. Top of the cliff. Both holding their boards in their right arms. The afternoon wind carried their words out to sea. Bill was a mountain. He lowered his big shaggy head and struck the guy in the chest, left-handed. This guy dropped his board to the dirt, then joined it. Like he'd been shot. Bill just stood there, growling and blinking. The man sat up, shaking his head, wondering how his universe had altered. Bill turned, walked to the notch in the cliff, went over the edge.

I was just coming in from an afternoon session. Kim was down at Second Point, where she had discovered there were a few other beginners and the waves were easy. Yesterday afternoon, an older, bald man had seen her struggling and paddled over. "Follow me," he said. "We'll ride one together." He pulled her away from the crowd, out onto the shoulder a bit. "Right here, just wait. Okay, here comes our wave, nobody's taking it, let's go. Follow me, aim your board a little to the right." They both paddled, both took off. The wave was just over waist-high. It caught Kim with a gentle but firm push, and before she knew it her board was sledding in a shallow free fall to the right. She just hopped up. The man was just ahead of her, looking back. "Yeah!" he cried. I watched the sweet wave lap at her legs. Out ahead of her was a paradise of smooth green wall. Her board, somehow, stuck to it. She got ahead of the white break and simply glided, hands up and spread wide as if she were embracing the sky. She rode it behind the bald man all the way across the bay, forever, a lifetime. Probably a third of a mile.

At the end he smiled broadly at her. Because he knew what she was feeling. "That's it," he said. "You're a surfer now."

So last night, at dusk, the nighthawk time, I invited our neighbor with the Sprites over for a quesadilla to celebrate and we sat again on the three lawn chairs in a row, watching the unnumbered colors streak the west. Jay told us he was a librarian from San Francisco who quit surfing for ten years because he didn't like all the aggression in the lineup. Not so much how others treated him, but what he himself turned into in order to catch a lot of waves.

"It was changing me."

"Yeah, I understand totally."

"But I loved it too much. I missed it. I found a way to be out there and be kind. I learned to sit just inside and pick up the leftovers." He smiled. "I actually catch more waves." I turned and looked at him. Unbelievable aspiration for a surfer: *To be out on the waves and still be kind.*

During the day, the fifty-odd surfers at Scorpion split up between Second and Third Point, roughly 30/20. The beginners went to Second because it was much easier to catch, tended to be smaller, and when you were done with your long ride you could pick up your board and walk around the beach back to the point. The bottom was soft sand and shallow, so mild that you could almost wade out to the takeoff point. It was almost as safe and easy as surfing at a wave pool.

Better surfers liked to come down here, too, because of the sheer fun. Relaxing. The ride went on forever.

One morning I walked down to Second Point with Kim and we surfed together. We were sitting down from the crowd, waiting for a wave that no one wanted. Often, these were as good as the best, they just developed later, and were a bit smaller. An old pickup drove down the sandy ramp onto the flat beach. A big Mexican man got out. Big, like hefty, generous-bellied, thick across chest and shoulders. And the color of a walnut. Shaped like a walnut, if a walnut weighed 230 pounds and had short legs like tree trunks. The man stood in the sun blinking for a moment, watching the wave. Then he slid his long longboard over the tailgate and walked into the water. No leash. He paddled right through the knots of the crowd, his board surging as if motorized. His arms were almost as stout as his legs; they moved powerfully in a two-cycle rhythm, independently from the rest of him, which was very relaxed. He smiled broadly at everyone he passed, his teeth blaze-white, his black hair gleaming. He went right to the point, right out past the farthest surfer in first position, far enough past him not to raise any hackles. Who, after all, could catch a wave way out there? It was way past the break, in smooth water. Might as well sit on a lake. The bigger the wave, the farther out it breaks, and no set waves today had been nearly that big.

He galumphed into sitting position on his board, making

his own waves. He seemed very unconcerned, three notches past nonchalant. His round head turned side to side as he took in the cliff, the bay. Without haste he turned his board, took four Herculean strokes, and just like that he was standing. He seemed to conjure the wave beneath him. There it was. Nicest set wave all morning. The crowd stared. Here he came, set like a rock, like an Easter Island statue, flying toward the masses. And then he lifted his back foot. The tree trunk of a man lifted it delicately behind him and spread his arms. He did the swan. It was one of the most extraordinary things I'd ever seen. He was sailing down the wave, through the awestruck onlookers, arched back on one foot like a diva.

He smiled at everyone. Then he dropped his foot, turned backward, and rode like that for a while. Beaming as he passed, hands to his chest in prayer. He was some kind of aquatic monk, something spiritually ascendant, rotund with grace. He crouched and effortlessly stood on his head. His board sliced down the everlasting wave as if it had a mind of its own. He rode on his head looking forward and backward. At the end, with a nimbleness shocking in a man of his specific gravity, he replaced his hands with his feet and stood up. Ta-da. Rode the perfect wave to the beach. Stepped off, picked up the board, walked to the truck chatting to little Mexican kids as he passed them, and drove back up the ramp to the road.

We laughed. I felt a warm smile roll all through me. The surfer had transformed the morning. Some teenager yelled at Kim, "It's yours!" and she caught his wave. I went back up to the point below the lighthouse and caught the wave of my life.

I was floating next to Jay the Librarian, thirty yards down from the big group of surfers at the point, and here came a firm, steep, muscular, rising dark berm of ocean. Someone outside had tried for it and messed up. I saw him wipe out, and then I saw the wave coming at the two of us, clean and huge and empty. I stared.

"You, Pedro," Jay said.

"You mean that?"

"You better hurry up."

I spun and dug into the water as hard as I could, thinking, *Angle right, angle right, if you're gonna catch this, angle right. Lift your chest, lift, lift, dig! Harder! Now drop! Drop head to the board.*

My chin hit the board so hard I got a bruise. The board dove like a bird. Falling. Away to the right. *NOW!* I popped up possessed. Fastest I'm sure I'd ever made. And I was standing. Oh, man. Out ahead, to the right, was this steep dark wall. It looked too steep. It was going to collapse any second. I could see the lip quivering, unable to sustain itself. When it fell I would be swallowed in white and that would be it. Without knowing where the impulse came from, I weighted heels, released the pressure of the right edge against the wave, and turned down. I sped straight down the face of the wave. The rush was spectacular. At the same time, the wave was breaking, falling white, crashing above, about to bury me. I crouched—someone had told me that made you faster somehow—and rocketed beneath the tumbling whitewater, racing it to the right. I had the speed. I aimed for the lip again without thought and shot upward, arcing like a bird peeling out. I felt like a swallow. That's how swift and free. I'd made it! The break was thundering behind me. Let's do it again. Release, free fall, skate the bottom out ahead of the break, turn up, hit the lip. This time I experimented with a more radical turn off the top, kind of letting my body lead the board, rotating torso left and letting it fall, and incredibly the board followed. It was my first real surfing turn. This is where one transforms into another animal. Like swimming with the sea lion.

Finally I slowed—time ebbing back, the cliffs, the brightness returning, the bowl of sky, sphere of the world. The wave was dying out, breathing her last, a low crumbling, a release. I lifted my arms and fell backward into the shallow water. Hoisting the board, which now felt to me less like a Bruno 9–0 than a set of wings, I walked over the sharp lava rocks in the shallows to the beach. Climbing the slippery smooth blocks of stone, I came up over the edge of the cliff, where Leesa and David grinned at me from their lawn chairs. I knew how long my ride had been because I had timed hers the other day: about forty seconds. Really long.

"Nice ride!" they said in synchrony.

I smiled at them. Without irony. Without anything. Kinship and glee.

A shout came from behind me. Like a bark. That's when we all turned and Big Bill swung and the smaller man sprawled on the dirt beside his own board. Another barked invective and then Bill walked away, disappeared through the break in the bluff.

That night I saw him in the bar, drinking at a table alone. One beer after another. Didn't look perturbed, just massive, implacable, ringing with a self-imposed isolation.

The restaurant was crowded. Most of the surfers congregated there in the evenings to drink Coronas and eat overstuffed burritos. And check e-mails; the house had two laptops they kept on the bar and rented out, two bucks for fifteen minutes of wireless time. Tonight, a group crowded around a tall dark girl who expertly worked the keyboard and brought up screen after screen of satellite images. She sat on the stool in a bikini with an Indian sari wrapped diagonally across her torso. She wore black rectangular glasses. She sat very tall, not pretty in the sum of her parts, but she gave off an air of insupportable languor, in the way of very successful models. She traced her finger on the map. Kim and I got a table, ordered Sprites, and I wandered over. I could hear flies hitting the blue zapper behind the bar.

"How close, bro?" said a boy in nothing but board shorts and a Dos Equis.

"Yeah," said his buddy. "Ground zero or what?" They held their beers to their stomachs and craned over the group.

She turned her head slowly, chin high, and looked at the guys like they were two bugs who were interrupting her lecture and should sit in the back of the class. That was all. She didn't deign to answer. She actually cleared her throat. "As I was saying, the path projected here is simply an aggregate of wind-speed probabilities for any quadrant at predetermined distances from the center of the storm's current position. That's what these different colors represent. Right now we have a forty-five percent probability of hurricane-force winds early on the day after tomorrow. That is, seventy-five to ninety-five miles per hour."

"Yeah, but is it gonna rain, bro?" said the boy, tenacious. He was a surfer. If you don't keep paddling for the peak of a wave, you've ceded it to another guy. "I mean, are we gonna be able to get outta here, cross the rivers and shit?"

Her long fingers came to rest lightly on the keys like a pianist's at the end of a piece. She studied the boys for a moment, raised one mordant eyebrow, unconsciously touched her glasses back to position as she wrinkled her nose, turned back to the screen. Silence. Everybody waited. She spoke to the local fisherman behind the bar in rapid, colloquial Spanish and he nodded, smiled, slid open the ice chest, and brought out a dripping Pacifico.

She twisted her head, stretching her slender neck, and let it settle in perfect balance at the top of her spine. "This is currently a Category Three storm," she said softly, making everybody lean forward. "Attendant rains could be on the order of ten inches in twenty-four hours. That would be enough to cut the roads, yes. If the projected track proves out. The storm could deteriorate or shift direction."

"Shit!" The two boys raised and clacked their bottles. "Sick! We better get the fuck out of here tomorrow!"

On the way back to our table I bumped into a young Australian surfer musician I'd talked to the night before. His name was Colin and he had a band called Beerfridge in Margaretville, wherever that was. "Who is that chick?" I said.

"What? La *Profesora*? She's been holding court right there all afternoon, mate. She knows words that are only legal at university."

"Yeah, but who is she?"

"Some biologist. Been coming here for a couple of years. Doing a study on manta rays or something out at some island. She knows all the fishermen. They don't charge her for Internet, either. That cunt in the corner is her squeeze." He pointed with his beer. Sitting there with the hooded watchfulness of a bouncer was a muscle-bound Latino with black braids down over his shoulders, earrings, eyebrow studs, skull rings, black tank top, and nonstop tattoos. He looked like an outlaw biker gang enforcer, like my youngest sister's high school boyfriend Claudio.

"That guy surfs?"

"Oh, yeah, they both do. Not bad. Longboarders. Me and Maggie are over there, come on and join us."

"Okay, we will."

That night an errant wind slapped the canvas. I couldn't hear the bats. We lay in the dark and talked about getting out ahead of the storm. I argued for staying put. The waves were too good, we were learning too much. Plus, we could just as easily get pummeled on the way back south.

"What's the worst that can happen?" Kim said.

"The hurricane could flip over the Beast, maybe carry it over the edge. We could land on top of La Profesora. Her legs would stick out."

"C'mon. Do you think it's dangerous?"

"Yeah, maybe. Tomorrow after surfing we could look for a room in a house."

She digested that. "Good idea. Remember: precious cargo. You are a married man now."

La Profesora's prognostication had its effect. I got up later than usual, which meant after sunrise, feeling groggy. I knew from my experience on a ship in Antarctica that pressure drop affected my sleep; we are all walking barometers. I made coffee and wandered across the bluff. Half of the trucks were already gone. Other campers were packing up. Nobody wanted to get cut off out here. Most people had jobs. There were masses of dark clouds over the hills inland, and flocks of terns were crying along the cliffs. I wasn't sure if that had anything to do with the storm.

It must have been stirring up the sea. I walked to the edge with my mug and saw the waves at Third Point coming in clean and tall, just overhead. A dozen surfers already out, but not the twenty or thirty of the past days. That was good.

When I paddled out I found Big Bill right next to me. His hair was still dry. His eyebrows lowered like two storms. His mustache drooped with a dangerous indifference.

"Peter," I said.

He grunted, kept an eye on the incoming waves.

"It's like *Key Largo* around here," I said. "Stuck in the hotel with the hurricane coming."

Bill swung his heavy head. "Great movie." His voice was like a D9 picking up road base. "Edward G.'s apotheosis. Completely overshadowed Bogey. Never better, in my mind."

Did Big Bill just say apotheosis? I can't even say that.

You just did.

I didn't mean to.

I smiled. Tightened up my voice, drawled out one side of my mouth like there was a cigar stub stuck in it, " 'I want more, see? Rocko wants more, more.' Or maybe it's more like *Treasure of the Sierra Madre.* All of us waiting in the hole."

"That was a passion play, wasn't it? Book's even better."

"Yeah?"

"Yeah, the author, B. Traven, interesting story. Nobody ever really knew who the sonofabitch was. German anarchist, British prison. Showed up on the movie set impersonating his own agent. Course, John Huston had his suspicions."

"Huh." Here came a set. We could see it coming, we were in position, and we both turned our boards. Bill would take the first. No better time than now.

"Hey, Bill," I said. "Did you knock that guy down yesterday?"

"Fucker owes me. Did all kinds of construction for the asshole and he says I didn't do the work. Fucker better pay." He rocked his board forward and took off on the cleanest, sweetest wave.

The clouds massed over the water. The wind came up. By dark it was shoving and scooping the canvas sides of the camper into a filled sail. The Beast was beating upwind. Just after dark the air cooled and the first raindrops pattered against the sides.

We huddled down into our flannel bags and waited for the storm. We had loaded everything, so that if the wind got bad we could drive off of the exposed bluff. We had looked for a room, but the gringo couple that owned the campground wanted $100. I had tried to explain that we just needed a safe place to throw down our sleeping bags for the night. Nope: $100. Screw that.

The patter thickened into a steady downpour. It drowned out the rush of the waves. It lashed the canvas. The Beast shuddered. We waited. The rain was so loud we gave up talking. I reached out and felt for the keys on the plastic ledge. They were wet. I put my hand against the cloth; it was wet and cold and the wind pressed from the other side. It was like pressing palms with the storm. Not too bad yet, not enough to run. The volume of the rain, the sound of it, rose. Didn't seem that was possible. If I listened closely I could hear voices in the roar. A rising and falling of harrowing force. Nothing I would lash myself to the mast to resist.

Our bed shook. With the next whomp of gust, I had an image of the storm as a great beast nosing and sniffing the van, the bluff. My pulse quickened. I had the keys tight in my palm, ready to jump. We were already wearing shorts. We could drive away right now, to someplace more sheltered. I thought of the water streaming off the rocky road that led off the bluff, that would be okay; but the soft sand track out to town could be getting swamped. So many of the greatest decisions in our lives boil down to when to stand and when to flee. So simple: Now? Now? Or now?

Big storms do what waves can do: they draw us taut like a bow. Leap? Or hold?

I usually loved storms. Now I was scared. Had we waited too long? I held Kim's fingers tight in one hand and the keys in the other. The temperature had dropped so quickly it was like another season, but not one that I knew; a season of night that smelled of gusted salt and mineral earth. Shhhhhhhhh. Between the battings of the wind I thought I could hear the enraged surf. Maybe not. It might have been my own thumping blood.

As suddenly as it began, it stopped. The deluge subsided to gentle sweepings of rain. We lay in the sleeping bags and listened. Could this be the eye? Was that the full brunt of the hurricane? Didn't seem likely. We slept. When we woke, the sky was a washed blue streaked with high thin horsetails and the waves thundered in just overhead high, row after row.

APEX

We had been surfing now for seven solid weeks. Every day. Except for getting married, not a single day off. Sometimes twice a day, often two or three hours at a stretch. Everywhere we went we were usually the most beginner of the beginners at every break. Almost. I was seeking out faster waves now, where there were no real beginners. But I kept myself in the role of neophyte. Kim struggled, building strength and timing.

We surfed another two days at Scorpion Bay, with a post-near-hurricane swell that sent in head-high perfect rollers, and then the waves dropped off just as if someone had shut a spigot. The points were like a lake. We packed up and drove back to Pescadero. When we rolled in to Jaime's surf camp on an afternoon in late September I felt spent and happy. We fell into the swimming pool and floated around, relieved not to have to watch for set waves. An hour later Jaime said, "Peter."

"Huh?"

"You look tired."

"I do?"

"Around the edges. Nothing serious. Thought you'd want to know."

"Thanks—Jaime?"

"Yes, Peter."

"Even through the screen?" We were talking through the little window of the shower door. The communal shower was twenty feet from our *palapa* and I was taking the first hot wash I'd had in two weeks. "You can tell I'm tired through the screen?"

"You ought to go down to the Costa Azul," Jaime continued. "Give yourself a break. It's—" He stopped. He was standing outside the shower door and our faces were a foot apart, separated by the screen. "Are you naked?" he said.

"Yeah."

"That's frigging weird."

He was wearing his goofy tennis visor, blinking at me. I started laughing and couldn't stop. "Wash behind your ears," he said, and walked away.

The Costa Azul is between Cabo San Lucas and San José del Cabo, in the tourist corridor at the very southern tip of Baja, about an hour away from Pescadero. We decided to try a reef break called Old Man's because it was supposed to be easy. This whole coast had been devastated by wall to wall condos and resorts. We had to park the Beast in a steeply sloped pocket of a parking lot crammed between hotels, where she balanced precariously between a Hummer and Mercedes SUV.

We followed the pedestrian steps down into a gully, went through a tunnel to the beach, which was more like the front patio of a hotel. Hotel employees with big arms and red uniform T-shirts rented out surf boards while spectators in bikinis on reclining chairs ordered drinks from waiters. We allowed our eyes to drift out to the wave. Must have been forty pink-faced longboarders bobbing out there, all gringos. No, there were three local kids. One guy was clearly teaching a class; he was paddling along his line of surfers and exhorting like a drill sergeant, urging one after another to take off, giving them a shove. Surfers who knew how to surf were catching the bigger waves farther out and slicing through the crowd of hapless human flotsam as they bombed down the line. Well, okay. Surfing is one of the fastest-growing sports in the world; in some respects, this was the future. We waxed up, waded in, jumped on, and paddled out.

For a few minutes I sat just outside the crowd, waiting for something bigger and wondering why Jaime had sent us straight to Kook City. And then a set wave rolled in and I knew why. It was a revelation. The wave itself was lovely. It was a right. It came in from the south and heaved up against the reef, bulking itself to impressive heights, and then it developed slowly, like a patient lover. For once, I left Kim alone; usually, when we are on the same wave, I yell all sorts of coaching tips and inspirational slogans, urge her on like a soccer husband. She hates it. She gets mad and paddles off and won't talk to me. This time I watched her with a kind of awe as she paddled around the group of kooks, keyed off the breaking peak of the midsized waves, got herself in a priority position, and took off. Chest up, trimming perfectly, then driving her head down and popping up. She zipped away on the longest ride, making it all the way to the shallow coral ledges. All I could see then was the back of the wave rolling away, and just over its lip, slinging toward shore and sliding right, her fencer's back hand; sometimes it gestured with the twisting birdlike flourishes of a flamenco dancer with castanets. Sometimes I saw an occasional black braid flying as she arced up to the top of the wave. Remarkable. Then she'd paddle back out and do it again. She did not look fatigued in the least. She paddled steadily, with easy strength, chest up. When she caught a wave, she parted the flock of beginners like a peregrine diving through ducks. Fuckin' A, that's my girl. I was so proud.

I paddled way way out, far beyond the beginners where one other confident surfer waited for a much bigger set. Eventually one came and I caught a ride that rivaled the Scorp in length, long and easy and smooth. I turned on the face and slalomed through beginners.

Back in the blazing parking lot, we loaded up with a fatigued happiness, a kind of shared pride we hadn't yet had before, and it was special. We high-fived.

"Alto cinco."

"Alto cinco."

All the work. The tumbles, the fear, the newness, the strain and exhaustion—it was paying off. Slowly, in its own time, surfing was giving back to us.

The next day we packed up, left a lot of our stuff in Jaime's room, and headed over to La Paz for our flight home. Dang. Just when we were getting the hang of it.

THE COVE

I had to go home to tend to other work projects. They also involved the ocean and, in particular, the fate of its largest inhabitants. I had seen whales in Antarctica swimming in great numbers, the spouts—the small misting breaths of babies and the tall jets of the big adults—staggered out to where an iceberg marked the edge of the world. Hundreds of humpbacks, swimming close by us, unafraid. Pairs, mothers and juveniles, cruising by, playing, rolling, fins, eyes, flukes— the exhalations in small explosions, sometimes groans and whistles. I thought how these whales make over 620 social sounds, how they can call each other by name, how they have three times the density of spindle neurons that we do—specialized brain cells that are thought to be responsible for empathy, grief, love, language. How their population is less than one one-hundredth of what it used to be before industrial whaling, how they tangle in abandoned fishing gear and

drown, are struck by ships, starved by warming and pollution.
They are critically endangered and I was trying to expose how
the Japanese want to target them in their illegal commercial
quotas, rip them with explosive-tipped harpoons.

I learned more about how the oceans are dying and how
all of us, every nation, every individual, contribute. The heedless abuse, rampant overfishing, sloppy energy use everywhere,
me among the worst, leading to carbon emissions, leading to
warming, to acidity, to the wholesale death of reefs and plankton. The sea cannot defend herself.

Then, when we were about to fly back to Mexico, I got an
e-mail from a guy who had been one of *National Geographic*'s
top photographers for eighteen years and was now making a
movie about the dolphin-killing cove at Taiji. Trying to expose the slaughter and shut it down. His name was Louie
Psyhoyos and his film company was called the Oceanic Preservation Society, or OPS. He had backing from Jim Clark,
the billionaire founder of Netscape. He had read some of my
writing about whaling and he wanted to meet me.

Kim and I drove up a leafy, prosperous street against the
foothills of Boulder. Louie's wife, a former ballerina, motioned us across the backyard, a field, really, scattered with
apple trees. In back was a studio. We stepped through the
sliding glass door into a room lined with bookcases and large
plasma computer screens. It was like NASA in there. Someone hit a switch and electric shades hummed up and let the
clear late autumn light stream through the windows. Six or
eight guys, all in their twenties and thirties, in black T-shirts,
stepped forward to shake my hand. Louie introduced himself. He was a commanding dude, tall, broad-shouldered,

with a lean face, crew cut, and intense green eyes. Maybe early fifties. I looked around the room. There was an esprit de corps, a quiet confidence and seriousness among the men that made me think of the French Resistance. Louie said they were going back into the cove in a few weeks. Dave Rastovich, perhaps the most famous surfer in Australia, was going to bring a bunch of celebrities to Taiji and stage a "Paddle Out" ceremony, basically a surfer's funeral, in the middle of the killing cove, and OPS was going to film it. The celebrities were going to charge the cove and hold the ceremony for murdered dolphins, whom they considered the original surfers. Hayden Panettiere, the young star of the TV show *Heroes,* was coming, as was an Aussie television star named Isabel Lucas, and Karina Petroni, the top U.S. woman surfer.

Louie asked if I wanted to come.

"How do you film in there?" I asked. "I've heard that access to the cliffs around the cove is all blocked with razor wire, that they have armed patrols and they tarp off the inlet when they are killing dolphins."

The men glanced at each other, smiled. Louie said, "We get in. We've been in twice now. We go in at night in all black. We have carpet to go over the wire. We have FLIR, military-grade forward-looking infrared cameras, to spot patrols. We have comm. George Lucas's lab, Industrial Light & Magic, matched the rocks in the cove and made us floating waterproof rocks that hold hot-rodded cameras that can film for eleven hours. We plant them around the cove. We have remote-controlled cameras that look like birds' nests. We rappel onto ledges way up on the cliffs with high-def cameras and when day breaks we change into full camo." Louie smiled at me. "If you come, we'll supply the face paint."

OPS. Now I understood the name. "We'd like you to paddle in on a surfboard with the rest, wear a helmet cam and mike." He crossed his strong arms over his chest. "Of course, you might get arrested. Do you have time to see some footage?"

Kim and I sat on a small couch in front of a large flatscreen. The shades hummed down. The screen came alive and dolphins began to die.

Thirteen fishing boats traveled over the water in a wide arc. From each, from the starboard side, extended a long pole into the water. Whalers banged on the poles, forming an acoustic net. Ahead of the boats, swimming fast, in panic, ran a pod of dolphins, twenty-five or thirty. Sleek, blowing rapidly, distressed. The boats herded them into the coast, into the funnel of a rock cove that quickly narrowed. Behind them, open boats ran two net lines across the mouth. The cove had two fingers. The panicked dolphins hit the net blocking off the one finger—"That's a public beach, believe it or not," Louie said—and turned. They were herded to the head of the second finger. There, divers in full black wetsuits and archaic round scuba masks and snorkels waited for them. They stood chest-deep in the water and grasped the exhausted, terrified animals in embraces that looked almost loving. They hugged and dragged them to the beach. Others, in wading boots, set the nooses around their flapping flukes and brought them tight. The nooses were attached to a taut line that ran across the waterline of the small beach. Still other men, in slickers and rubber boots, approached the dolphins, who struggled, half exposed, on the gravel. They carried T-handled spikes. They set them behind the blowholes and shoved down with all their weight. The dolphins screamed and writhed. Blood gushed in a fountain. The dolphins tipped over and thrashed.

They began to drown, unable to right themselves to breathe, drowning in their own blood. A spiker would step over to the next animal and spike it, too. On down the line. The cove began to fill with blood. In a few minutes the entire inlet was crimson. Babies, hearing their mothers crying out, thrashed around in the blood. Then a boat motored through the rest of the pod. A whaler in the bow began to spear dolphins haphazardly from the bow. They leapt, crashed, bled. Tipped over, drowning. Pairs of living dolphins tried desperately to hold the wounded out of the water with their snouts, trying to let them breathe. They were speared, too. The animals writhing on the beach took twenty minutes to thrash and die. Some, still alive, were dragged across the gravel with hooks through their eye sockets.

The screen went dark. The light came on. I couldn't speak for the longest time and when I did, I said that I'd come.

The slaughter continued every year from September to March. In this cove, dolphins, porpoises, pilot whales, false killer whales, and other small cetaceans were slashed to death almost every day during the season, over twenty-three hundred in Taiji alone. Up and down the coasts of Japan, twenty-three thousand small cetaceans were killed annually.

A single man had been coming here to document the slaughter every year, trying to get the word out. So far, nobody much had listened. His name was Ric O'Barry, and he had been Flipper's trainer. He felt partly responsible for what was going on.

He told me that his popular TV show had engendered a worldwide love affair with dolphins. He said that dolphinariums, dolphin shows, and swim-with-dolphin programs had cropped up all over the world. He said it was a cruel industry that was driving the killing in places like Taiji.

"How?"

"Well, the fishermen who kill the dolphins are very poor. They sell the meat, but demand has been dropping and prices are low. But when they capture a pod, they cull out the prime females. They can get ten thousand dollars from a broker for a single dolphin. The broker in turn can get a hundred and fifty thousand from a dolphinarium."

"You mean like SeaWorld."

"Technically, since the Marine Mammal Protection Act was passed in 1972, nobody is allowed to import wild dolphins into the U.S. They say all their animals are bred in captivity. But they know that that's a shrinking gene pool. They work around it. A dolphin from Taiji will go to the Dominican Republic, and from there will be sold to SeaWorld as a nonwild dolphin. If it wasn't for this thriving captive industry, the drive hunt—what's happening in Taiji—would have died a long time ago."

O'Barry, now seventy, is not afraid of a fight. He had been a diver in the U.S. Navy's elite antisubmarine hunter-killer group. He had blown off a finger with a shotgun doing stunt work for the Bond movie *Never Say Never Again*. Despite harassment and threats from local police, from the Yakuza, the Japanese mob, from the whalers in Taiji, from just about everyone, he kept going back. He stood by the cove year after year and wept. He started an organization called SaveJapanDolphins.org and tried to tell everyone. He was so well known in Taiji that he often had to drive through town in a wig and a dress.

He told me, "This is murder. These are emotional, highly socialized, self-aware animals. I knew dolphins were self-aware thirty years before any of the studies confirmed it. In the show there was a dock. At one end of the dock was a house where the family lived and at the other end of the dock was Flipper. Well, the family didn't really live in the house, but I did. Every Friday night I'd drag a long extension cord and a TV out to the end of the dock and Flipper would watch *Flipper*. She loved it."

He said that aside from the killing, there was another issue. The meat, sold to school lunch programs, given to children, was extremely high in mercury. Independent tests by a Japanese lab had found concentrations three to thirty-five hundred times the levels deemed safe by the Japanese government. He said Japan had the potential for another Minamata scandal on its hands, referring to the disaster in the late fifties and sixties when thousands of people died from mercury poisoning, tens of thousands were sickened, and hundreds of babies were born with terrible defects.

I flew into Osaka. At a downtown business hotel I met up with the international group of activists and surfers led by Dave Rastovich, the charismatic Australian free surfer. One cold, rainy night with the OPS team, we drove the four hours to Taiji and infiltrated the inlet and set up cameras high on the cliffs overlooking the killing cove. All night, three of us huddled on a ledge while the rain swept in and a light on some far-off headland blinked its warning in lonely silence. Then, when morning broke, I stripped off all the camo and put on a wetsuit and paddled out on a surfboard with about thirty others to perform the surfers' circle, the ceremony normally held for a departed surfer, but now enacted to memorialize all the dolphins and small whales that had died there. No dolphins had been netted in for killing that morning. I was so relieved. And despite the somber feel of the place, it felt good to be back on a surfboard again, just paddling around. Except that now, instead of looking over our shoulders for a good set wave, we were keeping eyes out for fishermen and police. The ceremony was moving, it went without a hitch, and everybody drove back to Osaka feeling pretty good.

The next afternoon Ric O'Barry called from Taiji where he keeps watch on the cove and said a pod of thirty pilot whales had been driven into the inlet and netted in, and would be killed the next morning. I guess the whalers thought the international attention had come and gone.

Six of us went back. We drove most of the night in a crowded van. Just out of Taiji, in the first faint light, we pulled over and got into wetsuits. Now there would be blood. The fishermen would have spears and knives and they were known to get worked up and violent.

The OPS teams had set up earlier in the night—avoiding patrols, going over razor wire with rolls of black carpet—and they had rigged a battery of cameras. Taiji is all about whaling—they have a whale museum with an aqua park behind, where dolphins captured from the cove perform tricks and tourists eat dolphin sandwiches. They have smiling dolphin statues and pictures everywhere. Just at dawn we parked behind a life-sized bronze of a humpback with calf and waited for one of the hidden cameramen, who called five minutes later: "They're killing! Go!" We sped to the public beach where we had been two mornings before. The six of us grabbed our boards from the van and splashed into the water, and we began to paddle as hard as we could toward the mouth of the killing cove. The plan was to perform another surfers' circle before we were stopped by the fishermen or the police. O'Barry wanted the footage to air around the world.

We scraped over one net line and then it was forty yards of open water to the cove mouth. No boat appeared. We paddled past the rock corner and looked into the inlet. It was all blood. Thick and red, like paint. The dark bodies of two pilot whales floated in it, washed into the beach. And then I saw them: twelve or fifteen of the little whales pressed in panic against a far net.

They huddled tighter as we got closer. They circled in terror, blowing hard. We stopped, circled, and held hands. The blowing of the whales slowed. I watched the large dolphins, twenty yards beyond us, slow and mill. They spy-hopped, lifting their heads out to look. Small babies nosed out of the water to peer at us. They calmed down. Half of their group had just been butchered in this water, many crying for a long time before they died. These whales were in shock. But they seemed to sense that we meant them no harm. Rastovich wanted badly to cut the nets, but we could see another net stretched across the cove eighty yards out, and another beyond that. All of these whales would be spiked within the hour.

We watched the remainder of this pod of pilot whales begin to flow against the net, their backs silvering in the long sun. We could hear them blowing. I sat on my board and felt tears stream down my cold face.

A boat cruised around an outer point of rock, a long, open motorboat. The fisherman throttled when he saw us. He skimmed over the lines of nets and wheeled dangerously close, standing, yelling. He motioned for us to go. I looked around our circle. Everyone seemed calm. The whaler revved his motor and tried to frighten us with the propeller. He came so close to Hayden's leg where she sat on her board that she had to pull it out of the way. Furious, he circled once more and headed to the beach.

We paddled out, not in. Closer to the whales. It was a bold move, as the local cops must be scrambling. In Japan you can be held for twenty-eight days without being charged, and no one was looking forward to a free cell in Taiji. We were yards away from the pilot whales now. The little pod huddled against the net and we could hear them breathe fast, hollow blows over the slick water. We floated in the blood of their family. Hayden began to cry quietly. Then Isabel. Then Rastovich's wife Hannah.

Soon the boat sped out to us again, and this time there were four whalers aboard. They feinted with the prop. One yelled wildly, picked up a long forked pole, and jabbed it at the closest boards. He hit Hannah in the thigh, then shoved Hayden's board. Both women stayed calm, keeping their balance and holding the circle. Behind them I noticed the pilot whales going crazy, thrashing against the net. Enough, Rastovich said. "Let's paddle in. Stay against the rocks."

We ran from the water, threw the boards in the back of the van, ducked to the floor, and sped away. Forty-five seconds later sirens wailed and police cars flew past us, heading toward the cove.

Back in Osaka, we all changed flights and left the country before the authorities decided to make someone pay.

At home, I was amazed at the press the protest was getting. *People,* CNN, AP, MSNBC, *Ellen.* Hayden was everywhere, a real-life hero. Ric O'Barry, who stood by the cove heartbroken and alone for so many years, was thrilled.

When I tried to sleep the image returned: Those twelve pilot whales swimming against the nets, watching us. I watched them back. There is a lot I want to communicate. A baby lifts its head. They are wondering why we are there, but they don't feel threatened. A boat approaches. I hear the motor like a snarl. The whales circle tighter, faster. I lie beside my sleeping wife and weep.

I continued to be shaken by a grief whose power I can't explain. Perhaps it is that the little group of whales spoke, to me at least, for the whole ocean. The dying waters. At home I began to see the surf trip as more about loving the ocean than anything else. It was a way to know her better. It certainly wasn't *Endless Summer*. One couldn't do that anymore, the sheer lark, not in 2008. The joy and the rush were still all there, surfing was still surfing, but one couldn't do it without a simultaneous commitment to taking some responsibility.

NEW BODY

After Baja, the first nights at home in Denver were weird. I tried to sleep but could not hear surf coming in tatters on a shifting wind. I couldn't smell the salt. When I listened for the ocean's mood, the ceaseless wash against the shore, all I could hear were the furnace clicking on, the hiss of the gas jets, the old fridge. Kit-ten, the little black and white calico, purring. Not the same at all.

I lay in the big bed with Kim, our cat, and a surfing-toned body that felt strange and new. It was strong in a way it had been only a few times in my life. It hummed with muscular power, with the music of the sea, and it wondered why there was no answer. I woke up at six every morning, wide awake, ready to pick up a board and feel cold gravel underfoot. I woke disappointed.

We ended up staying in the States for two months as I finished other projects. I went to Japan, then needed another chunk of cash, so I took a quick magazine assignment, a profile of an Olympic whitewater kayaker who would soon go to Beijing, and as I stood in the freezing wind on the banks of a swift channel of the Potomac outside of D.C., watching him glide with power through his aquatic element, my new body ached for water. Not the chlorinated, imprisoned lanes of the pool I tried to swim in a few times a week, but the wild, surging, unpredictable body of the sea. She was struggling and dying and I was heartbroken and my body ached for her body.

DUNE

The world had changed when we finally returned to Baja. It was freezing. The taxi driver picked us up in a winter parka and ski hat. After checking into Los Arcos, we finally looked up an old acquaintance of mine named Tim Means who runs Baja Expeditions. He's a hulking man, bulky in the shoulders, with a salty gray drooping mustache and unkempt gray hair blowing around his neck. He is one of the most effective environmentalists I've ever known. He knows that the Sea of Cortez is one of the richest marine environments in the world, as well as one of its greatest opportunities for preservation. Jacques Cousteau called it the Aquarium of the World. Over twenty species of whales and dolphins are seasonal residents, and two hundred bird species and over five hundred species of fish call the gulf their home. On some islands, like Espiritu Santo, there are plants that exist nowhere else. Look at a map: a narrow, seven-hundred-mile-long experiment in what hap-

pens when a rich body of ocean and a teeming human population come together. The wildness of the west, the Baja side, is
made up of vast stretches of coastline, island-studded, mostly
unpopulated, abundant with coves and points, cliffs, rock islets, inlets softened by mangroves; the mainland side to the
east strung with port cities, fishing fleets. Unfortunately, the
experiment had been failing until fairly recently. The Mexican
shrimp fleets engaged in a kind of bottom trawling that rav-
ages the seabed and that scientists describe as one of the most
destructive fishing methods on earth; the trawling had de-
pleted shrimp stocks until they were no longer commercially
viable. Resort development was tearing out the last critical
mangroves and filling in estuaries. Beach houses and resorts
threatened bird habitat and endangered sea turtle nesting
grounds.

Tim's dream was to turn the whole sea into one vast marine park and wildlife refuge. An entire sea protected, with
commercial fishing allowed but strictly regulated to keep
the fish populations healthy and sustainable. He was already
working to establish protected marine zones, and areas with
strong protections for mangroves and other critical coastal
habitat. If there was anyplace in the world this could be done,
it was here; it is hard to monitor the Pacific Ocean, but possible to monitor the Sea of Cortez. Though boundless in its
beauty, the Sea was a place you get your mind around. All that
was needed was the full cooperation and commitment of the
Mexican people and their government.

Given that that wasn't going to happen all at once, Tim
was taking one patient, furious step at a time.

We called him and he met us at Rancho Viejo Restaurant, a taco joint a block up the hill from the harbor. He sat
at a table on the sidewalk next to the hissing grill. A waiter

slapped down a dish full of grilled whole *guero* chilies. Tim hulked over the rough wood and the plates in a faded Hawaiian shirt. He seemed bigger and shaggier than I'd remembered. He had the same undisciplined gray mustache and hair. The same laconic preference for long silences. Until he started speaking about the Mogote sand spit in the middle of the La Paz harbor. A developer from Colorado was building a resort out there, high-rise hotel, condos, golf course. Tearing up some of the last remaining mangroves in the harbor. The developer was putting the golf course on sand, too, where there should never be a golf course. Tim said the bigger buildings were already sinking because they were built on sand. I asked the name of the developer.

"Bobby T——. I think he's from Denver, where you're from."

I knew the guy.

Then he told us that the public campaign to stop the big development out at Balandra, the mangrove cove we'd passed on the way to our wedding in the water, had been successful. The developers were going elsewhere. The issue had resonated with the people of La Paz. It was a conservation issue, but also an issue of sovereignty: the public was fed up with losing one public beach after another to resorts that catered to gringos.

Tim told us that Espiritu Santo Island had won UNESCO World Heritage Site status, meaning that it was protected under an international regime and would remain wild. The few fishermen who had camps on the island would be allowed to stay, and various groups were now working out the protections for fish and other wildlife around the island.

Tim could not make the whole of the Sea of Cortez a reserve, but he was chipping away at his dream an island, a cove, at a time.

"You two should hang out awhile," he said.

"I—uh—we're pretty eager to get back to surfing," I stammered.

"Well, you can stay at my place while you get ready to go across."

It was a generous offer. Tim was a famously private man and we felt honored. It was an offer we couldn't refuse.

Means's house was surprising. He was a man of standing in La Paz; wherever he went—restaurants, the marinas, the hotels—he was recognized and treated with respect and affection. One might expect a man like this to live in a fancy house. Understated, perhaps, but sumptuous. What kind of house would Jacques Cousteau live in? Something with a view over the ocean that he loved, something with rooms open to light and breeze, with patios and a desert garden. Okay, that's what I would have wanted. Anyway, you might expect a guy like Tim Means to have a sweet pad. He did, but it was nothing like we'd imagined.

I thought it would overlook the harbor. As we pulled up, I saw that the house stood on a grimy wide side street of concrete-walled modest houses, with a junk car shop across the way. It was a mile from the water. A sign for Grupo Tortuguero stood before the shaded bungalow beside it. Tim helped start the organization: groups of local fishermen and others up and down the Mexican coasts dedicated to saving sea turtles. The same fishermen that were wiping out turtles with careless practices were now patrolling beaches nightly to prevent poachers from robbing nests of eggs, and carefully transferring eggs from those nests into nurseries. It was an astounding grassroots movement.

We parked the Beast by the sign and approached the house. I stuck my hand through a slot in the tall heavy wooden gate and slid the bolt and the barking came up like a deafening alarm. A thud against the gate, then another. We heard clawing on the wood. Kim and I looked at each other.

"Do you have a piece of raw steak?" I said. "Isn't that what they do in the movies?"

Kim said, "We've got tortillas and beans. They're Mexican dogs, right?"

"Huh. Okay, I'm going in." I shoved on the gate and we squeezed through and were almost knocked over. Two thin Mexican mutts, one brown and one black, were on top of us, their licks covering our arms and faces. An old golden retriever seemed a bit embarrassed by her colleagues' lack of manners and politely licked our hands. A gray cat sat on an old chair by the door and blinked. Tim's house was two stories, set in a grove of drought-tolerant Palo de Arco trees, deeply shaded. Cool in here after the bustling, glaring streets of the town. An old hippie school bus, painted with fish and turtles, sat beside it.

I forgot to latch the gate. We heard it clatter and knock and turned to see the two mutts bolting through it. By the time I got into the middle of the street, yelling, waving, all I could see were a pair of insubordinate streaks blocks away. I ran after them, screaming my head off, terrified they'd get hit by a bus as they crossed avenue after avenue. I returned to the house ragged and upset, climbed into the Beast, and chased them down like a helicopter going after wolves. As soon as I pulled up on them and slid the door open, they smiled broadly the way dogs do and happily jumped in. VW vans were in the family. The brown dog hopped right up onto the backseat, on top of our clean towels, and lowered his head to his paws. The black jumped up into the passenger seat, furrowed his brow, and looked seriously ahead like a copilot. It took half an hour to wrangle them back to Tim's house.

Inside the house, it was blessedly cool. Tim had said there

was a good place to sit upstairs. We went up the narrow steps onto a covered rooftop. A couple of beat-up chairs sat by a low wall looking into the treetops over the front of the house. In the corner was a large sturdy cage. Inside was a giant iguana. A parrot squawked. Two cats slipped around our legs.

We were enjoying our reentry into Baja, but I was more than ready to go surfing. Tim took us down to the marina to see one of his new dive boats, a nice cabin cruiser, and we met his surfer son Carlos, who was putting down new decking. Tim said, "Carlos is taking a group out to Mag Bay for five days. Why don't you go with him?"

"Whale watching?"

"You know the drill." I did. I had taken my sister on a trip with them years before. We had slept by the lagoon on a windy sand spit in spacious wall tents on cots; we ate delicious food, drank coffee, went out in boats twice a day and ran around in the wild bay beside the nursing gray whales. Sometimes we could hear them blowing at night, and the explosive breaths rasped at my sleep. Dense fog rolled in over the dunes, and at dawn, walking to the water to pee, I saw the wraiths of coyotes patrolling the wet sand, and feral donkeys ghosting the mist, descendants of ones left by Spanish explorers and who had learned to become coastal scavengers. Once in a while a pair of whales bred near camp, pushed against each other by a helper, and their passionate waves washed up on the sand. A wholly dreamlike place.

Now I winced. I loved whales, but I wanted to become again an aquatic creature of my own. I needed to surf. I took one look at Kim.

"I've never seen a whale," she said, reverent, her big eyes glistening. My hopes for surfing very soon, as in the next few days, vanished like a whale spout in the wind.

"Well," I stammered. I guess my spindle neurons kicked in, the ones we share with gray whales, the ones that govern love and suffering.

Magdalena Bay was across the peninsula and to the north. We drove back the way we had come twice before, through the cardón cactus hills, the stony basins covered with yucca. We drove back through Constitution, where the local cartel supported the gray whales. On the other side of the bustling town we hung a left, west, toward the coast, followed the expedition vans down a flat sand road beneath a defunct telephone line, every third or fourth pole crowned with the giant stick nests of ospreys. We drove with the windows down, elbows stuck out, the oven air pouring in, and the clouds of dust from the cars ahead sticking to the sweat on our necks. The dust thickened the small hairs on our forearms so they looked like fur. Over the engine, we could hear the osprey chicks peeping, the malevolent heads of their mothers peering at us over the twig parapets.

We pulled up to a flea-ravaged fish camp on the edge of the lagoon. Way across, maybe five miles, we could see the line of canvas safari tents that would be our home.

Over the next few days it was cold, windy, choppy, and we got into open boats and followed whales with their calves in the early morning, and before sunset. I was chomping at the bit to surf, but was happy in any event just to be back on the sea. After the months on a surfboard being buoyed and rocked and tumbled, I could appreciate anew the whales' ancient choice to take to the water. Also, I liked being near the massive creatures again. Whales are like us, just bigger and better. Like us, if we weren't bent on killing everything and each other, and they are so big and powerful they are halfway to being geographical. A reef, a ridge, a whale. Get too close and they are an earthquake. The mothers nursed their calves, gently nudged them away from the boat. Turned half on their sides so they could fix us with one dark intelligent eye. Kim adored it. She just wanted to be close to whales. She wanted to study the glossy backs mottled with whale lice, the barnacles on a flank, the notches and scars in the great flukes as they came lazily out of the water. She was enthralled. When a male breached just ahead of us and crashed down on his side, I thought she'd faint.

Carlos led the expedition, and he knew a lot about gray whales, and was thoughtful and attentive to his clients. But I recognized a fellow surf-obsessed. Nothing explicit, but there were little clues, in the way the alien zombie invaders who look normal in a crowd recognize each other. The way he always seemed on low idle, engine just purring, slouching in the wind in his anorak, equanimous, friendly, shy, at the edge of the group with his coffee mug, expending energy with perfect efficiency, saving it. For the hunt. I could tell. It would take a lot to rouse this guy, and between surfs he rested in the easy way all hunters do. He told us that he'd taken a long mainland surf trip in his VW bus, and that he'd overheated so much he kept the heater on all the time to draw heat away from the engine, and that he tried to break down at good surf spots.

One evening I wandered away from the camp into a sea of haystack dunes. They tossed this way and that like a confused storm swell. I wound around in the troughs as though through a maze. Down in the low spots, sheltered from the wind, a thousand animal tracks in the sand told stories in measured, then frantic calligraphy. Here were the intermittent hops of a rabbit, here the tiny tank crawl of a beetle, here a strutting raven, here a coyote—meeting the rabbit, now an errant tuft of fur.

I climbed a ridge of sand to where I could look over the water of a lagoon and lay in the late sun on the leeward side of the dune, away from the stiff wind. The sand was warm. I thrummed with solitude and peace. Closed my eyes.

When I opened them the sun was nearly touching the farther sea. I blinked, shook the sand out of my hair, sat up, shivered. I gazed around. The lagoon was now a tidal mud flat stalked with slender-legged birds. The dunes—on the tops of the three closest hillocks, one on each, not a hundred feet away—were three coyotes watching me silently. My skin sprang with goose bumps. They were exactly the color of the sand in the red light of the last sun. They were big, well fed. Each lay still, centered between haunches, and studied me. I had no doubt that, were they to make a concerted effort, I could be supper. I grinned.

"Hi, guys." It wasn't much above a whisper, but the breeze was blowing toward them and they heard me. A couple of ears swiveled forward. Hello, I must be going.

I got up slowly and backed away. I didn't have waves but I had this. When I got to the bottom of the hill, into the sinuous trough, I took one last look over my shoulder and ran back to camp beneath the first high stars.

Four days into our week out on the bay, I told Kim we better get on the road. Carlos sent us back to the Baja mainland with a couple of his crew who were going over in an open *panga* to get more fresh water for the camp.

The Beast started up right away, but as we pushed along the smooth sand road under the line of ospreys I noticed the temperature gauge climbing. I stopped in the middle of the road, walked to the back, leaned against her rear end the way you would to a horse, reached down, flipped open the license plate door, checked the plastic coolant reservoir. Empty. Uh-oh.

I retrieved a funnel from under the backseat where we stored our tools, took our six-gallon jug of spare water back, and, while Kim held the funnel, poured almost a gallon into the plastic tank. I'd add straight coolant later to get the proportions right. Now I just wanted her to drink.

The temp gauge settled back to the middle of its arc, but twenty minutes later it was climbing again. I tried slowing down and it rose. I speeded up and it lowered for a few minutes—the faster air flowing by must have helped—and then she climbed again. I turned on the heater. She hesitated, dropped. Good. Climbed again.

We pulled over and this time I dug out a gallon of coolant and added half of it to the reservoir. This was not at all good.

We limped back to Tim's house and he sent us to a VW shop in La Paz just up the hill from Los Arcos. They went through the Beast. No coolant leak they could find. The owner, Rogelio, did say that if there were a breach in the head gasket and coolant was seeping into the oil and burning off in the cylinders, they wouldn't have found it. The compression seemed fine. I wasn't a mechanic, I wanted to get to the mainland, finally, and go surfing, and so I chose to find the whole assessment optimistic. My reasoning was: they didn't find a coolant leak, so there must not be one. Coolant might be leaking into the engine, but the compression was fine, so the engine was fine, so the whole overheating must have been an anomaly, just the Beast being the Beast, and we better get on the ferry. Right?

Not looking at reality head-on when a VW, especially a van, begins to overheat is like ignoring the sharp chest pains that radiate down your left arm and leave you breathless. That is definitely not just something you ate.

We drove the twisty small road north again out of town, past the mangrove cove of Balandra, to the big ferry terminal that sits a half hour from La Paz. We booked tickets for the three of us—the Beast cost the most—on the fast boat and in the early afternoon steered the Beast into the dark maw of the *California Star*, joining a snaking line of every kind of commercial truck and pickup and panel van. At three the whistle blasted, the thick hawsers were loosed from the dock, the big diesels churned and backed from the pier, and we headed out into a windy, slate-gray Sea of Cortez. We had apples and white cheese. We put on sweatshirts and rain gear and went out onto the upper deck and watched the sky flush as we passed the far side of Espiritu Santo, our marriage chapel, and we stayed out, leaning over the rail, pressing our hooded heads together until the sky darkened, and the booming thresh of the bow dropping into each trough was like a lullaby and made us sleepy. The second part of our adventure had begun.

Just When You Thought It Was Safe to Get Back in the Water

Kim was not feeling the same urgency to get back in the water. She never complained, but I could tell. This was a surf trip and she would try her best to learn to surf. I, on the other hand, was going berserk. We were so close. Just on the other side of this ferry ride was Mazatlán, and somewhere near Mazatlán was surf.

We sat down at a table in the large saloon of the ferry and spread out the map. We were landing in Topolobampo. Mazatlán was about a four-hour drive south. So, we would arrive in the middle of the night, sleep somewhere near the ferry terminal, and could be at a surf spot around Mazatlán tomorrow afternoon. On the other hand, the water this far north would still be cold. Not the worst thing to wear a shorty wetsuit, but after half a winter in Colorado, and chilly Baja, the idea of warm water and surfing bareback was appealing. Also, we didn't know any beginner breaks around Mazatlán.

We hadn't surfed in a couple of long months and we would be out of shape and rusty. I'd been swimming as much as I could, but I knew that even swimming didn't translate to strength on a surfboard. The paddling motion, while similar, is not at all the same.

We wanted to start somewhere gentle, someplace where we could stay awhile, camp, rebuild our strength and confidence. We needed a wave that didn't break on rocks or reef, that wasn't too fast or hollow. A sand bottom, something forgiving. We looked at the map. There was Mazatlán a few hours south. We traced our fingers along the coast. And there, farther south, within a day's drive, was Sayulita, a famous beginner's break that would suit all of our purposes.

The highway detoured through a busy market town south of Mazatlán called Escuinapa, the Crossroads. We needed bottled water before hitting the beach. As I pulled over at an open spot on the corner by a grocery store, we heard kids yelling. A bunch of tykes laughed and pointed. I stuck my head out the window. The back of the Beast was shrouded in a cloud of steam and smoke.

Damn. As I climbed down, I thought, *If we're going to break down, let's do it at a wave. Let's get stuck someplace where we can surf every day.*

Kim came back and looked from me to the steam. Arched an eyebrow.

"Out of coolant. Must be a leak. I think if we keep it full, we'll be okay." I turned to the clutch of boys. "Watch the van?" Forked fingers to my eyes and pointed at the Beast, nodded. They shoved in front of each other. "Yo!" "No, yo!"

"*Todos. Diez minutos.*"

We got a twenty-liter bottle of water, refilled the coolant reservoir, and she started right up. Sounded smooth. Okay. We'll get to Tepic this evening, get her checked out, then to the wave tomorrow.

We made it to the open highway. We cruised down it for a couple of miles. Freedom! The wind washing through the open windows, the vibration of the tires, the headlong flight into the districts of dusk! I wanted to look at Kim with a wild surmise. At last, we were on a surf trip. Then the Beast lost power and stumbled like a runner with a heart attack. I looked back. Billow of smoke. Worse than before. Pulled over again.

Now, this was more serious. We were on a highway. The sun was hanging over the dense dark tops of a mango orchard that ran to the horizon. Traffic was sparse.

Don't be on the roads at night. The bandits are worse on the mainland.

The admonition we had heard over and over.

"We've gotta unload the back," I said. "We need to look at the engine."

We did. Unloaded a wall tent, grill, boxes of surf wax, duffels of towels and sleeping bags, first-aid kit, patch kit, solar panel. Made a pile on the shoulder. The sun hit the trees. I lifted off the cushion, untwisted the latches to the engine cover, slid it out. We didn't need a mechanic to tell us that we were screwed: the main ribbed coolant hose was hanging free, dripping green blood, melted right off its coupling.

I looked at Kim. "Fuck."

Now I had several options, one of which was to lean against the Beast and cry. That's what I felt like doing. This was a toll road. There was no help out here. No cheerful local farmers rattling by who could take us back to town. No boisterous picnicking families who would feed us, hitch a rope to our bumper, and yank us back over that hill. On the other hand, if we left the van and hoofed it back to Escuinapa, night would fall on a deliciously packed, brim-full gringo RV; no doubt that when we returned she would have been gleefully stripped.

"Ting," I said.

"Ah, yeah?"

"What does coolant do?"

She looked at me like I'd gone mad. She whisked a mosquito off her face, bent a knee and scratched an ankle. "It keeps the engine cool?"

"That sounds right. It doesn't lube it, right? That's what oil does. Right?"

"I guess."

"We've got to try to drive back to that town. It's only two or three miles. Almost sunset right now. See, the coolant hose is busted. No coolant. But the cylinders should still have oil, right? So if we drive a few minutes and stop, let it cool down, it should run. Right?"

She stared at me. She has a dead-level, opaque expression that guards the door while she weighs two options; it always reminds me of northern steppes and the merciless choices of warfare: *Should I run this guy through with a dagger or kiss him?* "Rrrrright," she said, undecided.

"Okay, let's throw this stuff back in. Any old way. And try."

We made it three hundred yards on the first go. The temp needle wavered, then flew up like a hand touching a hot stove. The red warning light flashed. I pulled over. We waited five minutes. Started up again. Two hundred yards. Once the light flashed we had to get over right away. So far, no more smoke. We limped back north. Miraculously made it to the outskirts of the town. Now, if we could just get to a hotel, we were cool.

Got into a line of evening traffic crawling toward the town

center, between rows of parked cars. The red temperature light flashed. There was no place to pull over. Oh, shit. Horns honking, line of cars behind us.

"There!" Kim pointed to an empty curb ahead on the right. I went straight for it. Pulled in behind . . . a hearse loaded with flowers. Cut the engine. We were in front of a church, in front of the main gate, the wide steps. I looked across the street. A group of ranchers and farmers in pressed snap dress shirts and white palm-leaf cowboy hats stared at me without expression. Black eyes, black and gray mustaches. Very dignified. They were waiting for their buddy to be carried out of the church and we were in the way. I craned around and looked at the tail of the beast. She was pouring smoke.

The men's faces were blank.

"Perdón," I called across the street. *"Hay un hotel cerca?"* They wavered.

"Mi carro está muerto. Finito."

It was like a gust of wind hitting the men. I must have looked like such an idiot, in a cloud of smoke. They laughed. Everything dies. Especially VW vans.

The man at the desk in the lobby of the Hotel IQ was sympathetic. We had barely made the few blocks. He said his brother-in-law was a mechanic. He picked up the hotel phone and called him. "One moment," he said to us in English. "Please."

A guy in grease-blackened clothes showed up ten minutes later on a bike. He carried a screwdriver and a pair of pliers in one hand. Two tools.

"Mi cuñado," the desk clerk said with some pride. *"El mecánico."*

I had expected a tow truck; or a pickup with steel toolboxes along the sides. Two Tools leaned down into the engine, pried off the broken hose, got back on his bike, and vanished around the corner. The narrow street was in shadow and cool. At the end of it, where the church was, we could see a honeyed light warming the plaza. Two Tools was back. He carried a length of new black hose. He worked it onto its pipe, screwed tight the clamps, presto. Fixed. He took my funnel and refilled the coolant tank. Twenty dollars U.S. I gave it to him. I climbed in, slid the key into the ignition, cranked her. This time there was a groan, a death rattle, silence. The funeral procession passed us on the street; the older men nodded at us.

Two Tools licked his lips. *"Tal vez,"* he said, *"el motor."* Yeah, maybe. Good hunch. Before I could agree with him he had pedaled away.

I went inside "Do you have a room?" I said to the clerk.

"Por supuesto. Cuantos noches?"

I looked at Kim. She stared down at her watch as if she had seen a ghost. "What is it?" I asked.

"The Beast, Ting. She died at exactly four forty-four." The Chinese death number. "During a funeral."

Did seem odd. The clerk watched me, waiting for an answer. How many nights here?

That seemed like an existential question. Escuinapa, the Crossroads. The funeral. The surreal scene that had just taken place. The shimmering, slippery time of day, not afternoon, not dusk, the gold light on the plaza. I actually shivered. I looked at the man. Was there anything behind the polite, guileless smile? Was the Hotel IQ kind of like the Hotel California, the one in the song? Where the hell were we?

"One moment." I reached through the driver's-side door to the folded road map between the front seats, opened it, found Mazatlán, Tepic, Sayulita. Escuinapa was not on the map. Goose bumps covered my arms. I had this crazy thought that we might have had a fatal accident out on the highway, not just a breakdown, and that now we were in some sort of limbo town, halfway to heaven, where we could slowly get used to our new predicament. Listen, it's not that crazy. If it were such a stretch, Stephen King wouldn't scare you.

"What is it?" Kim said.

"Nothing." I turned to the clerk. "How about we say two nights? *Dos noches*, okay?"

He held my eyes, tipped his head.

I found a man to help us tow the Beast away from the hotel, out to an engine shop. He had thick strong hands, a bulge of muscle and fat on the back of his neck, ox shoulders, a proud gut. His short ginger hair was combed and oiled, his lips were fleshy, and his blue eyes bulged. It looked like his top front teeth had been filed flat across. Sergio. He ran the large junkyard on the outskirts of town, but for all we could tell he may have run the town as well. Everywhere we went in his Chevy pickup, people waved.

"Responsibilidad," he said, patting his chest. Rapid Spanish, the gist of which was, "We don't want a *borracho* to fix it and then she blows up again. Someone needs to be responsible."

This would take some days. In the meantime, Sergio picked us up at the Hotel IQ twice a day and took us to different places to eat. For Sergio the landscape was culinary.

On the first morning, bumping up a quiet dirt street of low concrete houses with barred windows and wrought-iron gates, Sergio coughed into a fist and said, "Pe-TER." He said it with great seriousness and gravity. He was about to ask a question that would determine the course of events.

"Sí?"

"Escuche." Listen.

"Sí."

"A ustedes les gustan tamales?"

I loved tamales. He was relieved. "Unnh," he growled, nodding to himself. *"Bueno."* Another block and he turned full in the seat and pointed out my window, cocking his wrist, straight finger, like an umpire calling a strike.

"Tamales de puerco," he said, pointing at a curtained window. He said it as if he were showing me a site of great historical significance. His bulging eyes widened with pleasure. His heavy face lit with joy.

"Wow," I said.

Two blocks later he pointed out his side at a green-painted house with a long table in the street. *"Tamales de pollo,"* he said.

After a week, the notion of actually getting to a beach and surfing seemed impossibly remote. Every day Sergio took us to the brick-walled yard where the Beast was being worked on. We were waiting now for a delivery of carburetor seals. And every day I went down to the Hotel IQ desk and paid the clerk for another night. Stranded. I liked the early mornings. I walked alone across the plaza and had *café con leche* at the same table, made by the same old woman, and watched the square and the town come alive, the caciques and blackbirds raising their ruckus in the old trees, and every morning I brought Kim back a cup to have in bed. We had given up trying to find out if the Crossroads actually existed. It seemed to exist. If this was some limbo between earth and wherever else, it could have been worse.

In the long evenings I sometimes accompanied Sergio on his rounds, picking up the junks of Escuinapa. Up a muddy lane, a terribly poor family sat all together in front of some single-room cinder-block shack. How had they gotten a hold of a car? Even one that didn't run? They sat on the step in the warm twilight and waited for the junk man, and they signed the paperwork and accepted the check from Sergio as if he were a god. He expertly backed the flatbed trailer up the hill, his crew jumped out of the truck, and, with help from half a dozen neighbors, they ran and rolled the defunct sedan up into the trailer for its last ride. I enjoyed these sorties. There was an esprit de corps among the junk men, a sense of some sort of nobility, as if they, in their noblesse, helped families survive, and helped others keep their sorry junkers running. Which was true. Definitely a prestige profession.

Sergio and I had fallen into an easy way with each other. We laughed a lot. He continued to feed us, fattening us up like Hansel and Gretel. I stopped counting the days and began measuring our time in town in approximate weight gain. He liked to host us for picnics out at the junkyard. It was sweet eating tamales among the dismembered cars, under a heavy, rising moon. If he bought me a meal, I bought the next one. I insisted. It was clear that he adored Kim. She made fun of him, calling his office "Restaurante Casa del Yonke." House of Junkyard Restaurant. He loved it. I don't think anyone in his life made fun of him. We had become friends. I had stopped wondering why he spent so much time feeding us, and rarely brought his son, Sergito, and never brought his wife. I figured it was kind of a vacation for the man.

I had never met anyone like Sergio. Here was a guy completely at home with himself, in command of his small country, a guy who gave his son a piñata a day. At pound nine, which was about day ten, the motor rebuilder told us the Beast was ready; it was time for us to go. I was sad. Sergio had been a prince. I had been expecting that somehow we would never be able to leave this place we never did find on a map. But it wasn't like that. We drove away, got on the big toll road, passed the spot where we'd broken down, and continued toward Tepic.

We hadn't been driving two hours when I was overcome with fever. My vision blurred. A terrible fatigue submerged me. I pulled over into a field and asked Kim to drive. Just follow this down to the coast, I said, and fell asleep.

I dreamed of waves. Cold black waves that exploded like ordnance and shuddered the beach. Ranks, tiers, out to the horizon, one giant looking over the next. They thundered in. An angry wind poured down off the cliffs to meet them like an opposing army and ripped the tops back in plumes of spray almost as long and bloody as the waves were high. But it was not liquid water, it was snow. The wind was shredding the waves into an ocean-borne blizzard. I stood on the beach, barefoot, holding a short surfboard. I was wearing nothing but shorts and was shivering. My teeth clattered. Those waves. They were the only thing I had left to do in my life. That was all I knew, standing there, while my ears sifted from the chaos the sound of boulders rolling on the seabed beneath the charging water

I woke up crying out, started up in the front seat. The van's AC was blowing into my neck and chest. Cold.

"Where are we?"

"Just passed Morelia. We're in the mountains. See, pine trees."

Kim was sitting up straight, driving with hands eleven and one o'clock on the wheel the way they teach you in driver's ed. "How do you feel?"

"Did you take driver's ed literally?"

"They showed us those horrible crash movies. After that I did everything they said except obey the speed limit." I looked at her. The things we never knew about our wife.

"I had a dream. Scary. Sort of. Can't remember much. I feel like shit."

We came out of the mountains onto a coastal plain of small farms. We had decided to skip Sayulita, go south of there where it would be less crowded. One more precipitous coastal range in front of us in a high humping wall. A bright orange steel bridge over a low-flowing river. Horses stood in the current. Palms and bright green cane along the banks, low fields of maize. We busted through the Sierra and hit the coast at Manzanillo. Skirted the town and found the coastal road north. Kim drove. I just wanted to curl up somewhere and sleep for a week. A narrow ribbon of broken pavement wound through the lovely hills of Michoacán. I remembered the tall cacti coming down to the beaches, the blue-water coves, the bocote trees flowering white, and the tiny hamlets. I had been here with Leonel Pérez a few years before, just after learning to surf from the Saint that first time. I had come to do a magazine story about the Mexican Masters champion and left even more determined to meet surfing one day on its own terms. Now I lay back in the front seat, closed my eyes, and let images of that trip roll in like waves.

Riding with the King

Kim drove and in my fever I remembered.

"Almost ready?" Leon had asked me that every morning. Since I was standing beside his two-door Chevy completely transfixed by the waves and hadn't taken off my shirt or waxed my board—and since it was still dark, and we hadn't had breakfast or coffee—I took it as a metaphysical question, like, *Are you ready to believe in a force much bigger than you?*

As I watched the tiers of surf near the Pacific resort town of Ixtapa, I realized that there were three things I now appreciated about surfing as a near-beginner: the raw beauty of waves; the anticipation of getting repeatedly thrashed; the possibility of one good ride, a kind of fleeting touch of grace. Also, my coach. I couldn't believe he was even standing up after last night's party.

Leon rubbed wax briskly over the deck of a board propped against his thigh. He was in training for the nationals in Baja's Ensenada in two months, and he couldn't bear to miss a wave.

He was honing himself like a weapon. He didn't wear a rash guard or sunscreen. His baggy shorts came below his knees. He was forty-six years old, short (about five-foot-six), broad-shouldered, and wiry. His ears were small. His nose, broken years ago, was slightly flattened. Even his buzzed hair was thinning, as if obliging a lifelong imperative toward sleekness. It occurred to me, watching him, that he was a man completely shaped by the sea.

Only four hours ago, Leon had been working on his second bottle of tequila *blanco*. Café tables had been shoved together outside his surf shop, Catcha L'Ola ("Catch the Wave"), behind the row of tall hotels lining Ixtapa's shore. A bunch of local surfers, four Texas longboarders, a pair of tourist police with shotguns, brothers and sisters of Leon, and two young women on holiday from Brooklyn were annihilating cases of Corona. The mother of Leon's two-year-old daughter was warily grilling redfish. Leon worshipped his daughter, whom he named Auramar—Aura of the Sea—but only tolerated the mother, who, he said, tricked him into having a child and once threw stones at his girlfriend. The fiesta was in honor of his forty-sixth birthday. Today would be another party.

"The waves look bigger today," I suggested.

"There is a swell coming. You are ready."

"I guess I am."

I was going to try a shorter 7–6 board for the first time, a personal threshold. I was Leon's age, and most guys who start surfing late stick with the more stable, less responsive long-boards. To hell with that: I was having a midlife crisis. This was my party and I could cry if I wanted to.

"You don't even look hungover," I said to Leon.

Now he looked up. He smiled—I could tell because the left side of his mouth lifted just a little.

"Practice." He tossed the wax to me over the hood of the car and nodded at the local kids carrying boards who were beginning to trickle in from the road. They had walked the last mile from the end of the bus route from Zihuatanejo, eight miles down the coast. They regarded Leon with specific awe: he would catch many more waves than any of them today, and have better rides, which was unnatural, since some of the younger boys had grandfathers Leon's age. Yet Leon was nonchalant about his status as the old master. "I just surf every day," he said simply.

I looked behind us. Out of the mountains, unbending slowly from dense groves of coconut palms, pushed the sweet water of the Río La Laja. The sun had not yet risen over the Sierra Madre del Sur, so the dark water reflected only a rose wash of dawn and the light of a single fisherman's fire burning on the sand. The river cut the beach and emptied into the sea where the surf broke over the sandbar. Even in the half-light I could see that the sets were easily head-high.

Leon straightened and turned toward the beach. And then, since he taught with the minimalism of a Zen master, he gave me the lesson of the morning. He was not at all like the Saint.

"Paddle toward the peaks. On that board, you have to be at the peak."

"Okay."

"Lock the car door."

"Okay."

Then he jogged toward the water.

It wasn't surprising that Leon didn't believe in holding a student's hand: all his life, his only teacher had been the thumping waves. As a small boy, living in a tiny village called Chutla, up the rugged Guerrero coast, he saw a neighbor who had been to California as a migrant worker wearing a T-shirt with a picture of a surfer shooting a tube. Six-year-old Leon kept thinking about that barrel. A few years later he began to see vans of American hippies with boards on the roofs passing on the narrow, potholed coastal road. "I was thinking," Leon said, pointing to his sun-burnished head, *"I want to do that."*

When his father, a traveling electric-appliance salesman, moved the family to Zihuatanejo—then a small beach town with one dirt road out to the highway—Leon stole a scrap of plywood from a wood shop and began boogie-boarding. When he was twelve he heard that an American friend of Jacques Cousteau's who lived across the bay had a longboard. Leon and a dozen other local kids asked to borrow it and took turns, and a local surf culture was born.

The same phenomenon of scrappy local kids hitting the waves any way they could was occurring up and down Mexico's Pacific coast. Unlike California surfing, born in the early 1900s, the sport in Mexico didn't have a direct pollination from Hawaii, with its centuries-old surf culture. There was no Duke Kahanamoku bringing showy exhibitions and aloha spirit; there were only wayward gringos. American legends Bud Browne and Greg Noll took some trips to Acapulco and Mazatlán in the late fifties, but, according to Nathan Myers, a historical-minded editor at *Surfing* magazine, Californians didn't start poking down the coast of mainland Mexico in significant numbers until the 1960s, after the Gidget movies and the Beach Boys craze had ignited the American surfing boom that suddenly crowded California's beaches. The majority of the first Mexican surfers were the sons of poor fishermen and hotel workers. I asked Arturo Astudillo, now fifty-two, one of the early Mexican pioneers around Acapulco, how he and his friends got their first boards. "We stole them," he said. He hung his head. "I am sorry. It was the only way."

By the late seventies, Leon, then a teenager, was shredding. He bargained with gringos for beat-up boards. He dripped candle wax on the decks for traction and made his own leashes out of surgical tubing. He began working in the booming new tourist center of Ixtapa. One morning, he and a friend named Antonio Ochoa paddled out into a wickedly fast hollow break beside Ixtapa's recently built breakwater. No one had attempted it before. They dropped in on an overhead, right-breaking barrel that blasted them through a tube like buckshot. The wind at their backs almost flattened them. They came back the next morning, and the next, and named it Las Escolleras, the Jetties. Then they began exploring northward, finding the Río La Laja break on the other side of a crocodile swamp.

They heard about a legendary Mexican surfer from Acapulco named Evencio García Bibiano, who everybody said was like a demon on the waves. In 1978, they went to watch him compete at the first Mexican national competition on the mainland, at a break in Guerrero called Petacalco, a fifteen-foot barrel that broke dependably twice a day. García, despite long nights spent partying, was beautiful, almost frightening, to watch.

Leon never missed a day on the waves. When he was twenty-four, he became a waiter at the club Carlos'n Charlie's, right on the beach in Ixtapa, a five-minute walk from the

Jetties. At Carlos'n Charlie's, every night is spring break, and Leon quickly became chief party maker. He wore his shirt unbuttoned to his waist, danced on the tables, judged bikini contests, administered a devastating sangria from a spouting pitcher. He knocked back tequila every night and was such a ladies' man that he is still called El Tigre. He dated models and TV stars, often didn't sleep, and, when the sun came up, grabbed his board and went surfing. When the onshore winds blew out the waves in the late morning, he'd nap for a couple of hours, then come back to the bar and load up the donkey with buckets of ice and beer.

"The donkey's name was Lorenzo," Leon said. "We shared free beers on the beach, for advertising. As soon as he saw me open the first beer, he chased me down. I taught him to drink. By the time we came back, he was drunk.

"Too much party," Leon admitted. After fifteen years in the fastest lane, he downshifted to a slower one, surfing with single-minded devotion and opening his shop. He, a sister, and two younger brothers started renting boards, giving lessons, and taking customers on day trips to nearby breaks. And once Leon got serious about competing, he won the nationals in his shifting age class—over-forty in 2002 and everybody over-thirty-five in 2004. There are few men alive who know the Pacific coast of Mexico as well as Leon.

I changed into a snug rash guard, locked the car, and picked up the 7–6 board. By now there were a dozen surfers bobbing thirty yards offshore. I didn't want to compete for waves today, but if I did, these teenagers—unlike the locals in California—wouldn't mind. They were tolerant, even encouraging. On one of our first days there when I collided with a local kid—my bad—he didn't emerge from the tumble yelling a bunch of fuck-offs. I said, *"Lo siento,"* and he shrugged and smiled, as if to say, *Don't worry, we all sucked at the beginning.*

The air was chilly. I turned down a smooth path toward the beach. Far out in front, I could see the swell form and break. I could see the small figures of four surfers.

At a tangled pile of drift logs, I unwound the leash from the board and secured the Velcro strap at my ankle. Then I waited for a little shore wave to break, jogged into the water, jumped onto the board, and started to paddle. The strong tug of the rip current pulled northward. I made it over a few steep swells and hit a low ridge of whitewater, paddling hard. It flooded over me, stopped my progress. I bobbed up paddling like a possessed turtle, shoulders burning, and when I shook my eyes clear, the only thing in front of me was a pelican and a head-high wall already breaking. Oh, shit. Duck-dive! Wait until the white pile is almost on top of you. Big breath. Rock the nose down hard with both hands, press the tail down with one foot . . . Yes! When I buoyed to the top, the wave was past. Dang. "Paddle again even before you can see," Leon had said. I did and made it over the next wave just as it peaked. And then there was only open, rolling water. Phew. For me, there was always this race to get past the break, always a little desperate.

I caught my breath and looked left in time to see Leon hunting the next set. While the other three surfers were just sitting on their boards, he was already moving, paddling smooth and fast, angling both toward deeper water and down the beach. Abruptly, he spun. He was just in front of a perfect peak, the rounded top of a glassy, inexorably forming mountain. No one else had seen it coming. And then he was an explosion of motion. "Everything moves," a local told me with a grin, describing Leon catching a wave: his arms windmilled, his feet kicked in a violent flurry. Leon had told me, "Paddle like your life depends on it." But what you remembered most was his expression: he looked like a gunfighter in the middle of a fast draw against five men. When the wave was steepest, hanging for a split second at its own angle of repose, with just the top beginning to fold, Leon was up, rocketing left down the wall with the speed of a diving tern. He was crouched, perfectly balanced, the wave ripping white down the line, un-peeling behind him and trying to devour him like a jaw. He stood upright and pumped, bouncing the front of his board for more speed, swung up to the stiff lip, and caromed down off it in another crouching swoop. I laughed out loud.

I was thinking, like the six-year-old Leon, *I want to do that.*

On my fifth day in Mexico, Leon and I drove the five hours down the coast to Acapulco for the Torneo Evencio García Bibiano, a Guerrero State selection qualifier that Leon would have to win in order to go to Ensenada. García, for whom the competition was named, was the legend Leon had first seen compete in '78. He was from Acapulco, and at a 1985 championship at Playa Bonfil, south of town, he used the home-field advantage and devastated the competition. He was a quintes-sential fearless big-wave rider and the first native to do aerials and floaters and 360s. On his last heat he already had more than enough points to take first place, but he had a few min-utes left before the horn, so he paddled back out for one more ride—just for show. Before a crowd of a thousand spectators he took off on a steep left and it closed out and collapsed. He seemed to kick out over the back side. His board flew into the air, then . . . nothing. The board washed onto the beach, and no one ever saw him again.

In a superstitious culture, García has become the resident spirit of Mexico's waves. Surfers will tell you with a straight face he was transformed instantly into a dolphin, who still patrols and protects surfers. He was El Campeón, the Champion, claimed by heaven, and every time a wall of green water rises out of the sea, a surfer may sense García's ghost gliding like a dolphin down the line. I met a twenty-five-year-old top surfer named Julio Cesar La Palma, whom everyone calls La Pulga—the Flea—and when I asked him if he had a hero, he blinked and put his hand on his chest. "Sometimes," he said, "I dream that Evencio García is surfing in my body."

If García were there on that Sunday in November, he would certainly have heard "Guantanamera" booming out of the giant speakers next to the judges' platform—not the old song but the hip-hop version by Wyclef Jean, Celia Cruz, and Lauryn Hill. Leon was out in the surf loosening up. I recognized him right away even from a distance—his bullet head, his constant roving back and forth, hunting. In surf, he rarely stops paddling, even between sets, his eyes on the horizon.

"*Guantanameeera . . .*"

According to the big posted roster, Leon's finals heat was coming up. At the top of some crumbling steps off the sand, wedged between a palm tree and a shaded slab of concrete covered with plastic chairs, where surfers were eating *sopa de mariscos,* seafood soup, was a beat-up white Chevy van with PRENSA painted in block letters across the front. It didn't look like any press van I'd ever seen. A wooden skeleton in sunglasses was chained to the grille. A faded xerox of a dog was taped to a window, with the words CUIDADO! PELIGROSO! I could see why: chained underneath were two tawny pit bulls.

A short, thin-faced young man with a sparse mustache hustled around from the back of the van. His loose hair hung down his shirtless back. He had skull tattoos and a skull pendant, and his official government press card hung on a necklace of shells and claws of black coral, along with a fancy Nikon. I introduced myself, and he ducked his head agreeably. *"Andale,"* he said, and pushed aside a bamboo curtain across the van's open side door. He sat against a bag of dog food, under a poster of Bob Marley.

Oscar Diego Morales, a.k.a. "Fly," was a roving reporter for *Planeta Surf La Revista,* a magazine by, for, and about Mexican surfers. It's slick and fun, splashed with Aztec design motifs, crisp action photos, and ads for Mexican beachwear. The second issue had just hit the stands. Oscar told me that surfing in Mexico was at a tipping point. It was growing more popular by the month. "Every time a good swell is forecast, more and more people come out," he said. Then suddenly, hearing a particularly irresistible riff from the speakers on the beach, Oscar leapt out of his seat and, bent over, began to do a crazy little dance to the music. He sat back down. I asked him how many dedicated surfers he thought there were now in the country, and he began, remarkably, to tick off each major break.

"Puerto Escondido, sixty . . . Acapulco, twenty-five . . . Ensenada, fifty . . . Mazatlán, fifteen . . . San Blas, fifteen. Nobody knows," he concluded. (Matt Warshaw, who wrote the seminal *Encyclopedia of Surfing,* estimates there are thirty thousand native surfers in the country, though Mexicans say there are far fewer.)

"What's with the skulls everywhere?" I asked.

"Skulls? Oh. No matter if you have green eyes, blue eyes, white skin—in the end everybody is going to be the skull. It's the true face at the end of our life."

As I left the van, a small pickup skidded to a stop at the end of the sand street, and ten shirtless teens with boogie boards and shortboards jumped out. Some had fade haircuts with long, red-streaked tops. Earrings, eyebrow piercings, blond-streaked ponytails.

"Hey," I called, "where are you guys from?"

Playa Princesa, a break a few miles up the coast.

"Are you students?"

Most of them worked as lifeguards and in restaurants for a few dollars a day. Another generation.

Back down on the beach, I found Leon. His final master's heat was about to start. He was with some other surfers in the shade of a *palapa*, stretched out in a plastic chair, drinking from a water bottle. He looked much too relaxed.

"Isn't your heat coming up?"

"In a few minutes. I am ready." I was more nervous than he was. I felt like a soccer dad.

We heard the blast of a horn announcing five minutes to go. Leon stood, stretched his arms back like a man waking up, grabbed his tiny board. How long can a warrior keep going to war? He reminded me of the graying soldier in *The Seven Samurai*, the one who would always survive on seasoned judgment, discipline, and patience. Then it occurred to me that I was Leon's age and I was just starting. What would I survive on?

Twenty minutes later, Leon won his final heat handily. He was now a Guerrero State champion, heading to the nationals. He also won the open longboard class. He shrugged it off. That night, after four days in Acapulco, we drove back up the coast to Ixtapa in the dark. We arrived too late to find a room for me, so I slept on the floor of his apartment, in a concrete block at the edge of the tourist zone, crowded by jungle. I slept under a shelf of trophies, a rack of six bagged boards, and a photo collage of Leon's younger brother Alejandro, who died in a motorcycle wreck fourteen years ago. The young man held a surfboard in half the pictures, was as handsome as Leon, and looked very happy. "His nickname was Karma," Leon said before he turned in. "Everybody loved him. He was a very good surfer. That is why we name the annual tournament in Ixtapa 'the Karma.'" I saw a flicker of emotion cross Leon's usually inscrutable face. Then he said, "You have been working hard. You can do it, the big wave. Practice more. Tomorrow I will take you north." Then he flicked off the light. I went to sleep listening to the calls of a loud night bird and thinking how everything is connected: Evencio García and La Pulga; Leon and his brother Alejandro; Antonio Ochoa and Oscar and me. And the waves out of the Pacific, which were now pounding the long, empty coast in the dark.

The next morning, Leon jostled me awake in pitch-blackness.

"Almost ready?"

"Are you crazy?" I could see his white teeth floating like a canted moon.

First we surfed Río La Laja, and then we started driving north. We passed through the industrial town of Lázaro Cárdenas, where the legendary tube of Petacalco used to break, before they built a dam on the Río Balsas. We drove into the desolate, lovely country of Michoacán. Tall saguaro cacti came down to the beaches. The road snaked over high bluffs and around rock coves that cradled blue water. We drove in third gear. The foothills were covered with white-flowering bocote trees, and rioting bougainvillea edged the dooryards of the sparse villages. It was like a more tortured Highway 1, but empty, with the Pacific crashing on the rocky points and fringing the long beaches with peeling waves. Mainland Mexico has twenty-five hundred miles of Pacific coastline— enough surf for a millennium.

Leon and I spent three days at Río Nexpa, where there was no phone or running freshwater, just a point break and a beach break going off all at once and a long, cupped strand with a few dozen thatch-roofed cabins built for surfers, each with a balcony and a hammock. On the second evening, Leon sat on the porch rail, drinking a beer, looking out at the ocean. I swung in the hammock, replaying in my head a long ride I'd had that afternoon. A surprising set had loomed, and I found myself in position, suddenly taking off on a fast overhead left and looking down at the pod of other surfers, who seemed far below. Some cheered. I popped up and crouched, and when I'd gotten ahead of the crashing white, I roller-coastered to the top of the lip and shot back down. The sensation was one of the finest I'd ever had. In my life.

"Look at the moon," Leon said. It was nearly full, rising out of the palms past the point. The sun was still a few degrees off the water, burnishing the tiers of breaking waves. A faint onshore breeze brought in the sound, a rhythmic thresh almost like breath. I didn't think he was waxing poetic—I knew what he was thinking: after the sun went down, there would always be the moon. He was already taking off his shirt.

"Aren't you tired?" I said. I think we'd surfed five hours already.

"A little. Almost ready?"

I stared at him. I burst out laughing. "What's my lesson for the day? You forgot to give it to me."

The left side of his mouth lifted just a little. "Surf whenever you can."

Opened my eyes. Kim was still at the wheel. Michoacán was still out the window. I sat up, turned off the horrid AC, opened my window to the turgid heat, inhaled the smell of the sea. Right away I felt better. Even dead I would feel better in the baffles of a stiff wind coming off the ocean. Consign me, then, to the sea.

"I can drive now, Ting. I know where we're going now. I remember this road from before."

"Feel better?"

"Oh, man. Finally. Look where we are."

"Not a tamale in sight."

"Thank God."

She reached out, searched out my head with a blind hand, stuck a finger in my ear.

THE RIVER

It bent out of the mangroves, the palm groves, the tall bocote trees flecked with white egrets. It widened into a generous lagoon before it coursed and riffled over the bar and crossed the beach. Emptied into the wild bay. Behind the river and the jungle of trees loomed the Sierra Madre. Felt old here, wild and ancient. A brontosaurus could lumber out of the palms, wade into the estuary, and he'd be at home. Except that a couple of fishermen who were casting hand nets in the brackish water would have heart attacks.

Squatting above the slow current, I counted three species of heron hunched on the mudflat of the far bank. There were skittering sandpipers, slender pink-legged stilts, a great egret long-necked and leaning on one leg over his own snowy reflection. In counterpoint, four soot-black cormorants at water's edge spread their drying wings to the early sun. Faces turned away, as if the exercise were distasteful. Their wings were ragged, their pose a parody of crucifixion, they were disreputable in appearance, and I thought as I watched and loved them that it was because they were diving birds who swam as well as flew, caught their fish in a submarine sprint, and I thought how most beings that straddled two worlds looked suspect to those who remained in just one. Why we were scared of bats. Of crabs and vampires and shamans. Why surfers have a badass rep.

Barra Llorona is ruled by birds. Almost every morning royal terns convened by the score on the beach above the lagoon. They all faced the same direction. If it was windy they closed their eyes. They seemed to be listening to a concert. Out along the surf line the squadrons of pelicans rolled in effortless single file. Three beats of the great wings, the line flowed upward, following the same precise arc as if over an invisible rise; then glide, sink to the swell, wings a millimeter off the water, never touching. When there were baitfish, the birds broke apart into a confusion of circling bombers who tucked wings and plunged with explosions of spray. So did the boobies. Smaller, grayer, they fell out of the sky with a fantastic and deadly corkscrew. Folded their wings on the way. Hit the water, one then one then one, like a rain of arrows. High over them all, arched, black, angular, fork-tailed, and crooked winged like a terror of prehistory circled the magnificent frigate birds. That's not my adjective, that's their name: *Frigata magnificens*. Wingspan of something like ten feet. Unlike most other pelagic birds, they can't settle to the swell and rest. They would sink and drown. The ocean is their mother but they can never sleep on her lap. Should they dive for a baitfish and get clobbered by a breaking whitecap, they are finished. Watching them work, I held my breath. It seemed unnecessarily dangerous.

Vultures ventured out over the river and onto the beach. Especially if there was a dead dog rolling in the tide wash. Pink headed, in the way of a raw wound, they landed on the dog. One hop, tentative, then a surge of whitewater rolled and washed the carcass and the birds lifted off, alighted tried again. It was clear they knew they were not seabirds. Not even shore birds, really. They just loved dead things and this dead thing happened to be awash.

We decided to camp in a palm grove on the south side of the lagoon. Lining out northward across the bay were a series of clean waves. We could watch them from our camp. Nothing else. No houses, no hotels. Just the curve of the shore out to the spuming cliffs of Punto Final—Last, or Final, Point.

It was late November. In another month the dry season would really take hold high in the mountains and the river would lose its push and no longer be able to vanquish the sandbar and release into the sea. It would become a lake. But now it still flowed unimpeded into the salt, met the dissipated surge of the breaking waves with a fine chop at low tide. It may have been knee-deep. At higher tide, or with a big incoming swell, it lay down and let the ocean flood in with the rhythm of the break.

The engine had barely shut off when I slid out of the Beast and walked for the first time into the shade under the coconut palms. I took one look at the river, the bay, the backing mountains, and my spirit went prostrate in relief. Here we were. Here was an actual wave. Here was no reason to move.

We set up our supersized screen room tent with the rolldown canvas walls and I spread out a tarp on the sand, still in a feverish daze from what I was recognizing now as a month of real stress. I lay out one of our flannel sleeping bags for cushioning and collapsed, plunged into a rocking, dreamless sleep.

When I woke, Kim was holding a real glass of fresh-squeezed orange juice. The sun had dropped nearly to the sea and was flooding through the screen, the gold color of the juice. In her other hand she held a thermometer.

"Where did you get that stuff?"

"Jean-Pierre."

"Oh."

"He's in the VW parked by the road. He's so cool, Ting. He's like sixty-something and he's down here from Quebec for the whole winter learning to surf like us. Here, lift your tongue . . ."

The orange juice was delicious, sweet, floating with seeds. The thermometer tasted like rubbing alcohol.

"You should see his rig. He's a builder in Quebec, he speaks funny English. He outfitted the whole thing himself. It's got a shower, Ting. Hot water. And this shaving mirror that extends off the back door. Isn't that cool?"

"Hmp—"

"Keep it under your tongue. He has a wine cellar in there—"

"Hmp?—"

"Well, it's just a little three-bottle wine rack, but he calls it the wine cellar. 'Ah, come wiz me, I show you ze wine cellar, ah-hah!' He's a hoot. 'Welcome to Café Jean-Pierre,' he says. He has an espresso maker, of course."

"Wumph?—"

"His girlfriend is coming to visit in a couple of weeks. She's like thirty years younger. They drove down here together, but she doesn't like the beach much. Here—"

She yanked out the thermometer, held it up to the blood

rays of the setting sun. I could hear a cacique in the palms, a strangled guttural shriek. I could hear the throb of waves. Where had we landed? Some kind of paradise. Complete with a New World Frenchman with a milk steamer. Praise the Lord.

"A hundred and one-point-five, Ting. Kinda high. Here, take some aspirin with the last sip. Good. You wanna go back to sleep?" I dropped off again. At some point I woke in deep dusk and I heard Kim laughing up by the road. Another voice: "You tink it not true, something like dat, I cannot believe my-self . . ." Through the screen I could see that she had set up our raft-trip table, the one that unrolled, with the screw-in legs, and set the lantern on top. I could see the shadows of two lawn chairs and the desultory curve of the hammock between two palms. A deep smile warmed my fluttery guts. Home. Home is sweet.

I slept for two days. On the third I woke in the early dark and shook myself off like a dog. Did a quick scan, checked all systems. Head? Check. No longer felt like an oven. Felt clear, cool. Stomach? Check. Hungry. Limbs? Weak, but steady. Looking for action.

I looked over at Kim. In the first wan light I could see ants crawling on her face and neck. Oh, boy, not good. I brushed and blew them off. She stirred, protested. Today we'd drive to town and buy two cots. Nothing wrong with cots. Marital relations are possible on a safari.

I shook her shoulder. "Hey, hey."

"Wanhproughhdf."

"Hey, let's go surfing. Remember that?"

"Frwbrdmh!"

"Great, okay. I'll get our boards. I'll wax yours. We have cereal, right? And powdered milk. In the blue cooler, right? You've been eating it. And coffee? Get up, Ting. Do your hair and stuff. Surf, Ting, surf!"

She burrowed down into the bag and covered her head.

The first morning back always takes a while. What had become in Baja an unconscious and swift rhythm of preparation was once again a halting stumble from board bag to wax box. From duffel—where were all those extra leashes?— to clothes container—somewhere in this one were our rash guards. Where did we shove the sunscreen? And then, while Kim put in her contacts and braided her hair, I had to stop and look again through the ringed trunks of the palms in a kind of dumbstruck awe. River mouth, sand spit, beyond them the whole curve of the bay. And now, in the first strong light, I could see a wave ripping in front of the *boca*, kind of dumpy, but farther north, out toward the middle of the bay, a clean left. The wave rose, shivered, crumbled, then sent a tear of white unreeling across open water. The line of spume caught the rising sun full-front and was lit like a cornice of snow. It reminded me of a Himalaya at daybreak. The early breeze, which I couldn't feel here but must have been blowing down the river valley and over the beach, was gaily spraying back the lip. Already there were half a dozen surfers bobbing out there, and I watched them catch the wave. It was fast, but not too fast—a three-month beginner on top of his game could probably catch and ride it. Looked about shoulder-high this morning. Perfect. I watched a longboarder paddle for one and catch it. Drop down the face, trim out dead sideways halfway down the wall of water, and ride it straight down the line, arrow-straight, all the way across the front of the bay, must have been a quarter-mile ride. Wow.

As I watched I saw a compact man walk through the grove with a funboard, maybe 7–6. He had thick gray hair and the slightly humped posture of men who have worked with their backs all their lives. He looked over, waved, smiled. Must be the famous Jean-Pierre. How cool to drop everything and come all the way from Quebec to learn to surf. To be sixty-plus and do that. I marveled. Hey, wait—it was just what we were doing. And I had felt ancient, beginning to surf at forty-five.

We had to paddle across the river. We hefted the boards and walked under the trees to a bank of tumbled stones. Mangroves crowded over them. We skirted the branches. A green heron, hunched on a limb, stretched in readiness for flight.

"Stay cool. Passing through." The bird eyed me with what could be malice, settled back. I reached out, touched a leathery leaf, tasted my finger. Salty. Amazing that these trees sink their roots straight into the tide. Many species deal with the extra salt by excreting it in a crystalline dust on the surface of their leaves. Mangroves are the nursery of the sea. Thousands of species of fish, birds, crustaceans, insects, and mammals shelter and breed in their roots and limbs. The forests clean the water by trapping sediment in their roots. Yet so few of these mangroves are left in the world. Coastal development has devastated them. Studies show worldwide mangrove loss of between 30 to 70 percent in just the last thirty to forty years. Half of what is left is in poor condition. At the same time, the estuaries they shelter are being radically degraded by pollution and engineering, or simply filled in and eliminated. I could hardly bear to think about it. This morning I wanted to start having fun again.

The river was cool. The water limpid. I could hear a cicada buzzing in the trees and the wash of the surf on the other side of the rising sand. As we cleared the bank and paddled out into the middle of the lagoon, the sweep of the Sierra inland was revealed. The mountains were high. Now, this early, they were shadows, a great rugged bulk shouldering a sky streaked with wisps of burning rose. We could see the deep cut, the long furrow in the foothills that must be the river valley. The first sun poured down it and lit the jungle on the far bank of the lagoon, which reverberated with green. Three egrets flew out of the trees, right over our heads. They did to the sunlight something different than the waves, just as white, but cupping shadow with each deep beat of their wings. Upstream, a dead tree stuck out of the river covered from end to end with preening pelicans. A frigate bird, circling high, peeled out and dropped, skimmed the lagoon, flicked a furrow in the water. Probably drinking.

Quietly, we paddled beneath it all. Clambered onto the sand on the far side and walked up the beach on gravel washed with foam. Small smooth stones, shiny and wet, beneath a steep cutbank of sand. We could hear them roll and sift with each rush of the inshore break—a deep crushing sound as the water pushed over them, a higher, lighter hiss as it sieved back. I couldn't keep from watching the bay: beyond the inshore chop the clean wave rose up and defined itself. It took the roughening touch of the wind across its face and frayed at the top, in spuming white.

We laid our boards on the sand and watched Jean-Pierre paddle out farther down the beach where he could more easily get around the exhausted shoulder of the wave. He paddled like a beginner, like we all do in the first few months—a lot of arm-waving and flailing but the board not moving very fast. Also, he lay with his torso on the board and his chin almost touching it, as if it cost too much effort to lift his chest, which in the beginning it does.

"See?" I pointed. "Looks like we might have an easier time going out up there. Where Jean-Pierre is going."

"Whateva."

"Aren't you jazzed, to get back in the water?"

She pursed and pushed her lips out like a little kid pondering whether to dump the flower vase off the side table. She rubbed her nose with the flat of her palm. "Let's see. 'Jazzed.' I just got—Hold on." She pointed a finger at one ankle at a time, up each leg, around to her back, to her ear. "Eight new mosquito bites. And we haven't even gotten in the water."

"Yeah, but there are no mosquitoes in the water."

"Whateva."

"C'mon, Ting, put your leash on, let's go. Follow me out."

"You're always rushing me." She was serious now, and mad. "I've got to stretch."

"Ting. First the hair. Then sunscreen every inch. Then stretch. We'll be lucky to get out there at noon."

I sounded peevish, I know. I should have been grateful she even agreed to come down here with me. I mean, she wasn't even having a midlife crisis.

I was becoming torn with frustration. The waves looked really good. In half an hour there would be more surfers, probably. Every cell of me wanted to charge into the water and get my first wave in months, but it would be very bad diplomacy to leave Kim standing on the beach to fight her way out all alone at a new break on this first morning. It would be outrageously selfish, bordering on dangerous neglect.

I bent down, strapped the Velcro cuff to my ankle, and picked up the board.

"I'll wait in the water," I said.

What an asshole. What I was really saying was: *if I were single and not married and not responsible for anyone else, as has*

*been the case for most of my self-absorbed life, then I would have
been out on the waves almost an hour ago.*

I glanced back to see what effect that last volley might
have had. She shook her head. When she's really pissed and
frustrated she doesn't make faces like white women do. Her
face becomes a disciplined mask, very still in all its parts, but
somehow energized, which might be betrayed by the flash or
luster of her eyes, or a deepening of her color. Some unsus-
pecting soul might interpret it as passivity or emptiness. Pity
that soul. I knew her well enough to hold my breath. I also
happen to think she is very beautiful when she is very mad.
The incandescent stillness, the meticulously harnessed fury,
had their charm.

I was not such a fool as to get her mad just for the fun of it.

She said, "That's like when you say, 'I'll wait in the car.'
Does it ever get us there any faster? Does it?"

I was half turned toward the water. I looked at her in her
tight long braid, her blue lycra shorts, and egret-white rash
guard—long-sleeved to protect her skin from the sun. She
had a terrible fear of how the sun would age and break down
her smooth unwrinkled skin. It was cultural. Chinese women
in Denver often went for walks in broad-brimmed hats. Given
this phobia, it was especially generous of her to come out here
surfing with me. I could see a couple of the eight new bites on
her legs where she had clawed them and made red, angry hash
marks. She suffers much more than me, than anybody I know,
from mosquito bites. She's not making it up. A bite I wouldn't
even notice swells up on her, turns hot and mean, lasts for
days. Once we did a long canoe trip on a wild river that flowed
into Hudson Bay. The mosquitoes up there are legendary. For
weeks before the trip Kim tried to change her body chemistry
to make it less delicious. Bananas, vitamin B, garlic. When we

flew in to Thunder Bay the Canadian customs official asked if we had any food or plants. Kim pulled out a string of garlic bulbs. Nobody had eaten a whole garlic bulb in Canada since it became a nation.

"Just this," she said happily. The man stared. Maybe he thought she was going to open an Italian restaurant. "I hear it's good for mosquitoes."

He looked at her a moment longer, pitiless. "Good luck with that," he said finally, and waved us on.

Now I looked at the streaks of her new bites and I relented. Sometimes I catch myself being a person I wouldn't tolerate for five minutes at my own kitchen table. Being a thoughtless, self-centered jerk. When it happens, when I catch that glimpse, I puddle on the floor—the beach—in shame. I wonder how she tolerates me. Couldn't she do so much better? There are a billion guys who would help her put on her sunscreen, who would learn how to French-braid hair and carry her board out here along with their own, and who would let her take all the time she needed to get situated in the water, just to have the privilege of her company on a trip like this. Instead of this maniac who thinks she needs to toughen up, who thinks every day is some sort of Outward Bound character-building exercise.

"I'm always on four-wheel drive with you," she said again, frustrated to the core.

I used to take that as a compliment. Now I was beginning to hear it as a plea to listen to her for once, to moderate my pace a little to accommodate a mate who was not me. We don't get to mate with versions of ourselves, unless we meet at the Olympics or something.

I put down my board. "You mean I'm being manipulative and pushy when I should be treating my very game surfer wife with the tenderness and generosity and compassion she deserves."

I could see, by the rise and fall of her chest, that she was breathing hard and that, whatever I'd just said, I'd said in the nick of time. She shook her head. It was not when she was at the height of upset that she let the tears come, it was when the storm was passing, when she felt safe enough to relax. Her eyes were wet now.

"That's right."

I trotted back to the rise of sand where I had been ready to abandon her. I touched her shoulder. "I'm so sorry."

She pouted. Not fake, real. Like a kid.

"I'm really, really sorry. You're so game. To do any of this. I'm such a dick."

She wouldn't look at me. "That's right."

Why couldn't I have seen that she was nervous? Probably really scared of getting back in the water in a strange spot after all this time.

"Ting." I hugged her. "I love you so much. I'm so sorry I get so—so mean."

She bent her head and pushed it into my chest, which meant she was on the verge of forgiving me. It was then, at this moment, that my love for her barreled in like a rogue wave and overwhelmed me. I'd never been with a woman who forgave me. Without exacting some flesh, or offering the words but keeping back the substance like a bad treaty. When Kim forgave me, she simply forgave me and moved on. She was much too light a spirit to carry around a grudge. It was so novel, so like a sweet and cool breeze. She was very patient.

"You're not mean," she said against my rash guard. "You're obsessed, thoughtless, and rude."

"Thanks."

She lifted her arms finally and squeezed me back. "Gentle," she said. "Be gentle with me."

"Okay." She lifted her face and kissed me. Her lips were soft. No lingering tenseness. She was just the loveliest thing ever.

"Okay," I said again. "Let's look at this wave and figure out a plan. Okay?"

She nodded.

I had done something right in a previous life. I was very lucky.

"I am Jean-Pierre," Jean-Pierre said when we paddled up. "I am glad to see you out of the hospital."

"Me, too." I thanked him for the juice, the thermometer, the aspirins. He was a strong man, wiry and densely muscled in his back, with trimmed gray hair and blue eyes.

"Well." He waved his arm in a broad welcoming gesture. "Another day in this paradise. If I learn to surf as well, then, so, it is a desert to the rest, eh?"

I laughed. "Dessert. Yes."

"I have not young gasoline in this engine," he said, patting his belly. "I am sixty-two."

"Sixty-two? You don't look a day over fifty." He really didn't.

He frowned, narrowed his eyes, looked at me sideways, not sure if I was mocking him. "Well, you say. My girlfriend, she keeps me young."

"His girlfriend is thirty-five," Kim said as if it were a point of personal pride. "Well, he wouldn't say exactly, but we played a game and I narrowed it down pretty close. Right, Jean-Pierre?"

"So you say." He shrugged, smiled. He was a trip. I was already glad he was camping next to us.

"Look at us, talking like chickens," he said. "Here comes a wave for us, not for the others." He turned his board. "Do you want?" he said with great courtesy to Kim.

She shook her head. "Not ready yet."

"I try." He said it as he was taking off with a great flail of his arms. He caught it. Stood up, hunched forward like a man charging out of a trench, and stiff, arms held out like a tight-rope walker. And went away down the line.

There were seven other surfers out there, four gringos, three Mexicans, and Jean-Pierre, who sat inside the rest, maybe thirty yards in toward shore where he could pick up the left-overs like the meekest wolf in the pack. Kim liked to get safely outside the break at a new spot and just paddle around on the rolling swell, taking in the sights. I guess it was her way of sussing it out. Maybe I would have benefited from the same kind of patience. I watched the other surfers catch the set waves and whiz by me on their way left across the face of the wave. I was on the shoulder, which meant that everyone was coming toward me down the line and the only wave I could get was the tail end of one they missed or let pass. By waiting down-wave at the far, far end of the lineup, you accomplished two things: you signaled respect for the locals—*See, I'm not barging into your scene like I deserve to surf or breathe the same air or anything like that*—and it gave you time to watch how the waves broke, where the peaks were, how the pack interacted. Did they all paddle aggressively toward the peak as it humped up and revealed itself—as in a competition? First one to get position wins? Or, as at most breaks, did they sit in a loose line and take their turns, paddling back to the end of the queue after they caught a wave?

Anyone who writes anything about surfing, or teaches it, always advises: when you get to a new break, sit down for half an hour at least and study it. Kim and I had just done that— for two minutes.

So now I vowed to be patient and study, sitting on my board. That lasted for three surfers. As the fourth was taking off on a beautiful, shoulder-high drop, I said, "Fuck it," and paddled out to where the rest were waiting.

As it turned out, I had a nemesis out there. He was somewhere in his fifties, large, with a gray beard and bushy gray eyebrows. I'd say his head was too big for his body, but then his trunk was thick and broad, with a big gut, too, that was not flabby in the least but seemed a perfectly proportioned part of the system of self-propulsion that was Otto. Eyes of indeterminate seawater, a flashing, darting, severe expression, hungry and full of secrets and mischief. He was Dionysian. He had an outsized voice that resonated past the roar of wave:

"Fuck! This swell is fucked up."

"How so?"

"If you can't see it, you wouldn't understand."

"Try me."

"Well, for one thing, it's coming from three directions. That's fucked up. Either peaks with no wall or it just closes out. Fucked up. You sit in one place but you might just as well sit over there. Again—"

"Fucked up."

"The sets come in from the south, past that rock at the end of the island. About 210." He meant degrees. "That's good. But then sets come in from the west and from the northwest. See, like that."

"That's really fucked up."

"Yeah, well, maybe here's one, I'm taking it."

Of course, I had position on him. It was just where I stopped to drift, I didn't mean to take the priority spot, but he took off right in front of me as if I weren't even there. Didn't even look over his right shoulder to see if I'd caught it. Nope, he took off like he owned the wave, which right then I guess he did. He had the strangest style. He dropped in like he was falling into disaster—body off balance out ahead of his board, right arm sticking way up behind him to counteract. Looked like a rodeo rider about to be bucked off. No way he was going to make the bottom turn, but he snatched his ride back from catastrophe and swooped up to the lip, then cut and turned aggressively all down the line. On his paddle back out I watched him stop to talk to Jean-Pierre, who sat at his spot inside just floating around, not catching anything.

I tried to make nice with Otto, but my overtures didn't get me far.

Me: "Nice ride. Late takeoff. The wave was breaking on your back, but you made it."

Otto: "Yeah, well. You do what you gotta do." Turns his board, begins to paddle away, an off-pink slab of a man on his pointy 7–6.

"Hey, Otto?"

Looks over his shoulder. I paddle after him. His expression is like a big dog who looks back and can't believe a little dog is trotting behind, trying to chase him down the street.

"Yeah?"

"Are you retired?"

"Nah, never worked. I couldn't get the hang of it."

"How did you—?"

"Trust fund."

"Ahh. But you surfed all your life?"

"Nah. I did a lot when I was a kid, growing up in California. But then I got into drugs and that kind of became my thing. Then I got clean and sober and came back to surfing. About twenty years ago."

I actually stopped paddling and sat up and stared at his retreating butt. "Oh . . ." I said, to the pads of his feet.

One after another the rest of the surfers in the lineup took off on long rides. And then I was alone, watching the open ocean and the undulating horizon. Watching for the lift of a bigger swell. And this feeling overcame me, a sense of focus I had not had for months. Intense, almost as if I could conjure the wave or the wave could conjure me. The connection with the sea I had missed so much. It came with a surge of relief. It had been way too long. And then here it came, a lifting of the dark water, a promising steepness, a long wall and no one else there. I pivoted, paddled like a maniac, remembered to drop my chin, and felt the lift and glide—release. Hopped up.

I made the drop, fell to the bottom of the face, then swooped up along it in a reflex bottom turn. Oh, yeah! I didn't rebel-yell this time like the kook of kooks, but was filled with glee. Kept it to myself. This was what I remembered: unadulterated joy.

Once, on my second day at the *río*, Otto yelled at me. I had just been paddling back to the lineup. He was zipping down the face fast. I had nowhere to go. Stop, sprint straight ahead, it didn't matter. Suddenly the wall was right over me and Otto was on me in a split second, unable to get around, wiping out. He came up foamy, disheveled, and irate.

"Look!" he barked. "You've got to get your shit together and learn to stay out of the way. You should be good enough now to figure that out."

I apologized and paddled away. But it burned. I felt humiliated and aggrieved. I mean, I had had nowhere to go, he should have turned around me. Also, it's okay to cut a beginner some slack. Especially if it's clear that he *wants* to be courteous, *wants* to learn and obey the rules. Who was this guy, to yell at me like he was the abusive father I'd never had?

I tried to shrug it off. One good thing about surfing is that even if you miss most of the waves and get yelled at, you still get tumbled and your body still provides you with boosters of endorphins and dopamines. I thought, *When you're on the pity pot and deep in your self-centered angst, what's the best way out of it? Service! That's what they told me in AA. Go be kind to someone else.* So I paddled down to where Kim was sitting beside Jean-Pierre and helped guide her onto a wave.

"Paddle! Paddle!" I yelled. "This one's for you! You can get it! Dig! Put your chin down! Down!"

She missed it and sat up, yelling, "Don't shout at me! It gets me all confused! Don't coach me!"

Well, that felt better.

I paddled back to where Otto was still dominating the waves. The guy hadn't let me get a wave all morning. If I was anywhere near him, he just dropped in on me cold like I had no rights, like there was never such a thing as surf protocol, as etiquette, as even a thing called simple kindness. At first I let him do it, figuring: new wave, new spot, new old muscles, and most of the waves I go for I miss anyway because my timing is way off. I had learned to just accept the fact that the good surfers around me were also keen judges of my ability, and if they didn't afford me any respect and took off right in front of me, it was because I didn't really deserve any.

But there were locals and there were locals. Otto just wanted every damn wave he could get and he didn't give a shit if anybody around him was struggling. In his book we shouldn't have even been there.

So Otto was local numero uno. This was typical of expat gringos who had staked out a wave for several decades. I learned to be wary of them. To stay out of their way until I was pretty confident that I would catch the wave I was going for. But when that happened, I knew I would have to carve out a place on the wave or I would never get a ride.

The next time Otto cut me off, I'd had enough. I just kept going and rammed him. He came up yelling that I'd hit him and I told him that maybe he better stay away from me from now on and stop cutting me off. It was the oddest thing: he was nice to me after that. Over the next few weeks I even began to appreciate his keen intelligence and humor, and he began to give me some of my most valuable lessons about reading waves, taking off, turning. Underneath his crusty surface he was solid and kind. I guess he just couldn't suffer complete fools. Go figure.

A few days later, I paddled up to a Mexican sitting on his shortboard staring gravely out to sea. The whole week we'd been there he had kept to himself, paddled silently by, reserved, hunting the peaks of the waves and finding them. His thick black hair was cropped straight across his forehead and he wore a short brush of a mustache. I introduced myself.

"Good morning, Pedro," he said in thickly accented English.

"*Como se llama usted?*"

"Johnny Be Good." He seemed vaguely amused. He was compact the way a tank is compact. He swiveled his head toward me and I was struck by lively green eyes. "Did you see the shark?"

"No. Was there one?"

"Right here. One . . ." He made a scythe out of air.

"Fin. You didn't get out?"

"No, Pedro. He does not bother me."

I didn't know how to take that. The shark does not ruffle Johnny Be Good because he is hard to ruffle, or the shark does not bother him in a more literal sense by biting his leg off? It seemed at the moment an important distinction. If the sharks here generally went about their own sharky business without sampling pieces of surfer, that would be good to know.

But the discussion was closed. Johnny pulled his board under him and took off down a textured wall lined out for a hundred yards.

That left me alone with my imagination and a sea of opaque dark water. What was I supposed to do? There was a shark around here. Or maybe it was just a Mexican psych-out. I didn't think so. Johnny had caught his own waves all morning and no one had gotten in his way. Otto left him un-molested. He had no reason to be blithe. So, should I paddle straight down to Kim and tell her and then proceed smartly to the beach? That would freak her out, probably for days. But then, I believed in the ethics of complete disclosure where it involved medical issues or top predators. But then, the shark did not bother Johnny so it shouldn't bother Kim and it would only bother me in the sense that I let it occupy a berth in the marina of my head; unless, of course, it chewed off my foot.

I decided to keep mum and keep a lookout, which Kim may not forgive me for after reading this. I sat on my Bruno torpedo-nose destroyer longboard and scanned the water, pretending I was looking for waves, but every wind riffle and benign silver bullet of a flying fish gave me a start. And then the big black thing popped up right off my nose, maybe twenty feet away. I jumped. Probably groaned. It was round as a melon. It had eyes. It looked like E.T. It was a sea turtle. She was curious. She appraised me and submerged and must have been, judging by her vanishing shadow, at least four feet long. That relieved me. I figured that where sea turtles were looking so relaxed there probably was no longer a shark.

Every morning, early, there was the same group out on the water: Otto, Jean-Pierre, Johnny Be Good, a few other Mexican guys, Kim, and me. A nearly full moon, still bright, sank into a rose haze over the sea as we dropped our boards into the slow water of the lagoon. We paddled across slowly, in soft cool water that shimmered with greens from the cane and magroves on the far bank. At water's edge I could see willets, sandpipers, egrets, a boat-billed heron, and a pair of yellow-crowned night herons, plovers, royal terns all strung out along the water. Tight formations of pelicans flew just over and the high, angular frigate birds. Small fish flipped the surface all around us like slow raindrops. The mountains brooding upstream. The shear and thud of surf. Right then, truth be told, paddling easily with Kim beside me on the glassy water, I didn't care if I ever caught a wave. Or ever learned to surf. Or ever wrote a book. The surface of the estuary tilted in sunlight. The air was cool. The feeding fish made soft flicks. The circle of our awareness expanded gently outward like the rings of a pond-tossed stone; and at the same time, with equal and opposite persuasion, the morning entered into us. I shouldn't speak for Kim. It did for me, and she stopped paddling, too, and we just drifted and listened. The sense of peace was so strong it seemed to ring like a sustained, resounding bell. I was happy. Love is a strange thing. At that moment it was undiscerning and pervasive. I loved Kim, I loved the willets, the coconut husk bobbing out to the salt, the crocodile that was somewhere around because they lived here, too. It struck me that taking in the morning lying down, spread out on water, was a completely different, more vulnerable experience than propped up and in command of two legs.

The waves were coming in with more energy, with longer intervals between them, which meant they were traveling from farther off, from their inception in storm. Some of the sets were overhead, about seven feet high on the face. Kim caught one of those, while Jean-Pierre yelled and cheered, and I could just see her high back hand zinging left down the rail of the lip, waving, grabbing at air.

The tenth morning I surfed until I could no longer lift my chest. I surfed until glass-off. There's a time in the late morning when the offshore wind lies down and the sea becomes dark and smooth. More oil than glass. A molten mirror that moves the light in sliding negatives, sheen and shadow slipping past each other with the undulations of the swell. Only minutes: the ocean holding her breath. Catch a wave in this hiatus and it is like skating down an oil-coated slide. Smooth. And then the sea breathes out. The wind has shifted onshore and it is gentle at first, barely texturing the face of the wave. The cresting lip no longer tremors and folds back while the rest of her body falls forward. Now she is all falling into herself. As the wind stiffens, the wave throws her hair forward and tucks her chin and curls over her tender womb. The wind presses on her back like a great insistent hand. With more and more force. Until she lets out a gasp and lies down.

Why surfers get up early.

ADDICTION

Surfing is an addiction. I read a book once called *Love and Addiction*. If I remember right, the author seemed to believe that these two powerful emotional states were deadly enemies, like love and fear. That one, in fact could not exist in the same room with the other. Lying there in the cot in the dark under the clamorous palms, listening to tiers of surf overlap each other, I knew that the two were compatible—like alpha wolf pups.

I was becoming addicted to surfing. I loved it also. With a deep, abiding, wholesome love.

Like all users, I was blind to the downsides of my addiction. If I pulled muscles, got sunburn or bitten by bugs, I didn't give a damn. Kim, however, was emphatically not addicted. She liked surfing sometimes, especially when the other surfers were nice to her and she caught some waves. But all in all she could take it or leave it. And she suffered from things I didn't even notice.

We slept in the screen room but bugs got in. They slipped in when we slipped out. As fast as we unzipped and zipped the door, they were faster. One or two mosquitoes harried our sleep. They ended up eschewing me and biting Kim. Every day we piled sand around the base of the walls so there was no gap on the ground. Kim had taken to dressing in long pants, long-sleeve shirt, wide brim hat with bug net when we lingered at Café Jean-Pierre at dusk. Still the no-see-ums and mosquitoes found a way. Before she walked the hundred yards of beach at dawn from the tent to the water, she slathered repellant all over her legs, arms, neck. For three minutes of walking. Still the sand fleas plagued her long calves, her vulnerable ankles, her neck, throat, ears, eyes. They mortified her by biting her eyelids. Her skin angered, swelled, reddened. She scratched and it bled and wept. A single mosquito bite could become a welt the size of a silver dollar. The itching magnified, crescendoed—should have, like all things that crescendo, ceased. No way. The nit of a sand flea, the ones that peppered my ankles as I walked to the water and forgot about a second later, they grew like miracle seeds in fertile soil. They bloomed lush flowers of itch and sting. When Kim undressed in the tent at night and said, "Ting, I have twelve more bites," pointing them out up and down her body, standing on one leg and bending back the other knee to point to calf and foot, leaning the fall of her hair away from her face to show me the swollen tender place beneath an ear; when she did this she was not being a wimpy drama queen; she was trying in some impossible way to quantify for me her suffering. On our sixth night she lay on the cot, spreading lydocaine on her legs, and began to cry. To herself, quietly. It tore me like a serrated knife.

"Ting, what? What's the matter? Are you okay?"

I knew what the matter was.

"I just can't bear it, Ting." She sobbed. "It just—they won't—"

Every day she came out with me in the horrendous surf, got pummeled on the way out, flipped her board back over, got back on, and kept coming. Every day she baked under the merciless sun on a sea without shadow, this woman who always wore a hat outside at home and was so careful with her skin. Every day she deferred to everyone else on the wave and got maybe one good ride. And followed me into places that were uncertain at best and sometimes scary, where drug deals happened on the beach and riptides tugged dead trees into the circling eddies of the vortex the locals called the Liquidora. She did all this because she wanted to accompany me on this adventure and because she loved me. She would much rather be at home skiing right now, or be dressed up in a space suit and performing experiments on the Mars surface for visitors at the museum. And now she was being tortured without surcease. She couldn't even take refuge in nightfall and sleep. It just tore me open. I felt flooded with compassion and rage. All I wanted for the whole universe was that her pain should stop. She cried. I was helpless. I didn't know how to stop this. I felt cornered, impotent, to blame. I panicked. I sat up on my cot.

"Do you want to go home, Ting? I think we should send you home. This can't go on. This is unbearable."

"And what?" she whimpered.

"I don't know. This is crazy. You are allergic or something. I don't know how you are going to be able to travel with me if you can't tolerate mosquitoes. Everywhere I go there are mosquitoes. I mean, this is serious. This isn't working out."

Wrong thing to say. I should have wrapped her in my arms. I should have taken her to a hotel, a hotel with an ice machine down the hall, and covered every inch of her with the tracings of soothing cubes. This was more like a threat, like blaming her for getting bitten. She took it as a punishment for frailty. She began to cry harder.

"What are you saying? You want to send me packing?"

"No, I—it's just I can't bear to see you like this. It can't go on. I—"

What a jerk. I was torn seeing her suffer, so what did I do? I took it out on her by threatening dire consequences for our relationship should she not be able to buck up and stop suffering so much. I had panicked some more. I had made her pain about me and then demanded that she assuage it. It was self-centered and awful. What the hell was I? What kind of monster of a husband? It was sordid, horrible. Suddenly I saw it. I saw her. On her back, covered with red spots and welts, and crying.

"Oh, Ting." I got on my knees in the gap and reached for her head and held it wet against my shoulder. "I don't want to go anywhere without you. We go where we go together. I'm sorry, I didn't mean that. You are so game and tough. I love you more than anything."

She cried. I didn't know how to soothe the itching but I could hold her and not be a jerk. I laid her back down on the cot and rubbed her shoulders and back and legs and feet, rubbing in the lydocaine and using the pressure to scratch all the itches and I did it until she fell asleep.

So little by little, with painstaking slowness, I was learning to surf and, even less quickly, learning what it was to love another person. Kim was teaching me that part. Kim demanded to be loved well. She would have nothing less. She would guide me, nudge me, let me flounder, set me back on the right track until I got it. It was astounding. I couldn't believe she loved me so steadily and forgave my lapses and gave me the nod to try again, better. I couldn't believe my great fortune in finding someone willing to go the distance with me, willing to stick around till I got it right. Last night, squeezed next to me on her cot, lying on her back in a respite from bugs because we had just combed the entire inside of the tent with a head-lamp and squished every mosquito pinned to the walls by the beam—she said out of the silence:

"You know you are in the presence of a goddess?"

She lay with her head on my arm, which was asleep. I looked at the shadows of the palm fronds in moonlight, shifting and whispering over the roof of the tent.

Her voice skewered my heart. It was without irony, simple, musical, a statement and a question.

Last night I guessed I learned that another definition of love was a simple negation, an opting out: when one refrained from being a jerk in situations where one has always been a jerk. Just say no.

Is it possible to love by simply not being an ass? I don't think so. But it goes a long way to clearing a space where love can happen.

The next morning Kim and I paddled out in the near-dark a good half an hour before anyone else, so that she might have a decent chance at catching a wave. Which she did. A nice long ride almost to the beach. I took out the fish, the short, fat brick, and wiped out again and again. I just couldn't get stable on the takeoff. But I spent a lot of time sitting, with Kim maybe thirty feet away. We let the swell lift us and set us down and we watched the gray over the mountains soak up color from a sun that was still below the horizon. It was a bit like sitting in rockers on the front porch. A sea turtle stuck up her black head nearby. An inconsistent breeze blew off of the river.

Sitting there at peace with Kim and the whole breathing circle of the dawn, I thought that this trip wasn't really about surfing. How could it be? By all accounts the ocean beneath our surfboards was dying.

Lifting and falling on our boards, I thought of all the certified genius economists who believed an economy could only be healthy if it grew over 2 percent a year.

I wanted to tell them, *Take off your thick glasses and come out on the waves with me one morning. I will show you how many less birds there were this morning than there were ten or even five years ago. I will paddle with you over to this dawn fisherman casting a hand net and ask him what his take is like this morning compared with twenty years ago, ten, five. I will take you to the harbor in town where the fishing* pangas *pull up with their daily catch and ask the same. And watch while they dump the plastic boxes into the tubs, and watch your eyes as you register the heap of eight-inch-long tuna and redfish where years ago twenty-pounders were more common. We'll go snorkeling off the islands to the north where the coral reefs used to be brilliant with the colors of myriad coral species and thousands of tropical fish and are now bleaching from rising temperatures and nearly dead.*

The oceans are dying. The oceans die, we die, too. It's that simple. Sixty percent of the world's population live on the coasts and derives a significant portion—at least 60 percent—of their protein from the sea. The oceans and their phytoplankton produce the majority of our atmospheric oxygen. It is just being understood that the oceans play a large part in regulating the earth's temperature through a complex interaction between biology and atmospheric chemistry (plankton and other ocean plants consume and then shelve for long-term storage vast amounts of carbon dioxide), and currents of both air and water are influenced by the ebb and flow of species.

I was thinking about this and watching the sunrise and keeping an eye out for sets on the seaborne horizon, and now and then looking over at Kim. I was thinking about the ocean, the mother of life, on one hand, and about this woman on the other. My slowly dawning realization was that if this journey was to be any kind of success, if my life was to have any real peace or joy, I needed to learn to love Kim. To really love her. And I needed to learn that much more than I ever needed to learn to ride any kind of a wave.

We got a call from Sergio, our friend from the town that wasn't on our map. He didn't ask, he told us: "*Yo voy. Llego Sábado.*" Sergio arriving, here, Saturday. I had to shake my head to make it compute.

"Wow, really?"

"*Sí, Peter, sí. Yo voy. Yo voy a surfear.*"

"You want to surf?"

"*Claro que sí! Porqué no?*"

I couldn't think of any reason other than that the whole concept of Sergio on a surfboard wasn't fitting into my head. "Wow. Okay. *Venga.* We'll pick you up."

On Saturday the sliding glass door into the customs area of the airport opened and there was Sergio. He was wearing blue shorts with an orange floral pattern, white sneakers, the official NFL John Elway shirt we had bought together in Escuinapa, and he carried a small green gym bag. He was bigger than anything in the airport except the jet; bigger than life. His eyes searched the rope line of greeters and when they found us his face lit up like a junkyard sun. I thought he might break bones when he hugged me.

"Sergio, you have to get your bag back in that hall."

He patted his little gym bag.

"That's all? How long are you staying?" I figured the weekend.

"Cinquo, seis dias. Ah, qué regalo ver a ustedes! Vamos a comer!" Let's go eat lunch!

That's what we did. We went straight to one of the fish restaurants that ring the stone harbor and I broke my taboo and ate commercially caught fish because Sergio didn't give me any choice. He took one look at the menu, ordered us both pan-fried fillets with garlic, and asked if we wanted lemonade. He ordered a Sprite for himself and appetizers and sat back in his chair surveying the beach and the harbor, the fishing *pangas* pulled up in the shade of the almond trees, the long sport-fishing wharf with the big hooks for hanging swordfish and marlin, and he smiled the deep, satisfied, unadulterated smile of a man who has realized his every dream and has just added fresh ceviche and shrimp salad.

"Salud, amigos." He raised his green can.

We had bought Sergio a guesthouse. It was a pop-up dome tent that we set up in the sand next to the big house, the twelve-foot screen room. We got him a light nylon sleeping bag and a pillow with Spider-Man on the case so that he would think of little Sergito. He was delighted. I don't know if he'd ever camped, but we knew he slept well, because his snores tore through the grove, competed with the roar of the building swell. In the morning he was up and at 'em, refreshed, drinking instant coffee like it was Starbucks. We couldn't be troubled with ice, with a melted pond in the cooler every day, so we had powdered milk for cereal, peanut butter and honey, crackers. Powdered sugarless Kool-Aid. Sergio called it *comida de bunker.* Bunker food. He liked it. He confided to me that if the end of the world came, we would be set. He held up a cracker and hard cheese with a big smile.

"Peter, Kim, *Comida de bunker fantástica.*" He toasted us and downed it, settled back in the hammock slung between two palms, where it seemed he could not imagine being happier.

"*Pura vida,*" he said. "I would have to work for forty years to live like this. *Una vida magnífica.*"

One morning Sergio announced that he was ready to try surfing. Kim and I exchanged glances. "That can be arranged," I said.

We decided that the best person to teach Sergio to surf would be my old mentor, Leon, King of the West Coast. His shop in Ixtapa was quite a haul from where we were camped, but I figured we could do it in three or four hours. I wanted to see my old friend anyway and we could spend the night with him. The next day, we woke Sergio up in the predawn dark and drove down there and treated Sergio to a late-morning lesson with Leon's brother Edgardo. We had warned Edgar of Sergio's dimensions. Edgar showed up at the beach with an eleven-foot foam board sticking over the tailgate of the shop's truck. He didn't have any booties big enough for Sergio's feet.

"*No problema. No te preocupes,* I am fine."

Sergio and Edgardo waded out into the whitewater. Edgar explained that he would push him, all he had to do was stand up. Sergio bellied onto the board and it sank. I blinked through the viewfinder of Sergio's camera. There was no way a mere person could submerge this board; it was a cargo ship. The nose broke the surface like a breach, like an animal struggling for air, and Sergio pinned it to the water with his flailing mass. For a moment it looked like he had succeeded, and then both the board and Sergio capsized. The big man struggled up out of the foam and without pause tried again. Edgar braced the board. I had never seen Edgar look scared.

Sergio bellied and wriggled onto the board. Here came a terrific surge of whitewater. Edgar shoved. In one of the greatest gestures of athletic willpower and courage I have ever seen, Sergio managed to bunch his entire being, his bulk, his mind, heart, massive shoulders, ham hands, expansive feet, into one animal lunge. He lunged. Upward. He landed with his feet on the board. The whitewater cascaded in a wall behind him. The nose of the great board lifted out of the water. I snapped the picture.

One of the luckiest action photographs ever snapped. I mean, I believe it to be on par with Robert Capa's picture of the shot Spanish loyalist.

No one need know that all the movement was on a trajectory of disaster. In that split second Sergio was a man standing on a surfboard with a wall of crashing wave behind him, his knees bent, a dazzled expression, hands thrown out for balance, and the nose of the board angled stylishly up out of the foam as if he were about to execute a classic longboard bottom turn. In that split second he was a surfer. Which was all he really wanted. We had the photo—enough of surfing. It was time to eat.

Leon's surf shop was the same as I'd left it—a riotous island of palms and bougainvillea, a covered patio hung with shells and

driftwood mobiles, primitive paintings of surfers on waves.
It occurred to me again what a strange town was Ixtapa. It
was not really a town at all, but an insta-resort dropped onto
the coast in the late seventies, a constellation of towering
hotel zone, plaza, restaurants, condos, golf courses, marina,
all mostly built within a decade over a filled-in tidal swamp
and wetland, and with the sole purpose of attracting tourism.
Leon, who spent part of his youth five miles to the south in
Zihuatanejo, remembered when it was all wild swamp and
mangroves, filled with crocs, waterbirds, raccoonlike coati-
mundis. When he and his friends were exploring the coast
northward for new surf spots they had to wade and paddle
across much of what was now covered in concrete, gift shops,
Señor Frog's, a dolphinarium. Sitting at one of Leon's outdoor
tables, I looked across the tourist plaza, with its gazebo in
imitation of real towns like Escuinapa, and wondered about
the trade-off. The estuary and swamp where Ixtapa now stood
in its glory was once home to countless species of birds, crustaceans, mangroves, and fish. The problem wasn't so much this
one resort, but that the same kind of development had occurred up and down the coasts of Mexico, was still occurring
wherever there was a pretty river mouth, a bay, and financing;
and the phenomenon was being replicated all over the coasts
of the world. It was the reason we had lost, by some estimates,
70 percent of the world's vital mangroves, and it left precious
little habitat for the littoral species, the crabs, fish, herons, willets, crocodiles, that depended on them. The same was true for
beaches. People can't stay away from a beach, as we had seen.
The sea turtles of the world need undisturbed beaches where
they can wallow out of the sea and lay their eggs unmolested.
Vacationers, surfers, beauty seekers everywhere were one of
the reasons sea turtle species worldwide were in a precari-

ous struggle for survival. Drinking a cold orange Fanta with
Sergio and Leon and Kim, I thought about these things, and
how I was part of the problem as a surfer who wanted a campground to sleep in, or a surf camp, a restaurant or two, an
airport to fly in to.

I took a deep breath and shook myself off, looked at Sergio, who I'd bet a million pesos wasn't thinking anything
about any species at all except what fish to eat for lunch. He
was beaming.

"Did you like surfing?" I asked him.

"Oh, Peter, *esta lindisima*." Beautiful. Sergio lived in the
brutal, shadowless light of the complete positive. The Corona
he held looked tiny in his big fist. He gazed around—for lunch.
There wasn't any in sight, so he began to orchestrate a meal for
us, seamlessly assuming the role of host in Leon's home.

He sent Lili, Leon's elegant sister, to the supermarket. He
peeled off a couple of five-hundred-peso notes and gave instructions for some type of fish, chilies, onions, tomatoes. Lili
came back from the store and Sergio asked for a knife, plates,
cutting board. Leon called other sisters and brothers. He sent
a boy for more Coronas. Sergio began chopping. He chopped
while he talked. He cut and squeezed limes. He sprinkled in
diced chilies. he spooned a dollop onto the back of his hand
in the pocket between thumb and forefinger, tilted his head
to the sky while his palate absorbed it as if asking God for
guidance. He added salt. By now there were fifteen guests.
Sergio was in his element as the host. He asked one person
for hot sauce, another for a bowl, a spoon. People came in and
out of the kitchen in the back of the shop bearing whatever
he needed.

"Oye, otro plato, por favor." He pointed his fat finger like
a magic wand. He spread his hand wide to signal enough. I

sat amazed. Now he and Leon were doing shots of Don Julio tequila, comparing it with Don Porfirio. I didn't even know Sergio drank. But no one, *nadie,* could party like Leon. He was still El Tigre. The music poured from the outdoor speakers and the levels in the bottles dropped like a lowering tide.

And then, two hours later, Sergio served everyone ceviche. It was superb. He had made enough for twice as many people, which made everyone happy because it is easy to eat twice as much ceviche. We cleaned the platter. I looked around. Leon's expanded family—sisters, brothers, cousins, nephews—Sergio, Kim. Ruddy faces, laughter. The little niece who liked to sweep around everyone's feet. For a minute life was so simple and sweet.

The day after we put Sergio back on the plane, a swell came in from the southwest and churned our sea to chaotic foam. From the tent, we could see lines of violent breakers strung all the way across the middle of the bay where no waves had ever been. The morning wind blew back their tops in long streamers of spume that would have been festive if we had not entertained the thought of paddling out among them. Kim didn't, I did. I stood on the bank of the river taking it all in. The morning seemed to be composed of nothing but waves. A swell so big it made shallows out of what once had seemed deep outer bay and pushed against them and broke in tiers miles out— some submerged reef I had never seen before. I crossed the river and stood on the sand of the beach and looked straight up into the onslaught. Beneath my feet the sand shuddered. There were so many explosions that they merged into a throbbing white rush that cracked now and then like thunder.

I went back to camp and put on my rash guard, paddled

back across. I passed Frank, a surfer from Massachusetts who had ventured out and turned back. He shook his head. "It's chaos. Good luck."

I walked down the beach, took a deep breath, and launched into a fast riptide. I paddled as hard as I could and cleared a steep wave fence, then angled the board south toward the river. I paddled and paddled. I saw Frank standing on the beach where I'd left him, but it couldn't be, that was way up the shore. I looked over my shoulder. A strong north-moving shore current was sucking me to Punto Final. I dug harder; I must have paddled for half an hour. Then Frank was in front of me. I had paddled against the current until my back was on fire and my arms felt like putty and I was in line with where I'd started. Except that I'd gotten outside the big break. I thought I had. Then I looked out to sea and here was a set coming. I mean a set as I'd never seen one. The face of the first wave was at least nine feet tall. The second one looked over it and the third seemed monstrous. Instantly I positioned myself to go after the first wave. It was more about self-protection, fight or flight: I just didn't want to meet that third wave in person. I rocked back on the longboard, pivoted, angled left, and as the first wave in the set barreled in I paddled like hell. Then it was beneath me. Then I was falling. Like off a cliff. Straight down the face in a drop like I'd never known. Then I was hopping up. Then the board was accelerating left, slicing across the face. The wave, the thundering maw, I had the sense of it, tearing and crashing just over my right shoulder. The lip of the wave was over my head. I flexed my ankles, weighted my heels just a little, and flew to the top of the wave. Lord, it was a face out ahead, tall and dark, but it had a slope, it was not a cliff, it was just like any other wave here but bigger. I swooped to the bottom, the whitewater engulfing my knees,

I held balance, then went to the lip and over the top. Rode whitewater from the next wave into shore on my belly.

One wave. The wave of my life.

On the beach, Frank shook his head. "Double overhead," he said. "I thought the current was taking you to the point. Glad it worked out. Nice ride."

"Thanks."

I felt bigger than myself. Not inflated, not big-headed, just proud and full of adrenaline and kind of incredulous that what I had just experienced had really happened.

"How long, how far did I ride it?"

"About seventy-five yards, I'd say. You made the drop, nailed the bottom turn, then roller-coastered."

"Wow."

We walked back to the river, paddled across. I looked upriver and saw a royal tern feint to the water, then peel upward in an effortless arc and catch the ruddy sun full on his snowy breast and I felt a great happy kinship overwhelm me. The tern and I didn't have much in common except that we were both in possession of warm-blooded bodies that got hungry, ate, mated, obeyed the turnings of the stars, planets, days, and seasons, and we both evidently had a blast soaring around on currents. Also, our heads followed our eyes and our bodies followed our heads—number one rule in motocross, kayaking, mating, surfing, diving for fish. Hell, we had almost everything in common. We were both surfers. I laughed out loud. Frank looked at me over the silky water.

"Nothing," I said. "That was just a rush."

With a good instructor, one can learn to turn a pair of skis in the first hour. Or hit a tennis ball over a net. With surfing, if you have an instructor who gives you a great shove as the wave lifts you, it may take days and days before you can reliably pop up and ride standing straight into the beach. Weeks before you have the strength to catch your own waves on a regular basis. Months before you can do it with enough control to get ahead of the break and begin to ride across the blue face of a wave. And this is on easy, soft, slow, forgiving waves. Come every day, give surfing the best of yourself first thing every morning, and you might have a chance over several months of beginning to actually surf. Maybe.

It's humbling.

We love surfers for the same reasons we have always admired doctors and pilots and firemen and shamans, for the same reasons we admire excellent soldiers: because despite themselves they have bowed to a force much greater than themselves, which in this case is the wave, and submitted to the gnarly rigors of its discipline. They have allowed themselves to be shaped and polished by the sea. They have given themselves up to this greater force, day after day, year after year. Crushed and punished, battered into something tempered and resilient, and sharpened to an edge by constant refinement. They are warriors in the best sense: by bending to the often brutal demands of surfing they have transformed themselves into beings who can respond to great violence with grace and humility. And beauty.

Nathan at *Surfing* magazine had warned me that surfing is not something to conquer in six months or a year. "It's a life path," he repeated.

I was just starting to get it—around the time I decided I would step up, or down, to a shortboard. Maybe there is some crash course in surfing somewhere. I guess I was trying to devise my own on this six-month odyssey. But if I had learned to surf in a month, and could pay for the wave pool and get a perfect hollow ride every time, then . . .

I would not sit dawn after dawn on an undulating swell and watch the pelicans glide on the cushion of what pilots call ground effect so that wingtips skim a hairsbreadth off the water. I would not fall into despair at not catching a single good ride in three days. I would not learn to watch, to wait for my wave. I would not get smaller and smaller before the brimming sea, even as my own skills increased.

I would be a man who surfs, not a surfer.

OBSTINATE AND SHORT

Deciding that surfing isn't really about surfing has certain advantages, especially if you're forty-eight, a kook, and you choose to take up shortboarding.

Shortboarding is really hard. I took calculus in college as a kind of character-building experiment; I thought that before I became a graduate of an institution of higher learning I should know how to calculate the volume of a can of beans. I never did figure that out—I just read the label that said twelve ounces and dumped the refrieds into a frying pan. But I did spend four hours every night doing assignments that were supposed to take an hour. I was a freaking English major who didn't even know what five to the negative one meant. I crawled into the professor's office on week three and begged him to let me drop the class. I told him it was all I was doing all term, that I didn't have time for anything else. The old bald bastard Sleznick got an impish smile and said, "What more could you want in life?" Well, I'd set myself the challenge and I guess he thought it was his job to not let me let myself down. He was a confirmed bachelor and a scout leader on the weekends and he had nothing better to do than help us all build character. I got a miraculous C.

Shortboarding makes that class look like drivers' ed.

"If you are over thirty and just learning to surf, you will be a longboarder all your life." The smug, patronizing words of a big sunburned beer gut in a sleeveless T kept ringing in my ears. He had been loading up his ten-foot Harbour board in the parking lot of Bolsa Chica, and I figured he was too stuck to get in shape, had spent too many years slowing his reaction time with toxic substances to ride anything but a floating oil rig and he didn't want to see a guy his age fly by him on a little board. Was that it? Or was it true? Other surfers in California had told me the same thing.

"Learn on a longboard. Then, as you get better, come down to something like an eight-foot funboard. Or even a seven-ten." That was the standard refrain. Well-meaning, I'm sure.

A funboard is a practical, no-nonsense hybrid. It's like a minivan. It has length, it has fatness, it has float, and sometimes it has, shamelessly, pretensions to a shortboard's pointy glamour. It's fun, you bet. You can paddle it if you are a little out of shape, and you can hop up on it if you are reasonably fast, but not that fast. Not fast enough for a you-know-what. You can turn it pretty quickly. You can have . . . fun.

I am not scorning it. I'll get one when the time comes. But I wasn't breaking my ass every day, surfing until muscles screamed and burned and arms became leaden and back muscles would no longer hold my head up, just to watch twenty-somethings from Orange County crank turns off the lip that were worthy of bats. I wanted to do that.

Which is pretty much how the first shortboards got developed in the first place: surfers experimenting with shorter boards in the late sixties and early seventies could do tricks and go places in the wave a longboard just couldn't go. Think about a big fast barrel like the Pipeline on the North Shore. A surfer wants to drop in and stay high on the wave and tuck right up into the tube. A longboard just won't fit there. It wants to drop down to the bottom of the wave where the surface is flatter. But a little shortboard, say with some rocker—a slight upward curving of the nose and tail—will fit high in the wave where it is most hollow. Add a hard-edged rail toward the tail that gives grip on the steep face and you have a tube machine. Also, shorter boards turn much faster, much looser, which to most surfers means: fun. In competition it means victory, and board design changed fast at the end of the sixties. In the 1968 World Surfing Championships in Puerto Rico, Fred Hemmings competed on a classic longboard and won, beating others on much shorter boards. At the next Worlds in 1970, Rolf Aurness won decisively on a 6–10 single-fin. My evolution as a surfer seemed to be haltingly following the evolution of the sport. At least in my dream. But I killed myself paddling the 6–4 that Bruno had made for me. I snugged into the lineup and watched everybody else go for every wave because I could not move the thing fast enough. I tried to take off as I would have done on a longboard, safely on the shoulder and away from the gnashing pocket, and watched wave after wave roll under me, heading for the beach without me, leaving like an unrequited lover arm in arm with someone else better positioned than me. I wore myself out taking off on these easy shoulders. Then in frustration I went right for the critical crest of collapse, I pivoted around just under the toppling tower, and got served. Got read to from the slamming book. Got baptized by five tons of loving water.

My shoulders cried out every night. I dripped salt water from my sinuses onto my dinner plate, all over my pillow. I couldn't hear anything anyone was saying because I had water and sand packed into my ear canals. I lived in kind of a numb daze. But I knew in my bones that if I didn't ride a decent wave on a shortboard before the end of the trip I would feel like a failure. I would have to write a book about how much I learned about getting whipped by the challenge I'd set for myself. I'd have to console myself by building a shack in Maine and filling it with Hudson Bay blankets and long novels and field guides like this midlife turkey I'd read about in the *New York Times*.

Was I a self-serious, middle-aged turkey? An SSMAT? I didn't really give a shit, as long as I could ride a fast overhead wave on a 6–4 shortboard.

Joseph Conrad wrote that convictions are merely justifications for our passions. I took that to mean that it is unwise to trust people bursting with conviction. *The worst are full of passionate intensity*—Yeats. I never do—trust them I mean. Even if they are convictions I agree with. In the same way, people who try to convince me that they didn't really want to get good at surfing, that all they wanted in life was to build the shack and get all Zen-y about it, I am suspicious of them; I think they are probably trying to put one over on me.

So if I tell you this surf trip is not about surfing, stay skeptical. It's a way of hedging my bets.

It's not. It's about love. Of a woman, of living, of the sea.

It is. One hundred percent. All about surfing.

I was coming to realize I needed help. Paddling that little frigging destroyer board around must have been getting me stronger. But the days were mounting up and the waves I actually caught and rode down the line on the 6–4 were pathetically few. In three weeks I could count them on one hand. And even those felt lucky. When I did actually ride a wave, Johnny Be Good and a local kid named Cole went apeshit. They fired salvos of encouragement: *"Andale, Pedro! Rápido! Tú puedes!* Bend your knees. You will get it!" That meant a lot to me. The gringo expats, mostly crusty men older than me, just figured that if I got better there'd be another person catching their waves.

In any event, a wave can be so gratuitous, so kind, only so often. I was getting my ass handed to me. It was time to go back to school. I needed a coach.

It wasn't hard to think of one. On an assignment a while back, I had met a pro surfer named James Pribram. We had quickly become buds. James, like me, loved to travel, especially into places and situations that were challenging and little-known. He also had a healthy streak of angry environmental outrage. He just couldn't bear that whole stretches of coast around the world were being lost to careless development and pollution, and especially that the world's great surf breaks were being destroyed one by one. When mangroves are torn up and seawalls built and river flows redirected, the hydrology changes and great waves disappear. Go extinct like the species of fish and coral that lie underneath.

James was known in surfing circles as the Eco-Warrior. He grew up in Laguna Beach, southern Orange County, and started surfing seriously when he was seven. It's all he ever wanted to do. Now he surfed all over the world, and tried to solve local environmental problems wherever he encountered them. At thirty-eight, James had boyish celebrity looks coupled with surfer toughness and a celebrity air. He was half Czech. Black brushy hair, keen gray eyes, medium height, and ripped. So, as he walked down the street of a little surf town in Chile, being filmed, it was assumed that he was a celebrity. He had no problem getting a meeting with the mayor, and starting a local campaign to stop an industrial plant from dumping pollutants into a rich lagoon important to local fishermen. A few months later the company stopped. It was ballsy, imaginative work from a surfer who looked like a teen idol. In Laguna Beach he wrote a column called "Surfing Soap Box" for the local paper. The themes were almost always environmental, and James had had a big hand in forcing the city to be more responsible about its oceanbound treated sewage. In response, the *Laguna Coastline Pilot* got reams of e-mails, mostly from gorgeous SoCal young women who told James that he was their hero. Living large, James, my boy. His Eco-Warrior show had been on Fuel TV and in 2007 he received one of the most prestigious awards in surfing that was not about some contest: the John Kelly Environmental Achievement Award, given to the surfer who did the best environmental work. Kelly Slater has been a recipient, as has Rob Machado. One man, one vision, many problems solved with real effects for the locals.

I called him. When I asked if he could tutor me on the shortboard, he said, "Yeah, good timing, really. I just got back from a trip. I could get down there at the end of the week and stay a week. Sound cool?"

"You bet. I need help bad."

I heard a quiet chuckle. "Surfing giving you a hard time?"

I hesitated. "Am I too old to be a shortboarder?"

James's laugh this time was a bray, a short cough of derision. For such a lame idea. "No, bro, you are not too old to be a shortboarder. That's all BS. A shortboard just requires some different techniques. You have to get used to the timing. We'll get you going. Don't worry."

I almost cried with relief.

Surfing at the End of the World

What a dude. James came through the customs line at the airport in baseball cap on backward and Oakley shades, carrying a board bag (short) and a day pack. Nothing else. He moved in a magnetic field of cool. Other travelers glanced at him, stepped back a half step to get a better look; they didn't know who he was but he was Somebody. I waved at him through the glass door. I couldn't see his eyes through the dark glasses but he lifted his chin a half millimeter. Cool.

It was a two-thirty arrival. We got to the river at four-thirty.

James said, "Nice." He looked across the *boca* to the tiers of wind-torn surf. "Let's go."

"Where?" I handed him Sergio's Spider-Man pillowcase.

"Surfing, where do you think?"

"It's afternoon."

"And?" His voice was Czech tenor and ranged higher when

he was incredulous or laughing at something I'd done that was particularly stupid.

"And the surf is all windblown."

"And?"

"Nobody goes surfing now."

"And can any of these nobodies really surf?"

"Well . . ."

That was the very first thing I learned from James: don't blindly do what everybody else does. James believed most people are sheep and consequently will always remain at a sheep level of achievement and consciousness. James believed in stepping back and seeing things for himself. We unslung the boards, paddled the lagoon, and walked down the beach. Despite the wind there was a swell running and waves were forming. Mostly they were crumbling and breaking in chaotic random peaks, sectioning in long dumps of white that left a surfer nowhere to go. We got to a wide mat of beach pea that grew across the spit between the lagoon and the surf. A few palm fronds had been stuck in the ground here, dried and brown, as a sun shelter for the local fishermen who worked the surf with hand lines. I stopped.

"We can go out here," I said. "The wave is that left out there." I bent to strap on my leash.

"Whoa, bud."

"What?"

"Were you going to look?"

"Why should I look? That's the wave."

James shook his head and emitted a high, derisive laugh. "You've got a lot to learn. Let's look at this thing."

I stood. The sun was hanging over the water, burnished and ready for a rest. The wind was stiff. James crossed his arms over his head to make a visor and just studied. After a couple of minutes I was going out of my mind. If we were going to surf, let's go. Sometime before sunset.

James picked up his board. "C'mon."

He started walking farther up the beach, toward the Liquidora, a circling, chaotic eddy of currents the locals avoided and which was particularly distempered this evening. It was foamy, peaking with colliding crosscurrents.

"Where are we going?"

"The best wave is over there, see?"

"Nobody surfs over there. That's right out from the Liquidora. See? You don't wanna go in there."

James shook his head again and smiled at me like I was a refractory kid. "You are my surfing son," he said. "You watch and learn. You don't even have a clue how much you don't know."

I was touched.

That afternoon James taught me that there was a good wave way over here north of where everyone surfed; that it was possible to surf and catch decent waves in the blown-out choppy evening; and that he'd paddle right around me and take every good wave away from me if I let him.

It was really hard for me to catch a decent wave. When one rolled in and I was perfectly positioned and it had a shape I could probably use, James would take it. I mean really take it. The guy could surf. From behind I'd see the nose of his board break over the lip, followed by an arm, a head, and then everything would reverse direction, sometimes in the air, as he snapped a cutback on one rail, and he'd disappear. He went down the line with aggressive, single-minded grace, like a predator running and bounding over rough ground.

When he paddled back out I said, "Why'd you take my wave?"

"*Your* wave?"

"Yeah, I was sitting right there, it was perfect."

"Son."

"What?"

"As soon as you stop moving toward the peak, you've ceded the wave."

"I have?"

"Yeah. Anybody else can go for the peak. If you want it, don't stop paddling."

"Yeah but this isn't Trestles. This is you and me. You're supposed to be helping me."

Now his grin was broad, warm. "I am," he said. "Here comes a wave. Go for the peak and don't stop."

That was something totally new. On the longboard I sat and waited for a wave. I paddled over to what I thought was the best position and watched the mountain of wave roll in, then I lay down, paused, adjusted myself forward or back on the board for the best trim, and finally paddled hard toward shore well out in front in order to get some speed before the wave got to me. Good strategy for a kook. Kook! I was ready to shuck the label like an old snakeskin.

James said, "Go! Go!"

I angled sideways and paddled directly toward the peak of the incoming wave, right at the crest where it first began to break, never stopping, and turned for the takeoff in one continuous arc. It didn't feel anything like sitting and waiting for a wave. This was fluid, dynamic. The 6–4 was responsive, and when the wave broke and slugged the board and washed my back I was already up and flying away from it.

We walked back up the beach as the sun hit the water in a collapsing pyre like a burning ship, and sank. "Did you see the fin?" James said.

"What fin?"

"Big-ass tiger shark swimming right by us."

"Why didn't you tell me?"

"I was catching my last wave in. Didn't you see me waving my arms?"

"No. But thanks."

Damn. This was tough love.

On James's second day, he, Kim, and I drove to a point called Barra de San Miguel. There was another river *boca* here and a very large estuary surrounded by undisturbed mangroves. The river emptied beside a high dry hill at the south end of a long curving bay. A fishing village and a few *palapa*-covered restaurants perched beside it, and a fleet of *pangas* was beached on the sand. Birds everywhere. I could see them all the way up the lagoon, frigates and pelicans, cormorants, egrets, and herons, all hanging out in the top of the thick mangrove trees, enjoying the nesting and shelter the way it should have been all up and down this coast. The wave here broke only so often. It had a sand bottom and was popular with beginners. Seemed like a good place for all of us.

I parked the van on the soft sand under some palms beside a restaurant and jumped out. Rash guard, one dab of sunscreen on the nose, wax the 6–4 destroyer with ten swipes, and turn for the shore. I was so stoked to practice what James had just taught me. Kim had barely gotten out of the front seat. I turned around for my coach. Where the hell was he? I saw him down the beach, by the cut in the sand where the river crossed it, looking out along the point.

"C'mon, c'mon, Ting, James is already out there." I leaned in through the open back door.

We were as locked into this tug-of-war as the Odd Couple. With as thick a skull as I have, I was just learning that it was a war I could never win. I could rant and tug all I wanted, but the tectonic plates, Kim's sunscreen, the volcanism and glaciation, Kim's bug dope and hair braids, the sedimentation, fossilization, mass extinctions, these would move apace. And at the end, millions of years would have passed, epochs, and she would look up, smile, walk to her longboard, and say, "Ready!"

But that didn't stop me. "C'mon, c'mon, James is waiting!"

She glanced around. "His board is still in the back of the van."

"It is? Oh."

I sensed an alliance growing. Both James and Kim seemed to be always telling me to slow down. I frowned. What was with all these slow people?

"Uh, okay, well. I'm gonna trot out there and go surfing. You've got your key. When James comes back you can lock up."

"Whateva."

I trotted out across the wide flat beach to my new dad. He had tugged his shirt off and placed it on top of his head in a white roll like a turban. He crossed his arms on top of it in his signature watch position.

Really cool people have a way of standing still that draws attention. They can make stillness enigmatic. Their charisma, in relaxed immobility, gathers around them like a cowl, like weather around a volcano. We wonder what they are doing.

"What are you doing?" I said to James as I squatted on the smooth pancake sand and strapped on my leash. The beach here was so different than at Barra Llorona. It didn't drop off a bench of sand to a steep soundboard of gravel. This was flat and gentle. The wave looked regular, relaxed.

"What are *you* doing?" James countered.

"I'm going surfing."

"You just lost your heat." He was talking about competition.

"I—I what?"

"You just lost your heat, bro."

"Oh." I was hurt. He forgot to call me "son."

"Where are you going to position yourself?"

I stood, looked out at the wave. "Right next to that guy on the green fish."

"He hasn't caught a wave since I've been here."

"Oh."

"You've gotta watch, son. Come to a new spot, stop and take twenty minutes to suss it all out."

"Yeah, but—"

"Where's the swell coming from?"

"Uh . . ."

"What's the period?"

"Uh . . ." I counted off Mississippis between the beginning of each break. "Eleven."

"What does that mean?"

"It's coming from pretty far out in the ocean."

"How big?"

"Chest-high."

"How often do the sets come in?"

"I, uh . . ." I shrugged.

He turned his head and looked down at me with a mixture of disappointment and a kind of incredulity—the kind of look you just can't stand to get from your dad. It was infinitely worse than getting yelled at.

"How big are they? Where do the set waves break?"

"Well . . ."

"How many waves in a typical set? Where is the wind coming from? What's it doing to the wave? Look at the texture there. Is it going across the face? Is it holding up the wave?"

"Um . . ."

"How fast is the wave? Where does it section?"

"James?"

"Yeah?"

"Do you really do this? Or are you raking me over the coals because I'm just not living up to your expectations as a surfing son? I mean, is all this like when you read the manual to your new toaster and it has five pages of safety instructions? I mean, nobody actually reads them, they just plug the sucker in."

He shook his head again, let out a laugh, confident and clear. "You wanna learn to surf? Or do you wanna always be a kook like that guy out there? I'm going to get my board. You watch. We'll have a quiz."

For fun that day James borrowed my Bruno quad-fin fish, the one that looked like a brick. He took off the two inside fins to give it more speed floating the white sections and to make it more challenging. By the time we paddled out, there must have been twenty longboarders clustered toward the inside, in front of the beach, and a few better shortboarders way outside, up against the point, waiting for the big set waves. James paddled past them. He paddled so far out you couldn't tell if he was a pelican or a man. Twenty minutes passed. I caught a couple of waves, but they were short lefts and I missed almost everything; I could never seem to generate any speed on the board. Kim went over into the pack of longboarders and was having the same trouble. And then a big set came in and I saw the pale figure way out on the point move onto it and into the break. The surfer accelerated across the face, being chased by the hissing, traveling line of white like a burning fuse. He flew to the top, veered right into the snowy maelstrom, and jetted out of it as if on fire. He crouched and generated magnificent speed straight across the face, went airborne off the lip, and landed back in the pocket. He jammed right toward the big crowd of surfers who waited for a shoulder to ride. James flew into them. They all just stopped. They stopped whatever the hell they were doing and just gawked, and James slewed through them like a slalom skier. When one clueless kook dropped into the wave without looking, right in front of him, James flew effortlessly to the lip and swooped around him. Anybody else I'd ever seen surf would have had a wreck. He kept going. He left a wake of astonishment behind him, an impression of raptor speed and beauty.

I kept trying. I caught a couple of little waves. After one short ride I saw James on the sand, taking a break, watching me with his arms on his head. I rode the whitewater in on my belly, got out.

"I figured out what your problem is."

"You did?"

"Yeah, I was watching you. I thought, *Pete's spending a ton of energy paddling, but he's not really going anywhere.* I watched. You're paddling all wrong. You're cupping your hand—"

"That's what someone told me in California."

"What did someone tell you?"

"They told me to cup my hands, extend my arm, and pull straight back like I'm starting a lawn mower."

James exploded. The most derisive laughter yet. "That's not what you do. You put your whole arm in the water. Relax your hands, let your fingers fall open. Paddle with your whole arm."

"Wow."

"Try it."

I went back out. Seemed to work. But before I could catch a wave, as I was sitting on my board, I saw James waving with both arms on the beach. Huh? And I saw Kim sitting on the wet sand. I rode back in as fast as I could, trotted up. Blood poured down on Kim's white rash guard.

A skinny Spanish tourist in a Speedo pressed a bag of ice to her mouth. James was holding her head and shoulders. She had tried for a wave and been tumbled. As she came up to the surface her board slingshotted back on the leash and smashed her face right between her nose and upper lip. Half inch higher, it would have broken her nose, lower and it would have knocked out all her front teeth. She was crying. I held her and murmured, "It's all right, you're gonna be all right, we'll go to the doctor in town. The bleeding's stopped, you're all right." I didn't know if it was true but it was the best thing to say and believe. Surfing was pushing our limits. I had pulled her into this.

We made a fire in camp. The night wind shirred the palms. Kim sipped Ensure. The doctor said the cut on her gum and inside her lip was pretty deep but unstitchable where it was. She'd have to endure antiseptic-soaked gauze placed under her upper lip and refrain from solid food for ten days. She looked like she'd had an overenthusiastic botox job, like Joan Rivers. She was a good sport.

"Cuj a vu wrrrr," she said.

"What?" we said.

"Cuj a vu mu wrrrr," she said.

"Oh, yeah, much worse," we agreed. I'd thought of it and thanked the wave god all evening. She was an actor and model and it could have really screwed up her face.

James lay in the hammock and chewed on a piece of grilled chicken. The moon was three-quarters full and made shifting shadows of the fronds. A night bird cried out. "You know, this is the first time in years I've traveled and just gone surfing for fun. No photographers, no sponsors. It's awesome."

He was as happy as Sergio had been, swinging gently in the same place. Except that the hammock and even the tree trunks looked less stressed out.

On James's last evening a sultry, premonsoon heaviness set in over the lagoon. It seemed to press down from the Sierra. The first leaden clouds moved past the peaks and a thick haze lay over the sea to the west. As the sun lowered toward the band of fog, it warmed slowly like reviving embers. The wind died. The palm leaves stilled and a languid heat overtook the mangroves and stilled the cries of the birds. James wanted to go surfing.

The bay was empty. No fisherman with nets waist-deep in the whitewater, no surfers. Kim had a no-surfing order from the doctor till her mouth healed and she'd driven to town to check e-mail. James and I paddled out. The sun lowered farther into a layer of blood-infused smoke. The water grayed. There was an easy, shoulder-high swell. We each caught a couple of waves. I could paddle a lot faster, now that I was using my whole arm, and my constantly inflamed right shoulder no longer hurt. I caught a short ride and paddled back out. It wasn't just the light––the short chop inshore crested and foamed and was the color of soot. So was the breaking wave beyond it. And the water was slick, windless, rippling like oil. It smelled like death. I sat on my board and looked around. My shorts slid on the greasy board. The sea palled, ashy under the smoking sun, swollen and malignant. It was portentous. It was the way I would have painted the end of the world. I looked inland. A column of greasy black smoke roiled out of the palms just upriver. What was going on? I slid back down onto my board and began to paddle against the current. On my second stroke my right hand came down on something large and fleshy. It slid away from my palm like something dead. Couldn't see because the water was so dirty.

"Hey," James called. "Something's wrong."

Yeah, I thought. *This is the apocalypse.* That's what it looked like. I saw no living bird etched against the sky, not a soul moving on the whole long beach. The smell wrinkled my nose. But worse was the way the water moved—not like the living ocean I was used to, but slack and unctuous. It slid off the crest like melted fat.

"Let's get out."

We both bellied in on the foam, which gave off a flat, fetid odor.

Walking back along the beach, we stepped over a dead sea turtle and a dead cormorant splayed on the wet gravel. We entered the palm grove where a few tents were pitched. Not a soul there. The few parked cars were gone.

"Did we miss the memo?" James said.

"Creepy. I always fantasized about an earth without people, but I'm not sure I like it much."

A woman stepped from behind a wall tent and waved, a simple action that snapped the world back in place.

We walked to our tents and laid our boards on their bags. "Damn." I looked around. "What do you think was going on?"

"Like a red tide," James said. "But gray. Sometimes if a lot of plankton die it can be like a death current. The water was really warm, did you notice?"

I had noticed. I thought how recent studies had found hypoxic, or low-oxygen, dead zones thousands of square miles in areas out in the middle of the ocean, caused by warming. (Warmer water holds less oxygen. Imagine opening a cold pop, the light rising of bubbles. Now let it get really warm and it releases its gas in a thick fizz.) A study led by Lothar Stramma of the University of Kiel in Germany discovered that deep water hypoxic bands are rapidly expanding and washing up onto continental shelves. Giant squids are one of the only species that seem to be able to live in the oxygen-poor waters. The study says that the trend eerily echoes a scenario that unfolded about 250 million years ago, when massive carbon dioxide emissions from volcanoes warmed the planet and stripped the oceans of oxygen. When that happened the earth shrugged off 95 percent of its biota.

As the oceans go, so do we.

THE WAVE THAT LIVED IN MY MIND

I had been thinking about a wave. It was a perfect right that swelled on the shelf of a shallow reef and hit a rocky point and jacked up in a green and overhanging wall that shot one dead-level barrel after another across the inside of the bay. It was in southern Oaxaca, almost to the Guatemalan border, at a place where the Pacific coast of Mexico inverted and caught the southern storm swell on its back and generated rights instead of lefts.

Nathan at *Surfing* magazine had told me about it, but I'd forgotten completely until Kim and I saw the movie *Absolute Mexico* at the surfing film festival in Huntington Beach during the U.S. Open championship when we had the keys to the beach and were camped below the pier. Kim and I had squeezed in with the crowd at the movie theater on the Pacific Coast Highway and dutifully sat with the Michaels and Bruno for what we'd thought would be another surf-porn fest.

I can't stand extreme sport movies, whatever the sport. But the wave in Oaxaca had been the site of one of the most extraordinary surfing competitions in history, a shoot-out between the world's top competitors and local hotshots on a consistent pipe that almost never ended. Some of these guys were covered up, traveling like lead inside a gun barrel for what seemed all morning. I watched and discovered that I was holding my breath. Kelly Slater was in the film, and Andy Irons. And some strong local surfers like Bobby Martinez who had the wave wired.

The competition was called the 2006 Rip Curl Pro and Andy Irons beat Slater, beat everybody. But what I remember was the wave, the way it loaded itself against the rocks, swelling and building pressure like a pulled bow and then shooting off the point like an arrow. I remember the color, the stone-blue that turned to glass-green inside the necked bottle of the barrel. The way the surfers changed color inside the wave like some reef fish and then exploded, nearly vanishing in light as they emerged and hit the shattering crystalline lip. The sound it made, the wave devouring itself, groan and thunder. It was such a wave to haunt even a nonsurfer, to haunt dreams.

After James left, I retired the 6–4 for a while, the one with four fins, and pulled out a standard 6–7 shortboard thruster, which was faster. It had the normal three-fin configuration designed for acceleration, especially when caught up in the whitewater of a section. With my new and improved paddle stroke I found that, for the first time in our two months at the river, I could really move. Which meant I was beginning to catch waves.

Just beginning. When I did, most of the time I just wiped out. I didn't pop up fast enough and got caught with a wave breaking on my back, or I popped up and went to the very bottom, skated through the transition and out into the flat ahead of the wall, not where I wanted to be. Like sliding down a playground slide and getting dumped into the dirt. And because I had not set an edge or a fin to help me generate opposing pressure—the thrust needed to swing back up the face—I just got buried.

One day Cole paddled up to me after seeing me wipe out a few times in a row. "Stay low," he said. "Keep your knees bent, you remember? What I told you? You are too straight. You'll get it. In a couple weeks you'll be having fun like the rest of us." He smiled. He could read the anguish of frustration on my face.

He held out a fist and bumped me. Later that morning, I did what he said and it worked—staying low allowed me to set an edge high on the wave and accelerate away from danger. I was so happy. With such slow progress, any small improvement seemed a triumph.

The board *moved* now. After two months of surfing every day for two or three hours, I felt like I was developing the instincts to catch the right waves the right way. It was the same with Kim. She had recovered from her cut and was catching waves now without help, making the extra power surge to drop in. Part of it was that all of our training was paying off: we were learning to read waves, and learning where to be and when. But part of it was sheer strength. Months of surfing hard every day had given us the strength we needed to begin to learn how to ride a wave. It reignited our desire to travel. The joy of breakthrough. Or maybe it was simple antsiness. We had been camped by the lagoon for almost eight weeks.

Whatever it was, I began to think about the wave in Oaxaca, wondering if I could ride it. I called Leon Pérez, my old mentor. He'd just had an operation in his gut, probably a result of three decades of hard partying, and he'd been out of the water for a month. It was the longest he hadn't surfed since he was fifteen. I'd seen him two weeks before and he was getting stronger, eating carefully, staying away from tequila and Corona, and impatient to get back in the water.

"Hey, how's the stomach?"

"Getting better. Little by little. I am surfing again. Taking it easy."

"You want to go to Oaxaca for ten days?"

"I was thinking about it."

"You were?"

"Yes. I need a break."

I thought about that. Leon surfed every morning of his life and caught many more waves than any of the younger locals, than anyone at all. He was the king of the breaks up and down the coast within an hour of Zihuatanejo. Hell, he'd discovered most of them back in the late seventies. He usually showed up at his shop after two, unless he had special clients to guide. He had arranged his whole life around surfing and answered to no one. I knew what he meant, though. He needed a break away from his convalescence, everything associated with the operation.

"You wanna go in a few days?"

"Yes. I want to see the wave at Barra. Also to stop in and see friends in Puerto." He meant Barra de la Cruz, the wave I'd been dreaming about. Puerto was Puerto Escondido, home of the Mexican Pipeline, the most famous barrel in North America, and an international scene.

"You're kidding. I've been dreaming about that wave! That's so weird."

"That's the way things work, Pedro."

"Okay, let's go."

"My truck is having some problems."

"Nah, we can take our van. We'll come down and pick you up."

It was settled. We'd go south to the perfect point breaks of Oaxaca with the King. It would be the climax to our trip.

LEON'S TREE

We spent the night in Ixtapa with Leon. His daughter Auramar was a rambunctious, pretty six-year-old who loved to make me hot tacos that got me screaming and begging for water. They were tacos that she made out of air, and my howls were theater, but they sent her into paroxysms of laughter.

Leon split custody with Auramar's mother, an attractive younger woman who had suffered some terrible things as a kid and was half crazy from it all. He adored his daughter even more than he loved the sea, which is saying something. Leon told us how he had planted a little palm tree for her when she was born, out there by the fence along the empty lot. It grew to the height of a man with a trunk a hand-span thick. One day he came back from a week of surf competitions and the tree had been knocked down and pulled out with a bunch of other brush. It lay in the lot desiccated and dead. All the fronds were brown, roots broken. Just a bare trunk. Leon freaked out. He called the mother. Auramar was sick. She had a fever and couldn't go to school. Leon thought the uprooted palm might have more significance than a memento destroyed; he feared for his daughter's safety. So he picked up the tree and he planted it back by the fence, this forlorn post, and he watered it and prayed. He watered it every day without fail. In the second week it sprouted one tiny green leaf. And

Auramar woke up and her eyes were clear and she went back
to school. He showed us the tree, taller now, almost eight feet,
and thick with green fronds.

We drove for fifteen hours, along the endless headlands
of southern Guerrero, hundreds of miles of surf. We drove
through small villages and palm and papaya plantations, with
always the rugged Sierra on our left as if to say, *This is another
dream. Your dream is the sea. Don't even think about coming up
here.* I wouldn't. Of all the mountain ranges I have ever seen,
from the St. Elias to the Pamirs or the Himalayas, the Sierra
Madre are the most forbidding—as unapproachable with
hide intact as the afterlife. Which is where you'd probably
go if you decided to drive up in there and wander around.
In those isolated mountain towns, rife with *droguistas,* xeno-
phobic describes the most mellow residents; everybody else
would really rather kill a stranger than give him directions.
It's easier, requires less thought. But the mountains were
beautiful, and they changed shades of blue the way the sea
does as the sun rises, becoming more and more substantial as
the day wore on.

   We took turns driving. There were two seats in the van.
The third person had two choices: to stretch out on a Therm-
a-Rest under the a stack of surfboards tied to the side, or to
perch in a folding camp chair between the front seats and yell,
"Tope!" every ten minutes. *Topes* are speed bumps, and they
are a highly effective speed-limit enforcement in lieu of state
troopers. Unless you're me. I think the suckers are put in by
the local alignment and shock shop. I didn't pay any attention
to them until we were right on top of one going fifty miles
per hour, and then Leon, dozing in back, would levitate two

feet off his sleeping pad and slam back down, and Kim would scream and her seat belt would keep her from cracking her head on the roof. I got yelled at a lot. It got so Leon would forgo resting and ride shotgun and shout warnings.

We drove down into the dry-season heat of southern Oaxaca. Rough coastal hills, big spreading ceiba trees at the edges of pastures, small villages of thatch-roofed shacks. We crossed long bridges over wide rivers that ran mud-brown and slow now with the first mountain rains, rains that hadn't yet gotten down to the low country. The rivers were lined with palms and cornfields and they emptied into the sea below us. Others were dry beds reflecting back the midday sun, and horses wandered the arroyos and banks. I loved being on the road again. We stopped for lunch at a roadside shack that canted in a billow of fragrant smoke and steam curling out of the open kitchen. The woman offered us two *platos del día*: iguana and armadillo. We had Cokes and drove on.

When Leon first surfed the barrel of Puerto Escondido the good road ended there. It was a fishing village with a small town center and the only route beyond it, south into Chiapas, was a dirt track. Not anymore. Puerto materialized out of the coastal farm country like some psychotropic Eurotrash dream of a Mexican surf city. The wide Zicatela Beach was flanked along much of its length by a jammed array of Italian restaurants, courtyard hotels with names like Flor de Maria and Santa Fe, organic cafés, smoothie dens, kitsch T-shirt stores, surf shops. Hip-hop and hard rock poured out of every other establishment. Luxury tour buses rumbled and idled at the curbs, and in among the herds of international tourists, like smoothly muscled predators on some herd-trodden savanna, moved surfers of every type. Long European girls in bikinis; sun-darkened locals with tattoos sprayed over shoulders and thighs, carrying their big-wave guns. Big, ripped veterans, eyes unfocused, minds blown out by decades of drugs and killer tubes, so skilled on their boards they moved on instinct, became engines on autopilot. And facing them all, with the distant boom of cannonade that rolled through the loudest of the music, was the wave, the Mexican Pipeline.

It just looked like suicide to me. We walked to a low whitewashed wall and stood looking across the stretch of white sand. I'd never seen anything like it. The groundswell rolled in and threw up a vertical wall just yards from shore. Then the whole wall dumped with an impact that shuddered the ground where we stood. Jeez. I couldn't even imagine going out there. Or wanting to. But every fifth wave or so the same wall tongued itself into a long, smooth, critical barrel. And that's when one of the brave surfers—there were only a handful out today—took off in a flurry from the lip to either make the drop or miss it. Usually three or four took off and two or three were skilled enough to pull back at the very last nanosecond. The one with priority threw himself off the face. Sometimes he surged ahead of the white bullet train of the collapsing wave and went to the lip. If he was really brave and really good, he dropped down again and put the brakes on by weighting his back foot and stalled, and waited for the onslaught of the barrel, and then he was covered up in the maelstrom and sometimes he emerged cleanly out the end and shot over the back of the wave unharmed. Sometimes he got eaten and the castle wall fell on his head and he disappeared and I found myself praying for his life. Just looking at the thing roiled my guts and made me want to find a bathroom.

Leon said it was pretty big now and the shape wasn't very

good, which was why so many we watched met disaster. He
shook his head. He was just recovering, not full strength, so he
probably wouldn't surf the barrel anyway, but especially now
when it was very dangerous.

We turned back to the street.

One of Leon's oldest surfing friends ran the most established
surf shop on the beach, Central Surf Shop. His name was
Angel Salinas and in the middle of talking to a customer he
caught sight of Leon and broke into a radiant smile.

"Discúlpame." He stepped from behind the glass counter.
He was a giant of a man, thick like a ceiba trunk, with a broad
round face and a bright smile and eyes that threw off light like
sunlight on textured water. His warmth was a weather pattern
that engulfed his surroundings. He spoke English in a bluff,
hoarse, happy tenor, the way you'd imagine a good-natured
grizzly bear talking. He reminded me of the happy bear at
Scorpion Bay. He first-bumped Leon and then crushed him
in a hug that would have accordioned stouter men. One of his
shop guys tactfully slipped over and took care of the customer
and Angel and Leo caught up in rapid Spanish. Kim and I
looked around. Everywhere there were posters of a big man
in a fierce wrestler's mask surfing the great barrel. And up on
the cabinets were mannequin heads with the same elaborate,
brightly colored masks. Cat eyes and fringe that hung down
around the throat and neck. They were frightening.

"Who is that?" I pointed to a poster.

"That's me," Angel said.

"He is the famous masked surfer of Puerto."

"Wow. What gave you the idea?"

A bearded man, fiftyish, came from behind a corner counter where he'd been working on a laptop. He was Ruben Piña, probably the most published surf photographer in Mexico. "We shot thousands of really good photos of Angel and submitted them everywhere. Nobody would publish them. Then he put on the mask, and wham. Everybody wanted pictures. *Surf, Surfing, Transworld,* everyone."

I asked Ruben if it was a racist thing. He shrugged tactfully. "Well, anyway. El Surfo is a sensation now."

Leon asked where we could get rooms cheap and Angel suggested right up the alley a block from the shop. That's where we went. The Beast barely made it up the steep drive. We got two flyspecked rooms with rattling fans and met Angel and Ruben for dinner at a pub on the front street. Leon was so happy to be among his old compadres. Soon the shots of tequila came out in crowded trays. I noticed that Angel drank only club soda. I could imagine the reason: get a huge, emotional surfer like El Surfo blotto and the destructive force could be as natural and unintentional as a tsunami. We sat near the front of the open bar, right on the street, and it was wonderful to watch how many surfers of all ages stopped by Leon's table for a fist-bump and a chat. Leon knew everyone.

Alejandro de la Torre came up the night street bare-chested and moving with a rhythm of a long swell. He wasn't tall but he was ripped like a body builder and his dark eyes were sad and his smile flitted across his face, revealing itself and gone as quickly as a surfer in a big barrel. A deep scar ran across his right cheekbone, knife or rock or thruster fin. His tawny hair hung loose down his back, partly covering the lat-to-lat tattoo of a stingray. The ray was partly filled in and part inked outline. I remembered him from the first surf competition I'd ever seen in Acapulco on that first assignment with Leon. I had met him again a week later at Leon's shop in Ixtapa and he had a little dog with him. I asked him where he got the pup. Alejandro tipped back his bottle of Corona to drain it and looked around. I ordered him another. He said, "La Pulga and me and a couple of others were in Puerto staying down at the hostel by the beach. We got stoned and we ran out of papers. La Pulga opened the drawer and they had, you know, the Bible in there, so we started ripping out pages and rolling joints. We got real stoned. I don't remember, maybe I fell asleep. La Pulga shook on me, 'Alejandro, Alejandro, wake up, it's the flood, man, wake the fuck up. God is punishing us for smoking the Bible.' It was true. The water was already under the beds. A big storm swell. Fucking really big. I grabbed my board and I ran out. The point was going off. I paddled out, there's this big rock, I paddled past the rock and I saw this bitch dog, man, she was putting her puppies on the rock. Trying to save them. I tried to get them all but a set wave came in. I held on to this little dude." He took a slug of beer and the shy smile shot across his face. He reached down and picked up the dog by the scruff of his neck and put him in his lap and gave him a sip of beer.

"What's his name?"

"Milagro."

Now, in Puerto, Alejandro came up the street in the rhythm of his own music and saw Leon and lifted his chin, angled over. He was amped, humming with the high-idle engine of so many surfers. The smile flashed and he met no one's eye. His scar throbbed on his burnished dark cheek, his hair was more sun-bleached. I wanted to ask about the dog, but figured there was no conclusion to that story that was not painful. He exchanged some words with the boys at the table, then, shirtless, went behind the bar. He seemed to work there, anything to keep surfing.

NIGHTMARE IN REVERSE

Two narrow lanes wound through the rugged, forested hills, now parched and thorny. Straightened along fields and pastures. At every crossroads a wobbly thatch roof on crooked posts, a stick fire under steaming pots, a flat stone *comal* for making tortillas. Heat. We stopped a lot, drank Nescafé, cold Fantas. Every side road turning down through the hills on our right led to a little-known wave that Leon had surfed as a young man. We were on the road again. After two days surfing an easy wave in a cove on the north side of Puerto, we were eager to get to the wave Leon and I had both been dreaming of. We had two weeks altogether for the trip, so no one was in any hurry. At another small side road there was a little sign that said ZIPOLITE.

"In the seventies there used to be a big nude beach down there," Leon said. "Hippies from all over the world."

Kim perked up. "I've never seen a nude beach. Let's go." Along the road, some evidence that hippies had stayed: A-frames and tree houses, signs advertising kinetic bodywork and aromatherapy. Espresso. How weird. We wound down to the coast, parked between a one story stuccoed hotel and a restaurant, walked out onto a wide beach. Empty. Kim was disappointed.

"We could get naked and take a picture," I suggested.

Kim shrugged. A lone gringo in a big straw hat with a woven satchel over his shoulder strolled toward us up the damp sand. We turned to go. "C'mon." I looked at Kim. Her jaw was hanging, eyes wide. What? She was following the progress of the man who had passed us. I looked at his pink and naked moon of a butt moving away. "Gimme the camera!" she said. "That guy is strolling up the beach completely naked!

Like he doesn't realize it. It's like one of those nightmares in reverse!"

Once we were back on the road, we detoured through Huatulco, a government-subsidized insta-hotel zone and marina carved out of a once-uninhabited bay. Leon said no one had lived here before, not even fishermen. Now it was miles of smooth and empty four-lane divided blacktop separated by a manicured median of planted royal palms and flower-box-trimmed bougainvillea bushes. With side roads leading to big luxury hotels, each with a beach, each with a hillside to ravish and climb. Condos, a golf course. We could see bits of the resorts as the road twisted and offered vistas of the bay. Tourists must have stayed here but the resorts felt lonely, hollow, disattached from the landscape like moon stations.

We drove on. The coast was more rugged. The little highway pitched and plunged, switched back. Crossed a high steel bridge over a shallow clear river crowded with tall old willows and palms. One rambling two-story concrete restaurant-house leaning above the bank. The river was a vein of vivid green pulsing through a parched country. The thickly leaved treetops bent and swayed in the afternoon wind pouring down the canyon. I felt happy. Two of my favorite people rode in the van with me. Over the days of traveling, we had developed an easygoing multicelled way of moving: if someone wanted to stop and pee, or eat, or get an ice cream, or rest, or drive, or look inside a church, the van nudged over and everyone was game, everyone participated with an easy willingness to shift gears. It was Leon's spirit, I think, that pervaded the organism of our van. He was not overly demonstrative or easily impressed, but he was truly mellow and tolerant and adventurous.

The highway, squeezed by forest, struggled up a grade. We spotted a tiny sign on the ocean side that read BARRA DE LA

CRUZ. We pitched down a new concrete drive that dropped like a roller coaster, twisted, and we could see the village below, a lush valley cradled between two headlands, a dark lake, fields of bright broad-leafed bananas. We caromed down through a *pueblito* of little concrete houses painted in pastels, wooden huts with thatch roofs, a whitewashed school, and a full-sized shadeless basketball court. The road turned to dirt and ended at the cone of a tall, round *palapa* roof with an elegant open restaurant beneath it, and a gate. The gate was a swinging bar. A sign informed us that surfers who wished to continue beyond this point must pay twenty pesos. Good idea; at least one poor village in Mexico was taking advantage of a natural resource sought after by an increasing flood of international surfers. A boy limped out from behind a shaded booth, wearing a clean white Quicksilver cap and Rip curl T-shirt. His right leg was twisted, and by the way he carried his right arm, high, fist clenched, I knew he had cerebral palsy. My younger sister has it, too. He came to me at the driver's-side window and asked how many we were.

"*Tres.*"

"*Sesenta.*"

"*Sí, bueno.*" I gave him an extra ten. His eyes widened, then he nodded and put the coin in the pocket of his jeans. He limped back and swung the gate and we passed through it onto a smooth new sand road that shot through pasture and banana fields and above the river valley on our left. We topped a rise.

"There," Leon said. "Pretty good."

I pulled to a stop in full view of the broad blue bay. A spur of ridge on our right, rashed with scrub and tall cacti, flowed down to the water and ended in a pile of protruding rocks. The wave, a right, barreled in off of this point. The wave heaved up against the boulders, unreeled fast in level lines of whitewater. Right now, simultaneously, three clean walls of wave, in three measured tiers, one behind the other, rolled into the beach. The closest in had the longest rope of white. A surfer worked the pocket of each one. A perfect right. Like Scorpion Bay but heavier and faster. Close to the rocks every other wave formed a hollow tube.

"Jesus." We all stared.

Leon smiled. *"Vámonos."*

Midafternoon was too late to have a good session most anyplace else on the Mexican coast, but not here. The wave was too muscular, too shapely, too clean to be knocked down by an onshore wind. It might fray, but it would stand up. The sight of it, from a mile away, did two things to me: it scared me, the kind of scare that made me want to find an outhouse; and it got me amped. I couldn't wait to run out there and get on it.

"The wave will be there," Leon said with a smile. He knew me pretty well by now. "Better to be patient."

Jesus, he sounded like Kim. "Yeah," said Kim. "Slow down, Ting. Remember what James said?"

"What did James say?"

She shook her head like I was a lost cause and began the geologic process of braiding her hair. We might not get out there till midnight. Well, maybe there would be a moon. Anyway, I couldn't just run off and leave my wife in the parking lot; not at this world-famous barrel.

Leon was remarkably mellow and methodical. He pulled out a 6–8 shortboard, something nimble but fast, and began to wax it. He stretched his shoulders, arms bent one at a time behind his head. Kim braided. The sun declined in the west. I was hopping up and down, almost running in place with my

Bruno 6–7. I couldn't wait to try it on a big fast wave. In the last week before we'd left I'd been catching more waves on this board than I was missing. I felt that I was edging onto a new plateau in my evolution as a surfer. Now would come a real test. Could I ride such a fast, hollow, powerful wave?

Leon wanted to find the local surf elder named Pablo Narváez. He was partly the reason we were here: he had met Leon at a surf competition in Acapulco and invited him to come down. I could feel the thundering of the wave in my viscera the way I felt the bass of a thumping band tugging my gut strings. But first things first.

Nothing about Barra was like anyplace else we'd been surfing in Mexico. The gate was the first thing. Charging for surfing. Outrageous, but fair in its way. These were poor people, and the wave was a resource. Technically they weren't collecting for the wave, but for use of the new road, which strung along the river and led right to the beach and a single shaded restaurant. A restaurant not owned by any grubbing vendor, but by the whole town. As was the lake we'd seen from above, which was filled with tilapia. Every Saturday the fishermen netted boatloads of the freshwater fish and distributed them to the villagers at the very low price of twenty pesos a kilo.

Communal living wasn't a trend here but a way of life. Barra was an "indigenous village." In the early sixties, the people, descended from the Chontal, had moved down to the rich valley at the mouth of the river Chacalapa from a flinty historical provenance up in the mountains. The Mexican government established a reservation for the Chontal and extended their lands down to the sea, granting the people a certain surprising autonomy. The town of nearly eight hundred had its own

police—an annually rotating job—its own bylaws, and held
real estate in common. Every third year all adult males had to
give a year of service to the town in various jobs, such as being
one of the twelve cops, working the fish, or helping to teach in
the school. Families were allotted the use of plots for farming.
Anyone could own a private business, such as the fine *palapa*
restaurant up by the gate, and these businesses payed no taxes.
The town council, which voted on all matters, was composed
only of the heads of households and only of men. It was this
august body that hired the boy with cerebral palsy to man the
gate, and which closed that very gate one day in 2007 to all
international surfers and "rented" out the barrel to wave oracle
Sean Collins and fifteen of his VIP friends for about $20,000
for three days. (Collins started the popular wave report and
forecast Web site surfline.com.) The "Goodwill Tour," as the
exclusive event was called, took place during one of the best
swells of the year and barred many surfers who had traveled
a long way to surf it. This was unprecedented in Mexico, and
the closing, and selling, of Barra created an uproar among the
surfing community.

Leon's friend Pablo was the king of surf in Barra. He surfed,
he guided surfers, he farmed, he was the most knowledgeable
ornithologist in this part of Mexico. He owned the *palapa* restaurant by the gate and at thirty-nine was a respected elder in
the town. He understood gringos, their proclivities and deal-
ings, probably better than anybody, as he had been leading
birding trips for rich tourists staying at the fancy hotels in
Huatulco for two decades. He said, "It is our right to close
the gate, to open it for anyone. Let people say what they want.
We will make our decisions. We will do what is best for the
community. We cannot stop people from surfing the wave,
but it is our road." He also told us that the community had

refused multimillion-dollar offers to sell their coast to developers. Having seen what had happened to the local people in places like Pescadero and La Paz—how they had lost control of their most precious resource—I understood that this was a decision of remarkable foresight.

We met Pablo in the shade of the beach restaurant, which was a tent over the sand, ten tables, an open kitchen. He had just come in from a session on the wave. He wore trunks and a red baseball cap. He had light skin and broad cheekbones, a tuft of beard on his chin. He spoke perfect English and was welcoming. He said there had just been a shark in the water. He and Leon set about catching up, but I didn't even try to follow the conversation.

The midafternoon sun beat on the white sand. Across the blinding expanse, up to our right, were the tumbled slabs and boulders of the point and the wave. The wave. From down here in the orchestra pit the thing was even more impressive. Scorpion Bay had been consistent, ruler-level. This was the same. But this was—this was . . . big. These didn't roll in and crumble, icing themselves with a frill of whitewater along their length like some vanilla log cake. Uhn-uhn. This wave took a deep breath as it approached the outer rocks and swelled into something more like a stampeding mammoth. More like a mountain. Then it curled, and when it curled it threw its whole top into the effort, it became vertical, past vertical, concave and hollow, sometimes tubular. When it passed the angle of repose, beyond which it could no longer live as a mountain, it relinquished itself to gravity with a geologic roar, a ferocious surrender. I couldn't keep my eyes off it. There must have been thirty surfers all clustered and bobbing at the point. I watched as one by one they jockeyed for position and took off. Most of them looked like pros. *This'll be interesting,*

I thought. The set waves may have been just over their heads, but they seemed much bigger because they were so heavy. The lip when it folded was thick, like a ridge of muscle. I couldn't wait any longer.

"Hey, I'll see you guys out there!" Pablo nodded, Leon and Kim exchanged what I like to think of as a glance of loving tolerance.

"*Ojo, Pedro,*" Leon warned. "Take a look."

I ran out onto the sun-blared beach, which sizzled like a skillet. I yelped and hopped all the way to damp, cooler sand. It felt like I had second-degree burns on the bottom of my feet, but I didn't care. I walked the wet tide line, over glistening piles of eely kelp and past little crabs skittering into their holes, without taking my eyes off the wave. I noticed how the surfers who were just getting in waited on the sand, then when the foam sucked back for the next wave they trotted out and took shelter in the lee of a lone house-sized rock just off the beach. They waited while the whitewater of the next wave surged around them, and then ran again for the beach of a tiny cove up against the spur of the point. From there they waded out along the projecting shore, in the shadow of the point, protected by the jut of rocks. Again they waited for the right timing, for a sequence of smaller waves, and jumped on their boards and sprinted right across the path of the break, sprinted out away from the rocks, angling to get around the crashing pocket and out fast to the steep shoulder. Okay. Easy. A game of angles. If you took a line too close, too straight up into the wave, you'd get nowhere and the most powerful part of it broke on you. If you paddled too far sideways, too parallel to the beach, the net of whitewater cast by the wave would unfurl and swallow you.

I ran into the shallow water, hugged the face of the first

protecting boulder like a SWAT trooper, holding a short-board instead of a rifle. Even the shallow foam surprised me. It charged in, faster than I was used to, and sucked out against my knees with real force. I had to hold the rock. So much energy here.

"Okay, cover me!" I said to the rock, and ran to the little cove beach. I stood on the sand and caught my breath. Leon had said to look. I looked. I had been looking. I got the idea.

I waded up along the point, bracing against each surge. The interval between each wave was barely long enough: a fast paddler could just get across between the avalanches of white-water. Okay, now! A big wave had just thundered by. I hit the board with my belly and started paddling like a madman up and away from the rocks. I sprinted as I had never sprinted before, and just barely cleared the next wave. It was like paddling up a cliff. Went over the back of the lip just as the ferocious jaws roaring in from my right got to me; the surfer in the pocket nearly grazed my feet. I dropped into the trough, into blue water. Whew. I slowed my stroke and took stock of where I was. I was still pretty close in to the point. Too close? Was this the impact zone? Nah.

In fact, here came a wave, right at me. It was a lot bigger than the last one. A kid out at the point missed it, wiped out. It was empty, steep. It had my name on it. Right? Definitely. Anyway, I had no choice. I was like an escapee caught by the spotlight in open ground. I pivoted, looked over my shoulder. Holy shit! The thing was huge. It was over me. It was breaking. I popped up at the same time as a sledgehammer knocked me full across my back and flung me away like a doll. I tumbled in bright champagne, hit the sand floor hard with a shoulder. I was bursting to breathe, but when I came up to burning sunlight I got shoved back down again with barely half a breath. I needed to breathe. Not gonna happen. I somersaulted, fought panic. *Relax!* My mind raced. *Relax! Relax and use less oxygen. Okay, okay!* When I finally sputtered to the surface I saw that I hadn't made it away from the rocks at all. I'd managed to turn right into the impact zone and tried to catch a catastrophe. I sucked air and tugged on my leash to retrieve the board. It felt strange. Really light. It reeled in with almost no resistance at all. I pulled in the back half of Bruno's 6–7. Jagged foam and torn fiberglass where the logo had been. I saw the nose bobbing into the cove, a helpless and poignant wreck. What an idiot. I swam after it. I saw a little local kid jumping up and down, running into the water, fighting with the current to snag it.

The boy was tiny, maybe six. When I got to him he was yelling, excited, holding up the nose, laughing.

"*Un regalito?*" he said. A gift?

"Nah, I want to see if I can fix it. *Gracias.*" It was my favorite board. I tousled his head. He grinned at me, handed me my small chunk of foam and fiberglass. I started walking off. I loved this board. It was the only thing short I'd been able to really move. But I had the 6–4 in the van. I remembered Leon telling me how when he was the same age, the only chance of getting a board had been a broken one from a gringo. I stopped and unstrapped the leash. "Hey!"

The boy turned.

"*Aquí. Tuyo!*" I gave him the two pieces. His eyes widened, huge. He couldn't contain his joy. He ran straight up to the brush, suddenly surrounded by five friends. "*Repáralo! Facil!*" they cried.

I went back to the van for the quad, and this time I made myself watch the other surfers for five minutes before I paddled out. Kim was sitting right where she should be, down the shoulder a ways, ready to catch any of the smaller waves the pros had missed. Leon laughed when I finally got out to him. "It's part of the game," he said.

Leon went straight to position at the point and fought for waves. He was courteous, but he hunted down every one, and he caught more than almost anyone. He tore down the line, making sweeping, effortless turns. He crouched and got barreled. He had that heedless beauty on the board. I sat just inside the big group at the peak and caught the few waves that someone missed. The speed, the stiffness of the wall and the lip, were a rush. I'd never surfed anything like this. It was wild out there. Giant bait balls of sardines deckled and thrashed the surface, while hundreds of small terns and a few widewinged frigate birds swooped over them.

Kim caught two long rides. I watched her when I wasn't trying to survive at the edge of the pack. She had the timing, the quickness, the strength, and she sledded down along the line on the fastest head-high waves she'd ever ridden. It was a triumph. Five months of surfing, total, and here she was. I almost burst with pride.

We shacked up in a room above Pablo's parents' house a block up from his restaurant. The room had been hurriedly added on to the roof to accommodate the new surfer traffic. The rest of the world had watched the same movie about Barra that we'd seen in Huntington, and a lot of them must have been inspired to pack their boards and book flights. Everybody in town was building bedrooms.

Surfing is a true meritocracy; you could be rich, you could

be God, but once you're out on the wave, you still have to earn respect and wait your turn in the lineup. You'd still get yelled at for pulling a dumb kook move like dropping in without looking. At Barra, locals who couldn't afford wax battled it out with Aussie semipros on trust funds. Off the wave, surf culture dictated that the rich wear the same baggie shorts and T-shirts and flip-flops as the poor. But then they got in their shiny rental SUVs and drove back the forty-five minutes to Huatulco to stay in one of the all-inclusive five-star hotels.

Not us. Kim and I had a spider the size of my fist hanging in the corner and it was better not to flick the bulb on in the rough bathroom in the middle of the night because the lightning evacuation of the roaches usually took place over our feet. We weren't there for luxury accommodations, though, and were used to these nighttime companions. For the most part, we wanted to sleep early. The plan was to get out just after dawn before most of the other hard-partying surfers. But . . .

One of Pablo's initiatives, after bringing in a lot of money from the surf competition and from Sean Collins's group, was to hire a music teacher for the school kids, and buy over twenty band instruments. Each child selected to take part in the band was given a strict lecture by the teacher on how it was a great privilege and that they had to take care of their instruments as if they were their own little brothers and work very hard so as not to impugn the honor of the town. These kids took their marching orders with the seriousness that only a ten-year-old with a tuba can attain. The whole orchestra got together every night on the veranda of the school and clashed out a din that shocked the nocturnal wildlife into traumatized silence. It sounded as if they were all tuning at once.

On the other hand, it was probably better than Leon's

quarters. The first dawn we picked him up at his shack, he emerged looking ragged.

"What's the matter?" Kim asked. "You look rough."

"My roommate," Leon said. Smiled sadly with one half of his mouth.

"Your roommate?" Kim's face lit with a sly, womanly smile. "That was fast. El Tigre. Rowwwr."

"Him," Leon said. "I think."

Kim's mouth fell open.

"Like this big." Leon spread his arms. "Iguana. He comes out right over the bed. All night I was afraid for my toes." He smiled. He knew iguanas didn't eat toes. He used to hunt them when he was a boy.

The wave at dawn was glorious. Suddenly I could really see it, empty of crowds, clean as sea glass, goose-bumped with the offshore breeze. The humps of the swell rolled in and accelerated as they hit shallower water and when they got to the point they heaved into a vertical wall and released. The sheer beauty, unadorned with surfers, was somehow like seeing a famous celebrity or model skinny-dipping in a mountain pool, without trappings or entourage, moving in the pure beauty of her God-given skin.

Leon and I both caught waves. I couldn't believe it. They were just overhead and fast and I made the drop just off the point and stayed ahead of the crashing pocket that was sometimes a barrel. Wow. I used the 6–4 destroyer and I was so excited. Kim had more trouble. The swell was building and it was faster than the day before and she got hammered.

Over the next few days the swell grew. The period between the waves lengthened and the sets grew to head-and-a-half-high, maybe eight feet on the front face. The increase in height was accompanied by a noticeable increase in power. Wading out along the rocks of the point and waiting for the lull to launch, I made sure that I didn't mess up like the first day. Next time it might not be only the board that broke. And as the waves got bigger, the crowd at the point got more aggressive, more impersonal. This was all business now. As I paddled out, around the shoulder, I had to be extra alert to make sure some set wave didn't bring a nearly breaking wall right on top of me—with a surfer on it. That was always the danger: that I might find myself pinned against the face of a set wave, not strong enough to paddle over it and get out of the way fast enough, and either get rolled by the break or sliced in half by an Israeli.

This felt like real surfing. All the strength I had built up over the past few months now had a reason to surge and galvanize. So did the judgment and the conditioning that asked our minds to be unafraid. It was tough with the big crowd at the point. I sat inside them and made myself be patient, forced myself to wait for a good wave that some pro screwed up. On the third day I caught a wave that was well over my head and rode it way down the line, yelling the whole way. On the fourth day the waves were bigger still, but Leon decided that we would head down the coast and find something Kim could do. I thought that was incredibly generous.

We got directions from Pablo to the "Lighthouse" and drove an hour down the highway, and up a maze of sand roads. The dry forest was lovely. Big oval leaves lay over the dirt track like any road in New England in the fall, except that these had fallen from desiccation rather than cold. The forest trail petered out into a vast sand plain of dry riverbed. An old rowboat sat bleaching and forlorn. Shallow pools lay stranded in the flats and the tire tracks divided, either way threatening to bog down in soft sand.

We got to a dozen fishermen's shacks at the mouth of the dry river, just pieces of corrugated steel and frayed plastic over posts. A few rusty pickups. Relentless sun and sand fleas. The bay was wide, with a rock bluff and a lighthouse at the far end, shimmering in heat waves. The water was smooth, mirrorlike, silvered blue in the long sun, the bay protected from the swell that was hitting Barra by a large headland to the south. This looked like a lake. The surface of the bay barely breathed, the swell was languid, small, the sound of the waves breaking on the shore soothing, inquiring. How could we possibly surf here? But it was somehow welcome, this respite; like a vacation from the pressure and power of Barra. We would just paddle around out there, find some little wave by the lighthouse point, enjoy the day and the scenery.

A heavy unshaven man in the nearest shack promised to watch the van, no problem. Leon pulled out his shortboard, a 6–8, so I took mine. I carried it and Kim's heavy longboard and we started up the beach, taking our time, breathing the windless air that was a cocktail of salt and dry forest rot and desert tang. We walked for half an hour, to the lighthouse, and we paddled out and tried the little rights coming off the rocks. They rolled across the whole inlet, so we could catch them almost anywhere, and Kim got a couple of long rides, which made me happy. A large dead leatherback sea turtle floated around with us in the middle of the bay, breaking the silvery shimmer with her lifeless shadow, and there was so little current that we could use her as a buoy marker, for she barely moved in the smooth water.

Hours later, exhausted, happy, wickedly thirsty, we walked into the fish camp just as several *pangas* pulled in with their catch. Leon asked for a large fish to offer Pablo, one that we could all eat it at his restaurant tonight. He held his hands apart, two, then three feet. The fishermen shook their heads. One balanced a tub on the gunwale, tilted it toward us. It was full of ten-inch mackerel and sierra. Babies.

"What about the big ones?" Leon asked.

Heads shook. "No. *Ya no*." Not now. What they meant was, *No mas*, not ever, but they wouldn't say it.

INCOMING

That night, before dinner, Pablo took Kim and I bird-watching. We walked along hedgerows of guanacaste, caoba, cedro trees, and through fields of pasture and bananas. Pablo was a terrific guide. He knew the local names for every bird, and the English and Latin. We saw tiny pygmy owls perched on limbs, watching us with swiveling heads that were barely big enough for the round black eyes. We saw flycatchers and a brilliant red-and-green-breasted trogon. Bright red tanagers. Pablo showed us the banana fields treated with chemical fertilizer. They grew quickly, he said, and fruited quickly, "But now look." The leaves were slack and burned, the plants stunted. He showed us another grown the traditional way, manured by cattle and burned off by fire. The trees were vibrant green and large. "You don't have to be a specialist to see the difference," he said.

I loved our walk, but to tell you the truth I was having

trouble concentrating. I was thinking about guess what. It's not that I was turning single-minded, but I knew that we had one more day here before we had to head back up the coast. Leon had to get back to his shop and begin planning a big surf competition that he was organizing, and we were booked to fly home in less than a week. The original concept of this trip was to see whether I could go from kook to a big hollow wave in six months. I had one more day. As if to oblige, the swell had been building without letup.

From the parking lot back at Barra, we could hear the roar and the deep bass of the waves exploding. Our last morning. Kim wanted to take a day off, so Leon and I got ready fast. He decided on his shortboard, but I unsheathed the gun, the 7–6 single-fin Bruno had made for just this.

The sets were coming in double overhead—faces of ten feet or more. They broke in heavy collapsing tubes, then ripped down the line with clean snowy tops that spumed back in the wind. We walked up the beach without talking.

"Ready, Pedro?" Leon said as we waded into the foam. "Careful. Be ready to move."

The crowd had thinned considerably from the previous days. We paddled straight to the point. All the waves were big. One after another, the surfers caught them. Leon turned and took off on a sweet hollow ten-footer. I tried the next, stalled at the bottom, and got swallowed, tumbled all the way into the shallows, grateful just to breathe.

I tried again and again. Took off on waves that were already breaking. Was I too eager? Impatience breeding impatience. It couldn't end like this. The wind was coming up, laying a low chop against the swell. It was coming off the ocean, straight into our faces. We had been out there for hours. It was getting harder and harder to paddle out because the waves were getting bigger and more serious and the stiffening wind blew spray into our eyes and stung and blinded us. Most of the surfers went in. Then I did, too.

Kim and Leon and I ate lunch under the tent of the restaurant and watched the sets roar in. I drank a Coke, finished an omelet. I convinced myself that it was okay. I'd caught something like a nine-foot face on my shortboard the other day. Pretty good. Pretty good for an old guy. Pretty good climax to our trip. I ordered another Coke and watched the wind drive over the backs of the waves at the point. They were so big they seemed to just shrug it off. They were big and empty of surfers and they heaved shoreward in relentless self-destroying ranks.

I stood up. I must have surfed for four hours already that day. Muscles fatigued, relaxed.

"See you guys in a while," I said. "Leon, you want to go out again?"

"No, too windy. I am tired. Hey, Pedro?"

"Yeah?"

Leon looked at me. He was the one who first taught me how to paddle for a wave, how to watch the peaks, be patient, but go. When you go, he had told me, go like your whole life depends on it. He looked at me, then the corner of his mouth came up in a half smile. "Take off at a good angle," he said.

I paddled out with my eyes closed most of the time against the burning spray. Squinted them open every few seconds to gauge the incoming walls so I wouldn't get annihilated. A flock of terns swarmed a bait ball. They cried and wheeled and dove. The buffeting and rush of the wind competed with the tear of the waves. It was kicking up foaming whitecaps. I sat, bucking on the chop, and watched the swell shatter against the farthest rocks thirty feet away. The wind drove the spume far up the onto the broken boulders, drove spray into the arms of cacti, and the bent and shivering brush. It seemed very wild out there. The waves, when they formed, heaved up from far out and reared dark and sudden and the size of houses.

Suddenly I found myself with just two other surfers. I'd been watching them for days and they were both world-class. One was Anglo, one Mexican, neither wore a rash guard, and they both had tattoos. And they were sitting inside of me. For the first time, I was the one farthest out, the one poised for a set. Nobody between me and the horizon but birds. The next wall rolling in was *mine.* It was a set wave, eleven or twelve feet high.

"Go!" one yelled. "It's yours." They'd been watching me, too. They knew I was a beginner who was trying hard.

I started to turn the gun. "I hope I can catch this!" I shouted.

"You got it! You got it!"

I paddled as hard as I could. I angled right, the way Leon had been coaching me, and thought, *Chest up, pop up fast!*

That moment when the wave overtakes you and the speed of the board is no longer from paddling but a force greater. Thousands and thousands of times greater. And the board accelerates. And it's faster than you can imagine. And the wave drops away like a cliff.

I popped up, amazed. I was standing and the wall of the wave lined out ahead of me, blue and clean. Without thinking I laid in a bottom turn and rocketed to the lip and came off it in a wide arc. Wow. I did it again. When I hit the lip the G force shocked me and buckled my legs. The board skipped down the face. I crouched: at the very bottom I looked up the wall. The double sense of speed and stasis. It blocked the sky. It was and ever shall be: mountainous, dark, quivering. And charging with breathless velocity, accelerating over me in a folding rush. Set the edge and swoop to the top, sheer flight, onrushing sky. Turn back. Another, tighter this time. The speed of it, the sense that the bay, the beach, the hills, flew to meet me. One more cut, try a more radical tighter turn, maybe a cutback, and—I lost balance. I wiped out. The break caught and tumbled me and rolled under and past. It didn't matter. I came up into the spangled sunlight yelling with pure joy. Looked back. I was a long way from the takeoff. Months of work and frustration, car breakdowns, broken boards, bruises, none of it mattered. I lay my arm over the gun and drifted in the whitewater. I could see the swarming birds in the blue air. I could see one of the two pros taking off on a steep wall.

The rip carried me south. *I'll drift,* I thought. *Rest. Let the current take me opposite the restaurant. Then I'll get out.*

Did I do it? I did it! Rode the wave. I loved it.

I loved the wave, the pros, the birds, the wind, Kim, the world, Leon, omelets, the wind, my arms—

SLAM!

Sudden tumble. Inside shore break. Underwater, and I heard a crack like pool balls. A scar, a blow. Back of the head. Explosion of black and light like cartoon lighting. Oh, fuck. *Do not black out!* I yelled at myself. *Do not faint!* That's death. Nobody out here, nobody can see. Struggled. Lunged for air. Breath. Reeled in the board and held it while feet kicked and scrabbled for the bottom. Stood, braced against the wicked current that tore down the shore and staggered out onto damp sand. Phew. Reached back, back of my head, and pulled my hand away covered in blood. Fin must have sliced it open. Stung a little, but mostly the torn scalp was shocked to numbness.

I laughed. I was alive. What a dumbass.

Get all cocky and fuzzy, pat myself on the back and forget where I am for one second and the ocean knocked me silly.

Pay attention.

For my own safety. Because it is the only way through. Because the things I love are fragile and only here for a little while.

Another inshore wave folded and thudded. The wind blew the spray over me. Closed my eyes, let it buffet and soak me. The wave shook the sand. Heard the thresh and boom and, very faint, the cry of a tern.

This is how I make a life. There is no next Thing. Just this—thud and shudder—and this

EPILOGUE

The afternoon of the Wave, I got six neat stitches from a doctor in Huatulco. Kim and Leon and I booked into a five-star resort for two nights to celebrate our trip. We wandered the shaded paths and read the little signs about the butterflies and birds; the hotel was all-inclusive and we ate everything in sight. A few days later Kim and I found a home for the Beast and flew out of Mexico.

I live on a lake in Denver. In the warm months, in the early mornings, before the boat rangers arrive, I paddle an old surfboard across it. Every once in a while I look over my shoulder and imagine a swell: the wave coming in, rising up to curl and break and carry me with the speed of a seal into certain joy.

ACKNOWLEDGMENTS

To my first readers, deepest thanks. Lisa Jones, Janis Hallowell, Helen Thorpe, Pete Beveridge, Rebecca Rowe, and Jay Heinrichs all read with great attention, speed, and fury. Lisa and Helen, you guys rock—you were always there with perspective, encouragement, and bang-on edits.

Nancy Carter, especially, gave of her love and profound insight in the hardest time. Thank you, sweet dance partner.

Ian King, you are a wrestler. And a keen reader. Thank you for your tremendous insight and attention. Thanks, too, to David Halpern for being there from the beginning: advisor, rigorous editor, friend; you are the very best ally. And to Kathy Robbins for years of support.

At the Free Press I'd like to thank editors Wylie O'Sullivan and Leah Miller. Wylie believed in this from the start and encouraged me when I was exhausted and waterlogged.

William Heller, a.k.a. Cuz, thanks for the help with the Spanish.

To Mark Lough and Sascha Steinway: I'm grateful for old friends with bent ears.

Several companies gave us important material support: Smith Optics has been great over the years. Thanks to Inno for the fine locking surfboard rack, to Jack's in Huntington Beach, and to Katin, for gear. Thanks to O'Neill, to Las Palomas Hotel in Tepic, Las Brisas Hotel in Huatulco, and most of all, to Mike Vavak at Ocean & Earth.

The whole undertaking depended on the kindness of many people. Nathan Myers at *Surfing* magazine was a great help, and a Guardian of the True Path. Robert Howson at Harbour Surfboards in Seal Beach gave generous hours of perspective and insight. Francesca Dvorak and German Agundez showed us a world nocturnal. Thanks to Lili Pérez and Edgardo Pérez for all the warm hospitality and help. To Pam Lough, too, for her generous hospitality, and to Lidice Ortiz for the same. To Helena Pless for everything. To Tony Garcia and his family for showing us the ropes. Terry Ann Watts, you were a champ. Jim Pyle, thanks for helping me retrieve the Beast from deep mango country.